VIBRANT
PUBLISHERS

I0028156

THE PROFITABLE GOOD:

A BOLD PLAYBOOK FOR SUSTAINABLE BUSINESS GROWTH

Fast-track your impact, revenue, and resilience with practical tools that make doing good the smartest move in business.

DR. TAMARA STENN

THE PROFITABLE GOOD
A BOLD PLAYBOOK FOR SUSTAINABLE BUSINESS GROWTH

First Edition

Published by Vibrant Publishers LLC, USA, www.vibrantpublishers.com

Paperback ISBN 13: 978-1-63651-666-0
Ebook ISBN 13: 978-1-63651-665-3
Hardback ISBN 13: 978-1-63651-667-7

Vibrant Publishers' books are available at special quantity discounts for sales promotions, or for use in corporate training programs. For more information, please write to bulkorders@vibrantpublishers.com

Please email feedback/corrections (technical, grammatical, or spelling) to spellerrors@vibrantpublishers.com

Vibrant publishes in a variety of print and electronic formats and by print-on-demand. Some material included with standard print versions of this book may not be included in e-books or in print-on-demand. To access the complete catalog of Vibrant Publishers, visit www.vibrantpublishers.com

Exclusive Online Resources For You

As our valued reader, your purchase of this book includes access to exclusive online resources designed to enhance your learning experience. These resources can be downloaded from our website, www.vibrantpublishers.com, and will help you apply essential frameworks to build sustainable businesses grounded in capability, purpose, and profit.

Online resources for this book include the following essential components:

1. Business Model Canvas: Starter Templates for Small Businesses
2. Writable BMC Template
3. Frameworks Worksheet
4. Neurodiverse Entrepreneurship Assessment Sheet
5. Reading Guide: Informal Entrepreneurship
6. Right-Side Connections Worksheet
7. Circular Design Decision Tree Worksheet
8. Collaborative Cost Structure Worksheet
9. Minimum Viable Product + Pivot Worksheet
10. Template for Designing a Blue Ocean Strategy
11. Blue Ocean Strategy Data Worksheet
12. Sustainability Leadership Mindset: Self-Assessment Worksheet
13. Social Enterprise Pitch Worksheet
14. Budgeting Worksheet

Why are these online resources valuable?

Ready-to-use layouts: Download, type, save, and revise your sustainable business model using these downloadable layouts designed for all types of new and growing ventures.

Business visualization: Visualize your entire business, including customers, resources, and finances, in one simple, intuitive format, perfect for refining your sustainable strategy.

Tailored methods: Explore diverse cognitive strengths and thinking styles that enhance business innovation.

Guided reflections: Use well-researched reading guides to sharpen your strategic thinking and grow equitable, purpose-driven ventures.

How to access your online resources:

1. **Visit the website:** Go to www.vibrantpublishers.com
2. **Find your book:** Navigate to the book's product page via the "Shop" menu or by searching for the book title in the search bar.
3. **Request the resources:** Scroll down to the "Request Sample Book/ Online Resource" section.
4. **Enter your details:** Enter your preferred email ID and select "Online Resource" as the resource type. Lastly, select "user type" and submit the request.
5. **Check your inbox:** The resources will be delivered directly to your email.

Alternatively, for quick access, simply scan the QR code below to go directly to the product page and request the online resources by filling in the required details.

Happy learning!

SELF-LEARNING MANAGEMENT SERIES

TITLE	PAPERBACK* ISBN

BUSINESS AND ENTREPRENEURSHIP

BUSINESS COMMUNICATION ESSENTIALS	9781636511634
BUSINESS ETHICS ESSENTIALS	9781636513324
BUSINESS LAW ESSENTIALS	9781636511702
BUSINESS PLAN ESSENTIALS	9781636511214
BUSINESS STRATEGY ESSENTIALS	9781949395778
ENTREPRENEURSHIP ESSENTIALS	9781636511603
INTERNATIONAL BUSINESS ESSENTIALS	9781636513294
PRINCIPLES OF MANAGEMENT ESSENTIALS	9781636511542

COMPUTER SCIENCE AND TECHNOLOGY

BLOCKCHAIN ESSENTIALS	9781636513003
MACHINE LEARNING ESSENTIALS	9781636513775
PYTHON ESSENTIALS	9781636512938

DATA SCIENCE FOR BUSINESS

BUSINESS INTELLIGENCE ESSENTIALS	9781636513362
DATA ANALYTICS ESSENTIALS	9781636511184

FINANCIAL LITERACY AND ECONOMICS

COST ACCOUNTING & MANAGEMENT ESSENTIALS	9781636511030
FINANCIAL ACCOUNTING ESSENTIALS	9781636510972
FINANCIAL MANAGEMENT ESSENTIALS	9781636511009
MACROECONOMICS ESSENTIALS	9781636511818
MICROECONOMICS ESSENTIALS	9781636511153
PERSONAL FINANCE ESSENTIALS	9781636511849
PRINCIPLES OF ECONOMICS ESSENTIALS	9781636512334

*Also available in Hardback & Ebook formats

SELF-LEARNING MANAGEMENT SERIES

TITLE	PAPERBACK* ISBN
HR, DIVERSITY, AND ORGANIZATIONAL SUCCESS	
DIVERSITY, EQUITY, AND INCLUSION ESSENTIALS	9781636512976
DIVERSITY IN THE WORKPLACE ESSENTIALS	9781636511122
HR ANALYTICS ESSENTIALS	9781636510347
HUMAN RESOURCE MANAGEMENT ESSENTIALS	9781949395839
ORGANIZATIONAL BEHAVIOR ESSENTIALS	9781636512303
ORGANIZATIONAL DEVELOPMENT ESSENTIALS	9781636511481
LEADERSHIP AND PERSONAL DEVELOPMENT	
DECISION MAKING ESSENTIALS	9781636510026
INDIA'S ROAD TO TRANSFORMATION: WHY LEADERSHIP MATTERS	9781636512273
LEADERSHIP ESSENTIALS	9781636510316
TIME MANAGEMENT ESSENTIALS	9781636511665
MODERN MARKETING AND SALES	
CONSUMER BEHAVIOR ESSENTIALS	9781636513263
DIGITAL MARKETING ESSENTIALS	9781949395747
MARKETING MANAGEMENT ESSENTIALS	9781636511788
MARKET RESEARCH ESSENTIALS	9781636513744
SALES MANAGEMENT ESSENTIALS	9781636510743
SERVICES MARKETING ESSENTIALS	9781636511733
SOCIAL MEDIA MARKETING ESSENTIALS	9781636512181

*Also available in Hardback & Ebook formats

SELF-LEARNING MANAGEMENT SERIES

TITLE	PAPERBACK* ISBN
OPERATIONS MANAGEMENT	
AGILE ESSENTIALS	9781636510057
OPERATIONS & SUPPLY CHAIN MANAGEMENT ESSENTIALS	9781949395242
PROJECT MANAGEMENT ESSENTIALS	9781636510712
STAKEHOLDER ENGAGEMENT ESSENTIALS	9781636511511

CURRENT AFFAIRS

DIGITAL SHOCK	9781636513805

*Also available in Hardback & Ebook formats

About the Author

 **Dr. Tamara Stenn** is an accomplished economist, educator, and pioneering innovator with over 40 years of experience in business and academia. As an Associate Professor of Entrepreneurship at Suffolk University's Sawyer Business School and a renowned Fulbright scholar, Dr. Stenn specializes in advancing sustainable development practices.

She is the founder and CEO of *The Sustainability Lens Game,*® LLC, an ingenious sustainability education company that brings innovation, fun, and resilience to organizations using applied learning and artificial intelligence. Dr. Stenn is also the author of *Social Entrepreneurship as Sustainability* and *The Cultural and Political Intersection of Fair Trade and Justice* along with numerous interdisciplinary papers in development economics, management, and entrepreneurship.

Her entrepreneurial ventures reflect a deep commitment to social impact: She founded KUSIKUY Clothing Co., a fashion brand that supports sustainable livelihoods for Bolivian indigenous women through alpaca clothing production; A Perfect Seed, a farmer-owned international cooperative that brings rare heirloom, quinoa varieties to the U.S.; and New Visions Advertising, an advertising firm specializing in zero-waste, socially responsible campaigns.

Dr. Tamara Stenn's courses empower students to tackle real-world social and environmental challenges using entrepreneurial thinking, hands-on collaboration, and sustainability-driven innovation. With tools like the *Sustainability Lens Game* and partnerships such as Sparkshare, students develop and pitch impactful social business ideas while exploring key aspects like gender equity, informal entrepreneurship, and prosocial motivation.

For more information about the course, please contact Dr. Stenn at:

Tamara.Stenn@suffolk.edu

https://www.linkedin.com/in/tamarastenn/

What Experts Say About This Book!

The book is both practical and fun, making it more likely to engage students, which is the key to learning. It's not a boring recipe book for the usual startup grind, but a way of approaching entrepreneurship that is not only about the bucks, but incorporates thinking about the other dimensions of our lives and communities, as well as making a profit.

– Drew Hession-Kunz, Lecturer in Entrepreneurial Finance, Boston College, Seidner Department of Finance.

The Profitable Good is an entrepreneurship textbook that offers a comprehensive and accessible exploration of building ventures through a sustainability lens. The book is grounded in the United Nations Sustainable Development Goals to show how responsible practices can drive long-term business success. It provides insight into all the critical facets and theories entrepreneurs must consider—from idea generation and analysis to operations and impact—while illustrating concepts through strong, practical, and relevant examples. Each chapter walks readers through the different thought processes of creating a business using a variety of activities that encourage analysis, reflection, and application, making the material easy to understand and highly pertinent for both students and practitioners. Clear, concise visuals further enhance understanding by effectively conveying key theoretical concepts.

Overall, the book is well-suited for undergraduate and graduate students, as well as aspiring entrepreneurs interested in launching a sustainable business, offering valuable guidance on the essential issues to examine before opening a venture's doors.

– Nicole O'Brien, PhD, MSc, BBA, Assistant Professor of Practice, Sawyer Business School, Suffolk University

What Experts Say About This Book!

The Profitable Good offers a clear and well-structured introduction to sustainability in business, organized around six major domains—Foundations, Customers and Channels, Operations, Financials, Value Proposition, and Leading Change. The progression is logical and intuitive, guiding readers from basic concepts (4Ps, SDGs, entrepreneurship self-assessment) to more advanced topics such as supply-chain ethics, sustainable financial models, transformational leadership, and communication for change.

The book provides a reliable, conceptually accurate overview of sustainability principles. The book reflects contemporary sustainability conversations—ethical supply chains, indigenous wisdom, stakeholder value, and regenerative practices. There is a coherent and engaging flow, moving from internal foundations to customer value, operations, financial models, and finally leadership. The pattern of concept → example → case study → quiz makes the learning experience structured and interactive. The case studies are diverse and carefully chosen to illustrate sustainability challenges across geographies and industries.

This is a well-designed foundational book that balances conceptual clarity with practical application. It succeeds as an introductory sustainability resource—accessible, relevant, and structured for anyone who needs both theory and hands-on exercises. The book delivers an effective, engaging, and pedagogically sound learning experience.

– Dr. Glory Enyinnaya, Academic Director, Department of Business Administration, Pan-Atlantic University, Lagos

What Experts Say About This Book!

The book is highly engaging and enjoyable to read. The use of the Business Model Canvas as a foundational framework is an excellent choice, as it provides a shared language that can be spoken and understood by a wide range of stakeholders. The selected examples are practical, engaging, and firmly grounded in the realities of communities. The decision to include a set of tips is highly commendable, as it adds practical value to the book and supports readers in applying the concepts presented.

The use of the Suma Qamana as a paradigm, alongside Permaculture, Solidarity Economy, the Blue Ocean Strategy, Circles of Sustainability and the Sustainability Lens Game as fundamental concepts, is very insightful. It makes it possible to explore and understand business growth in new ways and, most importantly, offers a fresh and invigorating perspective.

– Salma IDRISSI BOUTAYBI, PhD, Social Entrepreneurship Researcher & Doctoral Sherpa

Dr. Tamara Stenn's work stands out for its rare combination of rigorous research, human-centered insight, and a deep commitment to renewable economic solutions. Her leadership, clarity, and vision make her work in this book invaluable in shaping a more equitable and resilient future.

– Dr. Jeanette Landin, Professor of Professional Studies, Landmark College

What Experts Say About This Book!

As more and more individuals gravitate towards entrepreneurship for both profit and purpose, there has come to be a tremendous need for an intelligible, inspiring, and useful guide that lays out the central tenets of sustainable business venturing. With her new book, The Profitable Good, Dr. Stenn services this need in marvelous fashion. She fully fathoms and ably conveys a customizable message that sustainable entrepreneurship, like all business venturing, is a personal and professional journey. Beginners and experts alike will benefit from the frameworks, insights, and extensive practical advice. Dr. Stenn not only invites the reader to develop a personal road map, but also how to build a toolbox for successfully realizing financial, social, and environmental gains.

– Richard "Rick" Hunt, Ph.D, Dorothy Hottel Digges Professor of Entrepreneurship at Virginia Tech

Table of Contents

Preface

As a professor, entrepreneur, and social enterprise developer, I've spent decades immersed in the real-world challenges, theoretical models, and breakthroughs of building businesses that do more than just turn a profit; they strengthen communities, restore ecosystems, and empower people. This book, *The Profitable Good: A Bold Playbook for Sustainable Business Growth (The Profitable Good)*, is the culmination of this journey.

This book was inspired by a simple but profound question I encountered repeatedly in my work with students, startups, and mission-driven organizations: "How do I make sustainability practical and profitable in my business?" Too often, sustainability is treated as an afterthought or moral add-on, something noble but difficult to measure, implement, or sustain. I wrote this book to change that narrative.

Drawing from hands-on experience, academic research, and global case studies, this guide integrates sustainability into every segment of the Business Model Canvas. It offers a flexible, creative approach rooted in frameworks I've developed, used in my enterprises, and taught students to use in theirs—including the Four Ps, the Four Pillars of Fair Trade, and the Four Lenses of Sustainability. These frameworks help entrepreneurs of all kinds, from high schoolers with lemonade stands to global manufacturers, to build ventures that are profitable, impactful, and resilient.

There is more than theory here. This book is a toolkit of practical actions, reflective assessments, and design thinking methods tailored for learners and leaders who want to make a difference through enterprise. It empowers one to embrace their own strengths, including neurodiversity, and develop business models that align with both personal values and today's global goals.

Whether a student, educator, innovator, or changemaker, my hope is that *The Profitable Good: A Bold Playbook for Sustainable Business Growth* not only informs but inspires you. Because business, at its best, is a powerful force for good, and sustainability is the strategy that ensures we all thrive.

– Dr. Tamara Stenn
Boston, Massachusetts
2026

Introduction to the Book

What if a business could do more than survive? What if it could thrive by helping the world thrive, too?

The Profitable Good: A Bold Playbook for Sustainable Business Growth is a hands-on guide for students, entrepreneurs, business owners, and changemakers who want to build ventures that are competitive, innovative, resilient, and rooted in purpose. In a world facing growing environmental crises, widening inequality, and shifting consumer expectations, businesses that embrace sustainability are no longer niche outliers; they are the leaders of the future. This book shows you how to be one of them.

At its heart, the book is about integrating sustainability into every aspect of an enterprise, not as an extra task, but as a strategic advantage. Whether running a startup, managing a team, or exploring a business idea for the first time, *The Profitable Good: A Bold Playbook for Sustainable Business Growth* offers a practical roadmap to embed sustainability across operations, marketing, finances, leadership, and customer relationships.

Using the Business Model Canvas as a foundation, the book guides you step-by-step through how sustainability can strengthen each of the nine components of a business. You learn how mindful decisions around sourcing, staffing, and partnerships can reduce costs, build community ties, and open new markets. Discover how design thinking, neurodiversity, and inclusive practices can drive innovation, resilience, and social impact. And explore how global frameworks like the Sustainable Development Goals (SDGs), the Four Ps, and the Fair Trade Pillars can help any venture align with international standards and stakeholder expectations.

What sets this book apart is its accessible, experiential approach. Instead of overwhelming readers with jargon or abstract theory, it begins with a simple lemonade stand. From there, it expands into real-life case studies featuring companies like Patagonia, Equal Exchange, Green Mountain Power, and Tony's Chocolonely, enterprises that prove profitability and purpose can go hand in hand. At each step, you'll find actionable tools: reflective self-assessments, practical exercises, and creative challenges designed to make sustainability tangible and transformative.

The Profitable Good: A Bold Playbook for Sustainable Business Growth also recognizes that entrepreneurs come in many forms, with diverse backgrounds, skills, and ways of thinking. That's why it includes an entrepreneurship self-assessment based on the *Dueling Banjos* model, helping one identify their strengths and build supportive, complementary teams. One does not need to be an expert in sustainability; they just need curiosity, commitment, and the willingness to think differently.

By the time you finish the book, you will have a toolkit of strategies and a mindset that empowers you to:

- Understand how sustainability enhances long-term business success.
- Integrate sustainable practices across operations, from sourcing to sales.
- Identify new markets and attract socially conscious customers.
- Strengthen supply chains, diversify income, and build brand trust.

- Align with global sustainability goals and frameworks.
- Lead with purpose and authenticity in a rapidly changing world.

This is not just a book, it's an invitation to become part of a growing movement. Organizations today have a unique opportunity, and responsibility, to lead positive change. The tools and insights in this book will help organizations seize that opportunity and turn sustainability into a competitive edge.

The Sustainability Lens Game: Turning Theory Into Transformative Action

The *Sustainability Lens Game* by author Dr. Tamara Stenn is an experiential learning innovation that transforms complex sustainability theory into an engaging, hands-on experience. Developed from more than 25 years of research and practice in sustainable business (Stenn, 2025), the game bridges abstract concepts and applied creativity through design thinking, storytelling, and collaboration.

Integrating 64 micro sustainability tools, represented as "coin cards," with the 17 United Nations Sustainable Development Goals (SDGs) and the nine sections of the Business Model Canvas (BMC), the game generates nearly 10,000 potential sustainability solution combinations. Each play session becomes a unique exploration of systems thinking, problem-solving, and imagination.

In gameplay, participants reimagine viable enterprises — such as a dog-walking service, a lemonade stand, or the participant's own venture — into regenerative, socially impactful businesses. Players have two minutes to combine seemingly unrelated sustainability tools and SDGs into actionable strategies, using storytelling to explain how their business now operates sustainably within its BMC section. Every player takes a turn leading while others collaborate, mirroring the competitive–collaborative dynamics of real-world sustainability practice. Because there are no losers and every idea adds value, gameplay fosters psychological safety, creativity, and a sense of collective achievement.

A recent study conducted with 52 business students demonstrated the *Sustainability Lens Game's* effectiveness in building psychosocial orientations toward sustainability leadership (Stenn, 2025). Findings showed a statistically significant increase in personal responsibility for sustainability, with additional gains in motivation and intent to act sustainably. When a personal storytelling exercise preceded gameplay, participants demonstrated the greatest levels of emotional engagement and responsibility — supporting the idea that stories act as value-carriers and amplifiers of empathy (Creed, Ross, & Ross, 2021; Gillespie, 2022).

Players described their experience as "energizing," "eye-opening," and "hopeful." Beyond knowledge acquisition, the game helped them connect emotionally with sustainability challenges and see themselves as capable of meaningful action, key elements of transformational learning (Bryant et al., 2023). By blending analog gameplay with digital assistance from *Sustainability Sam,* an AI facilitator that prompts creative thinking and records player outcomes, the game creates an accessible, hybrid environment for both in-person and technology-enhanced classrooms (Hou & Keng, 2021).

Ultimately, the *Sustainability Lens Game* transforms sustainability education from passive theory into active practice. Each gameplay session concludes with a strategic Strengths, Weaknesses, Opportunities, and Threats (SWOT) analysis, examining the transformed enterprise's SWOT, along with reflection on trade-offs, actionable next steps, and a compelling elevator pitch. The game allows players to experience the interconnectedness of business, community, and the environment while cultivating empathy, responsibility, and innovative thinking—the hallmarks of sustainable leadership. It turns imaginative ideas into practical actions that build innovation, resilience, and fun into any venture.

More information, facilitation materials, and reflective blogs can be found at www.sustainabilitylensgame.com.

Who Can Benefit From This Book

The Profitable Good: A Bold Playbook for Sustainable Business Growth is designed for a wide range of readers eager to build ventures that are both impactful and financially sound. Early-stage entrepreneurs and start-up founders will benefit from actionable strategies to build strong, resilient business models grounded in purpose. Professionals and project managers seeking to integrate sustainability into existing operations will discover practical insights that can be applied immediately across sectors. Undergraduate and graduate students studying entrepreneurship, business, sustainability, or social innovation will find clear frameworks and hands-on tools that bridge theory and practice. The book can be used as a whole or by select chapters, depending on the users' needs and interests.

Educators, incubator facilitators, and business mentors will also find this book to be a valuable resource for guiding learners through sustainability practices using accessible language, relevant case studies, and real-world examples. Whether launching a first venture, growing an enterprise, or teaching others how to do so, this book equips one to lead with confidence, creativity, and conscience.

How to Use This Book?

The Profitable Good A Bold Playbook for Sustainable Growth is a practical guide designed to be used as both a learning tool and an action planner. Whether you're an entrepreneur, business leader, educator, or student this book provides flexible pathways to explore, apply, and adapt sustainability strategies to your unique context. Here are several ways to get the most out of the book:

- **Start with the Business Model Canvas (BMC):** Each chapter builds upon the BMC framework, showing how sustainability can be embedded in the nine segments of a business. If you're already familiar with the BMC, dive into the chapters that align with the segments you want to improve. If you are not familiar with the BMC, no worries, the chapters will carefully guide the way, introducing the BMC and how it is used.

- **Use the case studies for inspiration and analysis:** Each chapter includes real-world examples of purpose-driven companies. Use these as models, discussion prompts, or benchmarks for your own sustainability goals.

- **Complete the self-assessments and exercises:** Interactive tools like the Entrepreneurship Spectrum assessment and SWOT analysis help you identify your strengths and opportunities. These tools are especially useful for personal reflection, team building, or classroom facilitation.

- **Apply the sustainability frameworks:** The book introduces three core frameworks—the Four Ps, Four Pillars, and Four Lenses—to help you evaluate and design sustainability strategies. Refer to these throughout the book and use them to assess real ventures.

- **Align your business with the SDGs:** The book demonstrates how to map the United Nations Sustainable Development Goals to your business model. This approach helps you uncover new market opportunities and create measurable social and environmental impact.

- **Work through it sequentially or by need:** You can read the book from beginning to end as a full curriculum or jump to specific chapters based on immediate needs (e.g., customer development, supply chains, financials, leadership).

- **Use it as a teaching or facilitation tool:** Instructors and facilitators can use the book to structure workshops, team projects, or semester-long courses. Each chapter includes exercises, tips, and discussion questions to guide group learning.

However you choose to engage, this book is meant to be written in, returned to, and adapted as your ideas evolve. Treat it as your roadmap to building ventures that are not only sustainable but also successful by every measure.

Let's get started.

Note: *This printed edition reproduces visual materials in monochrome. Where color forms part of the original design or aids interpretation, full-color versions are available in the Online Resources.*

CHAPTER 1

Foundations of Sustainability in Business

Key Learning Objectives

- Understand the Business Model Canvas in representing the nine aspects of an enterprise.
- Discuss the power of the Four Ps of Sustainability, the Four Pillars of Fair Trade, and the Four Lenses of Sustainability, and how they contribute to the larger study of sustainability.
- Assess one's strengths and weaknesses, examining the seven stages of entrepreneurship using the *Dueling Banjos* method.
- Learn about the Sustainable Development Goals, how they pertain on a micro level to individual enterprises, and provide a place of new opportunity and growth.

In a general business context, sustainability refers to the practice of operating in a way that meets present needs without compromising the ability of future generations to meet theirs. The purpose of sustainability in business is to create long-term value by reducing harm, using resources wisely, supporting communities, and building resilient, ethical organizations that can adapt and thrive over time.

Sustainable businesses benefit through cost savings, innovation, stronger brand reputation, employee engagement, and access to conscious consumers and new markets. Communities benefit through ethical job creation, local investment, and inclusive practices. Environmental benefits include reduced pollution and waste, conservation of natural resources, lower carbon emissions, and the protection of ecosystems, helping ensure a healthier planet for future generations.

Business sustainability involves balancing three essential aspects: economic success, environmental responsibility, and social impact, often called the Triple Bottom Line. The Triple Bottom Line (TBL) is a business framework that expands the traditional focus on financial performance (profit) to also include social and environmental impacts (Elkington, 1997). It encourages enterprises to evaluate success based on three key dimensions: people, planet, and profit.

People includes the social impact on employees, communities, and stakeholders.

Planet refers to the environmental footprint, including resource use, emissions, and waste.

Profit is about the economic viability and financial performance of the organization.

The goal of the Triple Bottom Line framework is to balance these three priorities, ensuring that enterprise growth supports both society and the environment. TBL is a good starting point for sustainability. However, in this book, we will go deeper into the idea of sustainability, introducing multiple models, assessments, and examples to present a practical and holistic application of sustainability. We will take the idea of sustainability further by building deeper connections and responsibility. These connections extend beyond the confines of the enterprise, creating more options and actions beyond the Triple Bottom Line.

In Chapter One, we understand the concept of sustainability as something mindfully built into an organization to strengthen community ties, solidify supply chains, expand markets, diversify cash flow, and connect with customers. We explore the Business Model Canvas (BMC), a collaborative, design-thinking tool, used as a platform on which to build sustainability across an organization. We also discuss the development of sustainability in the context of a "Lemonade Stand," a simple venture that involves making and selling a beverage. As the Lemonade Stand evolves in this chapter, it serves as a foundational example for introducing key sustainability concepts and terminology.

We explore frameworks such as the 4Ps (People, Planet, Profit, and Purpose), the 4 Pillars (economic, environmental, social, and cultural sustainability), and the 4 Lenses (tools for analyzing enterprise health, innovation, and resilience). These frameworks will help you articulate your business vision, communicate with stakeholders, and align your ventures with global goals like the Sustainable Development Goals (SDGs). The chapter also includes a self-assessment of entrepreneurial stages, encouraging you to identify strengths and areas for growth as you go on to build resilient, purpose-driven enterprises.

Overall, the purpose of Chapter One is to ensure your understanding of sustainability in an applied learning context and to become familiar with the tools and methods used to identify and build sustainability. Let's begin with the case of the lemonade stand.

1.1 Introduction: The Lemonade Stand Transformation

Often, when working with enterprises and sustainability, people wonder where to begin. Existing businesses are complex, and new businesses are still developing. To make it easy, sustainability can be learned using a lemonade stand. This keeps everyone on the same page for starters and makes it easier to see how sustainability concepts can be used and function in more complex situations.

A lemonade stand is a simple venture that involves selling a homemade beverage outdoors on a summer day. Started and managed by children, often with guidance from adults, it is a classic example of a small-scale enterprise where raw materials are transformed into a product that serves a need and generates revenue. The Business Model Canvas provides a structure to study the different parts of the lemonade stand and to see what happens when elements of sustainability are added to it. Chapters Two through Five will go into more detail about how each of the BMC areas lends itself to a plethora of sustainability approaches. For now, in this section, we will understand the fundamentals of the BMC with respect to the lemonade stand.

Figure 1.1 The Business Model Canvas

The Business Model Canvas

| Designed for: | Designed by: | Date: | Version: |

Key Partnerships	Key Activities	Value Propositions	Customer Relationships	Customer Segments
	Key Resources		Channels	

Cost Structure	Revenue Streams

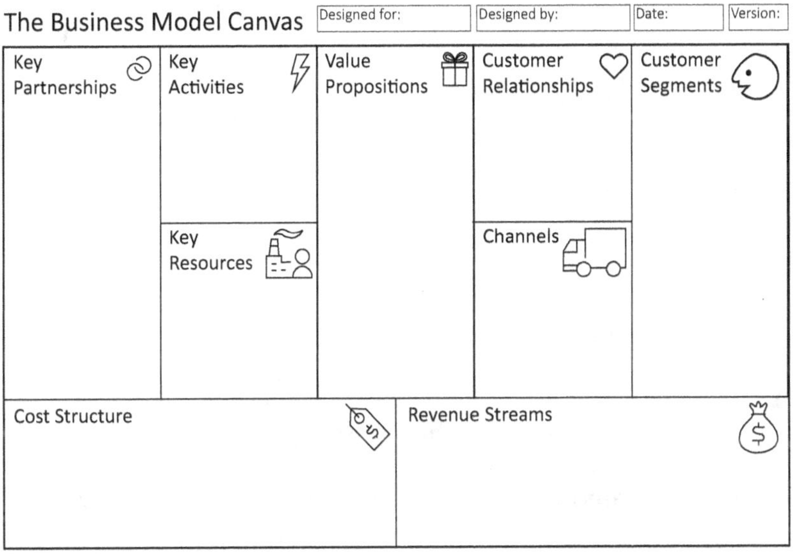

(Strategyzer, 2025)

The Business Model Canvas is a design thinking tool that builds conversation around business strategy and development.

The BMC, as seen in Figure 1.1, is a collaborative, design-thinking tool used by businesses and leaders around the world. It was developed in 2004 by doctoral student Alex Osterwalder, who crowdsourced the concept of business model development through a series of innovative workshops focused on strategy and development. His findings became the BMC as presented in his Management Information Systems doctoral thesis, *The Business Model Ontology — A Proposition in a Design Science Approach*, at the University of Lausanne (Osterwalder, 2010).

The BMC encompasses all aspects of growing and managing a business through nine segments:

1. Community (Key Partnerships)
2. Staff (Key Activities)
3. Materials (Key Resources)
4. Product (Value Proposition)
5. Sales (Customer Relationships)
6. Delivery (Channels)
7. Customers (Customer Segments)
8. Costs (Cost Structure)
9. Expenses (Revenue Streams)

As illustrated in Figure 1.2, these BMC segments can be clustered into three key areas with specific characteristics and purposes. The left side segments lead to more internal, logistical conversations examining how products are sourced and created. The right side segments are concerned with building outward connections and communications.

Figure 1.2 Three Key BMC Areas

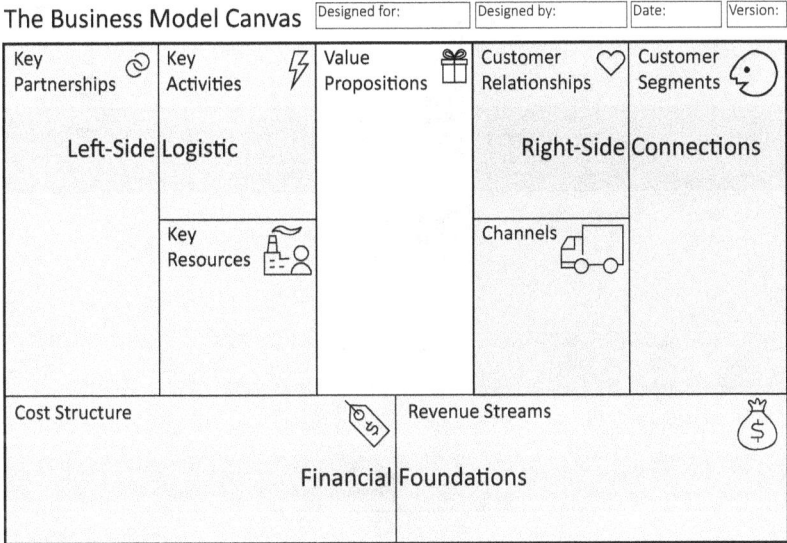

The Business Model Canvas

Key Partnerships	Key Activities	Value Propositions	Customer Relationships	Customer Segments

Left-Side Logistic — Right-Side Connections

Key Resources — Channels

Cost Structure — Revenue Streams

Financial Foundations

(Adapted from the Strategyzer BMC Model, 2025)

Considering the BMC as a brain, the left side represents the logical part, where detailed processes are analyzed and choices are made. The right side is the emotional and creative side, where relationships are formed. Both sides are supported by the financial foundation, the revenue and expenses of an enterprise. What remains independent is the central Value Proposition segment. This segment is the key definition of what is being offered and is influenced by all areas.

The following Figure 1.3 is the BMC of a simple lemonade stand at a farmers' market, with the challenge to make it more sustainable. Prompts define each category. Responses to the prompts are bulleted underneath.

Figure 1.3 Business Model Canvas of the Lemonade Stand

Key Partners/ Experience – Who, outside of your enterprise, helps you to meet your goals?	Key Activities – What you are doing, making, and/ or delivering?	Value Proposition – What makes you awesome. What does your product/ service do that no other does?	Customer Relationships –How do you maintain communica"on with customers after the sale?	Customer Segments– Exactly who is using your product/ service? Be specific.
•Farmer's market (Place to sell) •Suppliers (lemons, syrup, cups, etc.) •Food safety training organization	•Cut lemons •Make and serve lemonade •Set up and clean up **Key Resources**–What you need to get your product made or service delivered. •Lemons •Sugar •Ice and water •Cups •Stand/booth	Relate this to your Customer. Show the Customer need you are addressing. •Freshly hand-squeezed •Made on the spot •Local ingredients	•Listing on the farmers' market website **Channels**– How customers get your product or service. •Farmers'market sales	•Farmers'market visitors •Local residents •Tourists

Cost Structure (per market) – How much it costs: product, salaries, rent, materials, packaging, marketing, commissions. Be specific. •Labor: $90 (6 hours at $15/ hour) •Cups: $25 (200 with lids, 16 oz.) •Lemons: $120 (300 total) •Ice $30 (10 bags) •Maple syrup: $60 (6 quarts) **Total Costs: $325**	Revenue Streams (per market) – How you make $. Show the Return on Investment (ROI). •200 lemonades sold per market •$4.00 each •Total Revenue: $800 **Profit (ROI).**$800 revenue–$325 costs**$475 profit**

(Sustainability Lens Game, 2025)

ACTIVITY

Sustainability terms and tools are areas of rapid growth and innovation. While this book strives to explain most of the terms, if you encounter a term or acronym for which you need further clarification, do browse reliable sources on the internet for a better understanding.

1.1.1 Left-Side Logistics

The left side of the BMC includes Key Partners, Key Activities, and Key Resources. This side represents the heart of production and the internal functioning of an enterprise (Fig. 1.2).

Key Partners:

Reading Figure 1.3 from left to right, we start with the Key Partners. The lemonade stand has indirect business relationships with the farmers' market, suppliers, and a food safety certifier. These are organizations that help the lemonade business but are not a direct part of the company itself.

Key Activities:

This includes the human resource functions of the organization. These are the tasks that employees do to provide a good or service. In this case, they are setting up the lemonade stand, cutting lemons to prepare beverages, adding sweetener, and serving these beverages, while keeping the stand clean and safe.

Key Resources:

This component includes the raw materials that go into the production of the good or service. The lemonade stand uses lemons, sweetener, ice, water, cups, and the stand itself to produce and sell the lemonade.

How these components work together effectively:

In all aspects of production, from resources used to completed activities, these choices impact people, the planet, and the community. This includes decisions about sourcing materials, equipment, hiring, and worker pay. Even Key Partners, choosing who to associate with and how, create places of choice. In these choice points, is where sustainability actions grow, strengthening and expanding the enterprise.

When one looks at sustainability as mindfulness, opportunities on the left side of the BMC emerge. For example, to strengthen community ties (Key Partners), the lemonade stand could partner with a local organization by donating a percentage of sales to the organization. Simultaneously, this organization promotes the lemonade stand to its client base, so sales (and donation amounts) increase.

In the Key Activities section, jobs can be designed to support marginalized community members. This creates meaningful opportunities for them while fostering empathy and loyalty among customers. To strengthen sustainability, the Key Resources might include organic sourcing, which helps protect the environment from harmful agricultural chemicals. It also provides customers with a healthier beverage option.

As mindfulness of sustainability actions increases, engaging in such actions further transforms the lemonade stand. It is no longer simply making and selling lemonade; it is now giving back to the community, providing meaningful jobs, and supporting healthy food production. Thus, through this book, we will not only access a tally sheet of sustainability actions to take but also understand the how and why of a sustainability mindset. This way, anyone can learn the creative thinking techniques that transform enterprises and lives.

As the lemonade stand grows in its transformation of production, the qualities that make the product special expand. This is recorded in the Value Proposition segment of the BMC, which focuses on the benefits the product or service brings to the customer. Initially, the stand produced hand-squeezed, fresh lemonade with locally sourced materials. With the example of added mindfulness, it added community ties, jobs, and organic sourcing to its product value, thus creating a competitive advantage over other beverage stands in the market.

1.1.2 Right-Side Connections

The right side of the BMC includes Customer Segments, Customer Relations, and Channels. It represents the creative, emotional connections of an enterprise and is associated with sales (Fig. 1.2). It looks at how the Value Proposition or competitive advantage connects with customers.

Let's start with the Customer Segments component on the far right; an enterprise's core customer base is defined by current users. The lemonade stand's core customers are primarily the attendees of the farmers' market. This is correlated with the Value Proposition the market brings, which is made up of tourists and locals seeking a connection with area producers and fresh foods. To build more sustainability into the customer side of an enterprise, the Customer Relationships, Channels, and Customer Segments come into play.

For example, the lemonade stand can build on its sustainability efforts on the production side of the BMC, attracting new customers who seek organic beverage options. These customers may also be associated with the organization receiving donations, or may be allies of the disadvantaged workers. Thus, the lemonade stand has expanded its customer base, built on the unique aspects of its product, the Value Proposition. In this way, engaging in a sustainability mindset grows one's enterprise.

TIPS

- Start simple when exploring sustainability in business. Using a familiar example like a lemonade stand helps break down complex ideas.
- Think of the BMC as a brain: The left side (partners, activities, resources) is logical and operational, and the right side (customers, channels, relationships) is creative and emotional.

To continue growing the right side of the BMC using sustainability practices, Channels looks at how customers obtain the product or service. In the lemonade stand example, customers buy the lemonade at the farmers' market. The business is reliant on the farmers' market hours and traffic for all sales. This can be expanded in a sustainable way by including a carbon-free local delivery service using bicycles. Thus, the stand will be able to expand the distribution range of the product.

The Customer Relationships aspect addresses how customers are communicated with after the sale. Currently, there is no outreach provided by the lemonade stand. Stand owners notice that there is usually a short line of customers waiting for their hand-squeezed, individually made lemonades. This presents an opportunity to make a cut-out of an organic lemonade character with the stand's branding that people can stand by for a photo to share on social media. Creating ways for people to engage with your product or service and share their experience is a good way to build relationships.

Taking a larger view of the right side of the BMC with Customer Segments, Channels, and Customer Relationships, a more creative right-brain side of the BMC emerges where intuition, spatial reasoning, artistic abilities, and emotional processing come into play. This is associated with the marketing side of the enterprise. Expanding one's sustainability practices gives enterprises new markets to move into and messaging that sets them apart from the competition.

1.1.3 Financial Foundations

The base of the BMC comprises the Cost Structure and the Revenue Streams components. This represents the financial side of the enterprise and the foundation upon which it is built. Without a strong foundation of balanced costs and earnings, the enterprise will fail.

Cost Structure:

Adding sustainability elements to the lemonade stand gives it economic resilience. Currently, the stand sources its cups, lemons, ice, and sweetener from general wholesalers, paying cash. Employees are also paid a basic cash-based wage. Cash, however, is a liability. Costs of products can change, supplies can run short, the money itself can lose value, and cash is not creating value as it is waiting to be spent.

Relying solely on cash (monetary exchange) is like a farmer mono-cropping his fields. If the farmer grows only one product, for example, corn, and there is a windstorm, the crop is destroyed, and they lose everything. If the farmer had diversified and planted squash and beans along with the corn, the corn may have been lost to the winds, but the other crops would have been fine. The same holds true for an enterprise's finances. By diversifying how goods and services are purchased and paid for, risk is mitigated, new relationships are formed, and the enterprise is stronger.

One more sustainable Cost Structure solution for the stand would be to have a direct relationship with the family producing the organic lemons. Building a relationship with the family enables the lemonade stand to bring the family's story to the booth, show the single source lemons on the trees, talk about the lemon grove, the family, and their organic farming methods.

This creates a competitive advantage for the lemonade stand and attracts new customers who value the farmer relationship. Closer relationships also create a more reliable supply chain. If there were a problem with production or delivery, the lemonade stand already has a strong relationship with the producer, making it easier to work together on solutions. Shorter supply chains save money by having fewer distributors and mark-ups in the process.

Revenue Streams:

Revenue Streams benefit from a sustainability mindset by creating more ways for new customers to access the goods and services. The current lemonade is sold at $4 a cup, which might not be affordable for everyone. A buy-one-give-some model can be created where, for $6, someone can purchase a lemonade for themselves and a half lemonade for someone else. The half lemonade can be presented as a half lemon-shaped yellow Velcro coupon that is attached to a felt lemonade tree attached to the stand.

Customers who do not have the full $4 for their lemonade can take a half lemon coupon to help offset the cost. This option enables customers to feel good about helping others, appealing to people's empathy, and expands access to the lemonade to new customers. This story is good for sharing on social media, building the brand's customer connections.

In summary, using the BMC as a model and adopting a sustainability mindset, there are many clever, win-win ways in which an enterprise can be strengthened to provide benefits to the community, suppliers, and customers. These approaches can also increase the feeling of well-being for workers and help the enterprise become a leader for good, all while continuing to grow.

POINTS TO REMEMBER

- Sustainability is a mindset, not just a checklist. It involves mindful decision-making across all aspects of a business.

- The BMC's nine segments help visualize and build sustainability into every part of a business, from supply chains to customer outreach.

- Embedding sustainability can strengthen community ties, diversify income, and attract customers through meaningful storytelling and value-based branding.

EXERCISE

Complete a BMC for an enterprise you know or are thinking of starting. If it is a large enterprise with multiple products and services, choose a single item to begin exploring first. Keep it simple, like the lemonade stand example. As you progress in this book, you will have opportunities to grow and transform your BMC.

DISCUSSION QUESTIONS

- Sustainability is not easy. It takes extra work. One must have the awareness and desire to expand their way of thinking and implement it into an enterprise. What do you think is the motivation for someone to engage in a more sustainable business practice?

- The BMC divides an enterprise into nine parts. What other enterprise parts exist that are left out? What other business models map the facets of an enterprise? How are these different from the BMC? Looking at these models through a sustainability mindset, what opportunities do you see?

1.2 The Power of Four: 4Ps, 4 Pillars, 4 Lenses

Sustainability is a broad, vague term that can have many different meanings. Being able to discern the different types of sustainability areas and how they can be found and measured is the first step to identifying and building more sustainability into an enterprise. Becoming familiar with sustainability terms and models is also helpful for marketing, talking with investors or pitching, research, and academic study.

The following models: the Four Ps of Sustainability, the Four Pillars of Fair Trade, and the Four Lenses of Sustainability are unique frameworks that capture sustainability's multiple facets. These models can be used individually or together for guidance and impact.

1.2.1 The Four Ps of Sustainability: People, Planet, Profit, Purpose

The Four Ps model is built from the original sustainability model, "The Three Ps: People, Planet and Profit," a framework that evolved from John Elkington's "Triple Bottom Line" in 1997 (Elkington, 1997). The Three Ps provided an important step away from the narrow view practitioners originally had of sustainability, which focused largely on environmental issues. The Elkington's Three Ps was a groundbreaking model, defined as follows:

1. **People (Social):** The impacts of enterprise actions on employees, communities, and society
2. **Planet (Environmental):** The environmental impact of enterprises and their resource usage
3. **Profit (Economic):** Traditional financial returns

Although the Three Ps helped strengthen sustainability practices, there was another aspect that was often overlooked: an intrinsic motivation or "purpose" to operate sustainably. In the following text, we will understand the combined impact of the Three Ps and how it led to the fourth P, "Purpose."

The idea that an enterprise could engage in sustainable practices (often associated with higher costs and inefficiencies) while still maintaining profitability was new and not well understood. In the 1990s, products were marketed for their taste, look, and appeal. There was little awareness of the other side of production, human rights violations, environmental degradation, harmful chemicals, carbon outputs, and waste. The term conscious consumerism had not yet been coined.

Though there were fair-trade and organic options for goods, these items were on the periphery and hard to find. There was little mainstream awareness or demand. E-commerce was just beginning, and search engines like Google were still being developed. It would be another ten years before the first set of Sustainable Development Goals was announced.

A mindset change:

Nevertheless, it was recognized that enterprises play an important role in the future well-being of the planet and its people, and could "do good" while also doing well. Sustainability pioneers demonstrated this in practice. The non-profit organization, California Certified Organic Farmers, defined the concept of "organic" in 1973 and provided the U.S.' first organic farming certifications (California Certified Organic Farmers [CCOF], 2025). Similarly, the Dutch non-profit, Max Havelaar, sold the first certified fair-trade product, Mexican coffee, in 1988 (Max Havelaar, 2007).

Economically, it was considered "irrational" for consumers to pay more for products thoughtfully made (Doane, 2001). It was believed that this type of consumer was an elite subset that could not be scaled to any market significance. Over time, that changed. As certifications became more well-known and new companies chose to follow eco-friendly models, additional goods and services came online. Dr. Bronner's made organic soaps. (Dr. Bronner's, 2025); Equal Exchange produced high-quality chocolates from farmer-owned cooperatives (Equal Exchange, 2025); Ten Thousand Villages used its global church-based networks to source fair-trade handicrafts (Ten Thousand Villages, 2025).

Regulatory and market changes:

The internet grew easier to use with more consumer education being developed. Organizations such as Co-op America, founded by Paul Freundlich in 1982, produced the National Green Pages, a print book of eco-ethical businesses. They also hosted "Green Festivals," which are large regional trade shows where consumers could shop eco-ethical goods (Green America, 2011). Co-op America, now known as Green America, helped to launch now-established sustainability brands such as Clif Bars and Guayakí Yerba Mate in the 1990s.

Consumers proved they were on board. They desired to make a difference with their spending and demanded more choices and better goods. Soon, the Triple Bottom Line approach, measuring success through people, planet, and profit, was seen as a desirable option for all businesses. By 2001, the eco-ethical product category grew by 19% in a single year, being valued at USD 13.8 billion in today's dollars

(Doane, 2001). The growing market value of this category led to businesses with unethical practices joining in, too.

In the 1990s, Nike was cited for the sweatshop production of its sneakers, though by 2008, Nike was the world's largest buyer of organic cotton (Koszewska, 2010). Cosmetic companies in the 1990s tried labeling their products "organic" because they had water as an ingredient, arguing that water was organic. The United States Department of Agriculture (USDA) labeling law had to be adjusted to clarify that water was not an organic ingredient. In other cases, processed foods were labeled 100 percent natural and organic when they had just one small—or no—organic ingredient in them (Doane, 2001). New laws were developed to protect consumers from this type of deceptive marketing known as greenwashing.

Figure 1.4 The Four Ps of Sustainability

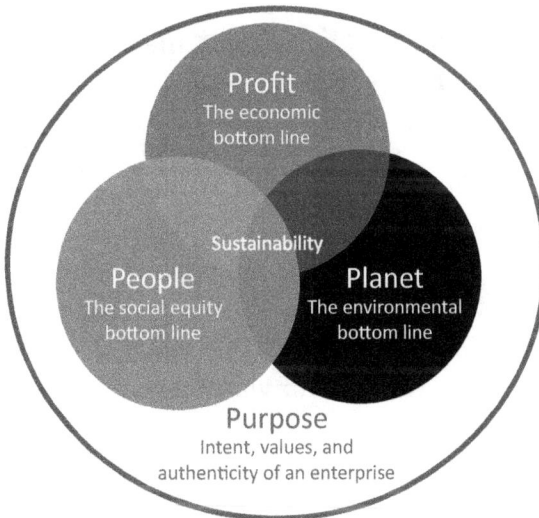

Profit
The economic
bottom line

Sustainability

People
The social equity
bottom line

Planet
The environmental
bottom line

Purpose
Intent, values, and
authenticity of an enterprise

Emergence of the fourth P: Purpose

These scenarios and developments highlighted the need to identify the intent of actions. This is where the fourth P, "Purpose" came in (Fig. 1.4). By emphasizing the intent behind an enterprise's actions, the purpose for them to engage in the Triple Bottom Line (the three Ps), the full extent of their sustainability is revealed.

According to the four Ps, for an enterprise to be truly sustainable, there needs to be a deep belief and desire to do well. There must be an intrinsic motivation to take the extra steps to check supply chains, source safe, clean materials, and minimize waste. The enterprise should also be motivated to reduce non-renewable energy usage and environmental impacts, and pay and treat workers fairly, all while building markets and revenue. Following the four Ps instills a sincere purpose on sustainability actions, building a sustainability mindset, authenticity, and a culture to do good.

1.2.2 The Four Pillars of Fair Trade: Institutions, Consumers, Producers, Government

While the Four Ps focus on the institution, the Four Pillars of Fair Trade take a deeper look into the supply chain and outsourcing. With 66 percent of U.S. businesses outsourcing, it has become a USD $970 billion market (Kumar, 2025; Deloitte, 2019). Outsourced jobs and production often take place in countries with less worker protection, lower wages, and reduced infrastructure for waste management and workplace safety.

Enterprises may either be unaware of the environmental or social injustices in their outsourcing and supply chains, or they may be motivated by low pricing and ease to choose the most economical options. The Four Pillars of Fair Trade discussed in this section help enterprises connect better with their supply chain and outsourcing procedures so they have safe, strong, and reliable relationships.

The Four Pillars of Fair Trade

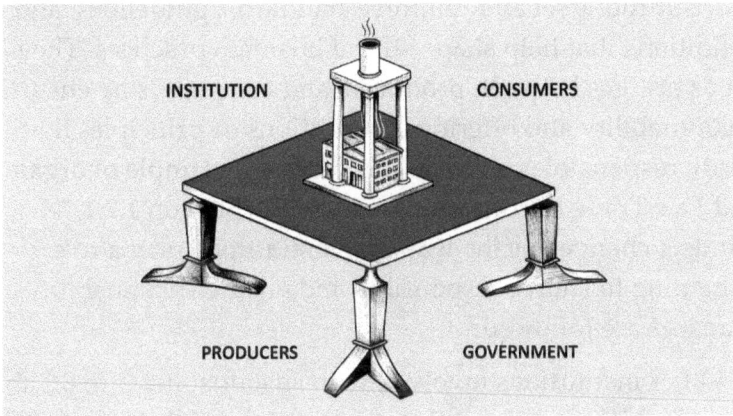

INSTITUTION

CONSUMERS

PRODUCERS

GOVERNMENT

(Stenn, 2013)

The four pillars of fair trade first appear in the book, *The Cultural and Political Intersection of Fair Trade and Justice*, which is a deep study of 20 years of fair trade production (Stenn, 2013). The four pillars are defined as institutions, consumers, producers, and government (Fig. 1.5). The idea of there being pillars is that the enterprise rests atop the four pillars; if all sides are in balance, the enterprise stays steady and strong. If one pillar is out of alignment, it affects the entire organization and can cause a weakness or fall.

1. **Institutions** create and enforce rules and standards, helping connect producers and consumers through certifications that ensure ethical practices.

2. **Consumers** support sustainable businesses by intentionally buying their products and services, providing revenue and validation.

3. **Producers** supply goods and services; businesses can support them with fair pay, long-term contracts, safe workplaces, and community investment.

4. **Governments** shape policies, back local fair trade efforts, and improve infrastructure.

Institutions set and reinforce standards, guidelines, and definitions that help shape ethical business practices. They act as bridges between producers and consumers by ensuring accountability and offering certifications or principles that verify responsible conduct. The previous example of organic and Fair Trade Certifications, covered in Section 1.2.1, "A mindset change," is the way that institutions play a role in helping to source responsibly and ensure sustainability practices are followed.

Other institutions involved with sustainability are B Lab Global which looks at entire organizations and missions; the Forest Stewardship Council (FSC) which ensures sustainable management of forests and timber; and Cradle to Cradle which looks at the waste and recycling aspect of production and produce lifecycle (B Lab, 2025; Forest Stewardship Council, 2025; Cradle to Cradle Products Innovation Institute, 2025). Institutions are an important ally in helping organizations to engage in healthy supply chains and outsourcing.

Consumers play a vital role in supporting sustainability by intentionally purchasing products and services from sustainable businesses. Consumers provide both revenue and validation for business efforts. Their choices are often driven by ethical and environmental concerns or cultural solidarity. They may also be motivated by a desire for high-quality or unique goods, or a commitment to building a better future. Through these conscious buying decisions, consumers not only sustain the economic viability of enterprises but also affirm and encourage their ongoing sustainability practices.

The third pillar, Producers, is at the heart of the fair trade model, providing outsourced services and supply-chain materials. An enterprise becomes responsible for producers' well-being when choosing to conduct business with them. Like any enterprise, producers also need to provide value, or they will not have sales. Because of this, enterprises, as customers, are in a powerful position with producers and can influence how they work.

Getting to know producers includes engaging in transparent, democratic business practices, as well as visiting work sites and extraction and processing facilities. Through reciprocity, enterprises can work to improve producer well-being by paying fair prices, engaging in long-term contracts, ensuring safe work environments, and helping with community and infrastructure development. Taking the time and responsibility to know producers and suppliers builds a closer relationship for the enterprise, ensures it is using eco-ethically sourced materials, and creates new ways of interaction.

Though often less directly involved, governments play a critical role in sustainable development. They influence policy environments, support local fair trade initiatives, and address infrastructure deficits (like roads and regulation). They are also occasionally involved with integrating fair trade principles into trade or development strategies.

When sourcing products and services from other countries, enterprises can help and step in where government support is lacking, especially in marginalized or rural areas. Together, these four pillars, institutions, consumers, producers, and government, form a mutually reinforcing system that sustains outsourcing and supply chain materials.

Each pillar plays a distinct role, and the interaction among them brings about justice, empowerment, and sustainability in global trade. Viewing sustainability through these pillars allows for a multi-perspective understanding.

1.2.3 The Four Lenses of Sustainability: Resources, Health, Policy, Exchange

The Sustainability Lens is composed of four interrelated parts or "lenses" that help individuals and businesses assess and enhance their sustainability efforts (Stenn, 2017). Inspired by Andean indigenous knowledge and global sustainability models such as Permaculture and Solidarity Economy, this lens is both a practical tool and a philosophical approach to sustainable enterprise development (Fig. 1.6).

Figure 1.6   The Sustainability Lens

(Sustainability Lens Game, 2025)

1. **Resources** look at where materials come from and their impact, including energy use, labor, and transport.
2. **Health** focuses on people's well-being, motivation, and sense of community within the enterprise.
3. **Policy** covers fair internal rules and efforts to promote broader social change.
4. **Exchange** deals with how products are shared and sold, aiming to give more power and access to underserved consumers.

Similar to the four pillars' Producers, the Resources lens focuses on where things come from. It goes a bit further than the four pillars in that it examines the origins and impacts of materials, including extraction, energy, and labor. It requires a deep understanding of supply chains, tracing materials back to their original sources, whether petroleum-based, plant-derived, mineral, or animal, and acknowledging everyone involved in their production and handling.

Resources look at the whole carbon and environmental footprint, including transportation, and embrace opposites. For example, taking a Resource perspective, a distinction can be made if recycled materials are sourced from a global supplier hundreds of miles away, heavily produced using local ingredients and a lot of energy, or locally produced but not certified organic.

The next lens, Health, looks closely at the human resource element of an enterprise. It represents the emotional dimension of an enterprise and how sustainability affects well-being, passion, morale, and community cohesion. It includes staff satisfaction and workplace joy, celebration and recognition, and the presence of safe, inclusive environments.

Health has elements of the 4 Ps, People, in it, but goes further to recognize the need to celebrate and look at the workforce as an extension of the local community. This lens bestows the enterprise with a key role in supporting the well-being of the community through the work it creates and resources it uses.

The Policy lens emphasizes action, governance, and engagement. It involves creating equitable internal systems and policies that reflect on outcomes and ethics, and engaging in advocacy and systemic change.

Policy is different from the four pillars' "Government," as in this case, the enterprise is promoting the policies it creates and follows for itself. In this process, it acts as an example for others while also educating consumers and building value. Policies could include incorporating employee voices in decision-making, adjusting pricing for sustainability, or engaging in transparent, participatory management.

Exchange refers to distribution, access, and market power. It reflects economic inclusion and access to goods and services, empowering marginalized consumers and creating diversified pricing. An example of Exchange could be an enterprise raising product prices to ensure worker well-being, then using strategies like bulk buying or barter to maintain accessibility for low-income consumers.

The four quadrants, Resources, Health, Policy, and Exchange, work together as a holistic, reflexive system that allows enterprises to grow sustainably, ethically, and inclusively. Together, these Lenses can be applied to the Business Model Canvas to apply sustainability concepts to each of the nine quadrants.

> **TIPS**
> - Use the Four Ps to articulate your enterprise's *why*—it's especially useful for branding, leadership decisions, and talking to investors who want to know your deeper purpose.
> - When analyzing your supply chain, apply the Four Pillars to evaluate how institutions, consumers, producers, and governments interact—and how your business can engage more ethically.

1.2.4 Summary—The Power of Four: 4Ps, 4 Pillars, 4 Lenses

The Four Ps, Four Pillars, and Four Sustainability Lenses are three distinct but complementary frameworks for understanding and practicing sustainability in enterprise. Each offers a unique angle:

- The Four Ps focus on internal values and purpose.
- The Four Pillars highlight external relationships and systemic roles.
- The Four Sustainability Lenses provide a reflexive, holistic view of sustainability processes.

The Four Ps (People, Planet, Profit, Purpose) emerge from the Triple Bottom Line approach and center the internal intent and values of the enterprise. They ask: *Why* does the organization pursue sustainability, and *how* does sustainability align with its mission and identity? The inclusion of "Purpose" distinguishes this model by emphasizing authenticity and long-term vision, making it particularly useful for branding, leadership, and strategic planning.

In contrast, the Four Pillars of Fair Trade (Institutions, Consumers, Producers, Government) shift attention to the external ecosystem of a business—particularly in outsourced, global supply chains. This model emphasizes balance and interdependence. It highlights the roles and responsibilities of all actors involved, ensuring that sustainability is not pursued in isolation but upheld through relationships, accountability, and justice across systems.

The Four Lenses (Resources, Health, Policy, Exchange) offer a practical and philosophical toolkit rooted in action and reflection. Inspired by indigenous and solidarity economy models, these lenses encourage users to assess sustainability through interconnected domains: environmental impact, human well-being, internal governance, and equitable access. They integrate both internal and external factors, creating a bridge between the introspective focus of the Four Ps and the systemic structure of the Four Pillars.

It's true that these models differ in scope and orientation: the Ps being values-driven, the Pillars system-focused, and the Sustainability Lenses process-based. Yet, they all share a commitment to multi-dimensional, eco-ethical sustainability. They reject simplistic or single-issue approaches in favor of more nuanced, inclusive practices. Used together, their value is magnified.

The Four Ps can guide the *why* of sustainability. The Four Pillars ensure integrity in the *who* of the supply chain. And the Four Sustainability Lenses provide tools for the *how*— enabling daily decision-making and innovation. Together, they offer an actionable map for enterprises navigating sustainability in a global, interconnected world.

As outlined in Table 1.1, by integrating values, systems, and operations, these models allow businesses to move beyond compliance and toward true transformation.

Table 1.1   Comparison of the Three Sustainability Frameworks

Dimension	Four Ps (People, Planet, Profit, Purpose)	Four Pillars (Institutions, Consumers, Producers, Government)	Four Sustainability Lenses (Resources, Health, Policy, Exchange)
Focus area	Internal enterprise values and mission	External stakeholders and supply chain relationships	Holistic systems and processes within and beyond the enterprise
Primary orientation	Why: Purpose-driven sustainability	Who: Key actors in sustainable trade	How: Action, impact, and systems thinking
Core strength	Clarifies ethical intent and business culture	Balances roles and responsibilities in global trade	Enables reflexive practice and practical evaluation
Scope	Enterprise-centric	Ecosystem of trade and governance	Interconnected internal and external sustainability areas
Key concepts	Purpose, value alignment, triple bottom line	Accountability, collaboration, justice	Impact, well-being, access, governance
Applications	Branding, leadership, investor communications	Supply chain transparency, sourcing, policy advocacy	Business operations, decision-making, and impact design

(Continued)

Dimension	Four Ps (People, Planet, Profit, Purpose)	Four Pillars (Institutions, Consumers, Producers, Government)	Four Sustainability Lenses (Resources, Health, Policy, Exchange)
Examples of use	Measuring mission alignment and social purpose	Assessing supply chain equity, fair trade sourcing	Mapping sustainability across the business model canvas
Similar to	Social enterprise mission statements	Fair trade and development frameworks	Systems thinking, permaculture, solidarity economy
Added value when combined	Sets intention and ethical foundation	Builds infrastructure for ethical engagement	Operationalizes sustainability through reflection and design

FUN FACTS

- Sustainability once seemed irrational to investors. In the 1990s, paying more for ethically or organically made products was considered a fringe idea; thus, some economists even called it "irrational." Today, it's a $13.8 billion+ market with mainstream appeal (Market.us, n.d.).

- The first fair trade product, Mexican coffee, was certified and sold in 1988 thanks to a Dutch nonprofit, Max Havelaar—named after a fictional character who stood up for ethical trading (Fairtrade International, 2025).

- Sustainability begins with awareness of choice. The Business Model Canvas reveals that every business decision—who to partner with, what materials to use, how to price products—involves a choice. This chapter encourages mindfulness in these choices as the first step toward embedding sustainability.

- Small enterprises can model big change. Using a simple lemonade stand example demonstrates that even micro-businesses can apply advanced sustainability strategies, such as ethical sourcing, social inclusion, and community investment, offering a scalable model for larger ventures.

- Financial sustainability is about more than money. Diversifying revenue through creative models like barter, story-based branding, or shared value pricing builds long-term resilience and customer trust. It also reduces dependency on unstable cash-only systems.

- Sustainability is a form of innovation. By adopting sustainability practices early, enterprises don't just comply with ethics. They also stand out through unique offerings, purpose-driven storytelling, and stronger emotional connections with customers.

1.2.5 Exercise

Select a product or service you purchased recently. Using the Four Lenses of Sustainability (Resources, Health, Policy, Exchange), evaluate how sustainable the offering is. Where do you see the greatest strengths? Which lens reveals the most significant opportunity for improvement, and what concrete action could the enterprise take to address it?

Solution:

Product: Reusable Stainless Steel Water Bottle

Resources: The bottle is made from stainless steel, a durable material with a long lifespan. Its production requires mining and high-energy processing, but it reduces long-term waste compared to single-use plastic bottles. If responsibly sourced and made with recycled metal, this lens is a strength.

Health: The bottle promotes personal health by reducing exposure to Bisphenol A (BPA) and microplastics from disposable plastic bottles. It also supports well-being by encouraging hydration.

Policy: The brand markets environmental values but provides limited transparency about labor practices or material sourcing. There is little public information about worker treatment or compliance with environmental standards in manufacturing, and an absence of clear certifications.

Exchange: The bottle is sold at a moderate-to-high price point, which may limit access for lower-income consumers. There are limited discount options or pricing alternatives.

Table 1.2	Evaluation chart: Sustainability evaluation of a reusable stainless steel water bottle		
Lens	**Strength or Opportunity?**	**Evaluation**	**Suggested Action**
Resources	Strength	It is durable, reusable, and reduces plastic waste.	Continue using durable materials; explore recycled metal sourcing.

Lens	Strength or Opportunity?	Evaluation	Suggested Action
Health	Strength	Supports user health and sustainable lifestyle habits.	Promote health benefits more actively in marketing.
Policy	Opportunity for Improvement	Needs stronger policy communication and internal governance.	Publish sourcing and labor standards; pursue certifications like B Corp or Fair Trade.
Exchange	Opportunity for Improvement	Needs to improve accessibility and pricing options.	Offer lower-cost models, discounts, or community programs to improve accessibility.

Key strength and opportunity:

The greatest strength is in the Resources lens—durable materials and reduction of waste. The most significant opportunity for improvement is in the Policy lens, particularly in transparency around labor and environmental practices.

Concrete action:

The company could publish a detailed sustainability and sourcing report, including labor conditions, factory audits, and material sourcing practices. It could apply to third-party certifications (e.g., B Corp, Fair Trade manufacturing) to build trust and accountability.

Note: The same exercise can be done for each of the sustainability assessment frameworks that we discussed in this section. We can also explore a comparison of how a product is understood differently within each framework.

In the next section, we will explore the role of entrepreneurs in sustainability and why understanding personal strengths and areas for improvement is essential for building sustainable ventures. While the Business Model Canvas and the sustainability frameworks provide powerful tools for analyzing and designing enterprises, it is ultimately entrepreneurs who bring these concepts to life. Their unique skills, perspectives, and decision-making styles shape how sustainability is implemented in real-world contexts.

By assessing your own entrepreneurial strengths and growth areas, you will be better equipped to leverage opportunities, address challenges, and design ventures that are resilient and impactful. This self-awareness sets the stage for meaningful action. It ensures that sustainability goes beyond a theoretical exercise and becomes a practical reality, driven by the people behind the enterprise.

1.3 Know Your Strengths: Entrepreneurship Self-Assessment

Sustainability in business starts with people, specifically, entrepreneurs who bring unique strengths to building and managing enterprises. However, being an entrepreneur means wearing many different hats. For example, an enterprise demands sales, marketing, customer relations, resource acquisition, production, staffing, administration, and accounting, with each job requiring different skills.

In addition, as an enterprise grows or matures, the required entrepreneurial tasks to run it also evolve. What's more, the agility and excitement of a startup slow down as an enterprise settles into more routine stages. This diversity of roles and evolving demands highlights why entrepreneurship exists on a "spectrum." Different skills and approaches are required at different stages, and no single type of entrepreneur fits every point along the journey. Let's explore this spectrum in greater detail in the following section.

1.3.1 The Entrepreneurship Spectrum

Good organizational skills are needed to keep an enterprise steady and moving forward. Further, innovation is important to push established enterprises forward as competition and change catch up. Sustainability is a disruptor in all such areas of an enterprise, creating new opportunities to change production, sales, partnerships, and also the interpretation of the bottom line.

However, not all entrepreneurs have all the necessary skills for starting and growing a viable enterprise. And no one person can master every aspect of a sustainable venture, whether designing ethical supply chains or reimagining customer relationships. Moreover, people are neurodiverse, meaning they see and understand the world around them differently. Some are creative big picture thinkers, others are more detail-oriented and careful.

Some people move fast, jumping into change and then making adjustments afterwards. Others take their time, analyzing data and testing outcomes before moving forward. Even people who are neurotypical, have a range of natural skills and interests that affect the way in which they approach and engage in different entrepreneurship stages.

This difference in seeing and approaching opportunity is known as the Entrepreneurship Spectrum. Identifying where one falls on the entrepreneurship spectrum helps one better understand their propensity to embrace change, and seek out and try new substantiality practices. The spectrum identifies entrepreneurship strengths and notes where outside talent, consultants, partners, and staff can help balance areas in which the entrepreneur may be weaker.

The entrepreneurship spectrum is also influenced by the fact that some people are neurodivergent, such as those with Attention-Deficit/ Hyperactivity Disorder (ADHD), autism, or dyslexia. They may often possess highly specialized skills in a few specific areas, such as abstract systems thinking, out-of-the-box creative problem-solving, or intense focus. Others, who are neurotypical, may have a broader range of more balanced skills but lack the ability to go deeply into any one attribute. Both experiences are valuable.

1.3.2 Impact of Neurodivergent Traits on Entrepreneurial Strengths and Weaknesses

It is often believed that neurodivergent people make outstanding entrepreneurs because of their distinct ways of thinking and approaching problem-solving. One remarkable case is that of Satoshi Tajiri, the creator of a renowned Japanese media franchise consisting of video games, animated series, and films, *"Pokémon,"* who was diagnosed with autism as a child. Tajiri channeled his intense focus and love for collecting into creating one of the most successful media franchises in history. His unique way of thinking contributed to the innovative mechanics behind *Pokémon* (Eldred-Cohen, 2021).

Another example is that of Paul Orfalea, the founder of Kinko's copy centers, who was so dyslexic that he rarely wrote or read anything (Orfalea & Marsh, 2007). But like many dyslexic people, he had excellent interpersonal skills and was an expert at delegating tasks. By building a strong, autonomous team, which Orfalea calls a family, building deeply personal relationships with vendors, and associating with college campuses, Orfalea became a leader in the photocopy industry.

Richard Branson, the founder of the Virgin Group, attributes his ADHD traits of impulsiveness, risk-taking, creativity, and problem-solving to his company's success (Branson, 2012). What started as a mail-order record business has grown into a multinational venture capital conglomerate. The Virgin Group now owns stakes in a diverse range of businesses across various sectors, from travel and leisure to health and wellness. It also has stakes in music and entertainment, telecoms and media, financial services, and space exploration ventures.

However, while the outwardly expressed neurodivergent traits helped people like Tajiri, Orfalea, and Branson to excel, there were large gaps in their entrepreneurial abilities that needed additional support in order for their ventures to survive. What makes these individuals stand out is the high concentration of strength they show in specific parts of the entrepreneurship spectrum. This strength can be a competitive advantage, but it is often followed by deep weaknesses in other areas.

Tajiri had an obsession with bug collecting and arcade games. This led to his unique ideas for *Pokémon*, but also made him difficult to work with since he was not open to feedback, nor interested in explaining himself; his obsessions locked people out. Orfalea's business can be chaotic without someone keeping track of his actions and writing things down for him. Branson has a hard time with the day-to-day details of running enterprises and hires others for routine management tasks.

1.3.3 The Seven-Stage Framework for ADHD, Neurodiversity, and Entrepreneurship

Not all entrepreneurs are neurodivergent, and not all neurodivergent people are entrepreneurs; though all people share a degree of neurodiversity, and everyone has a degree of entrepreneurship strengths and weaknesses. Professors Lerner, Hunt, and Verheul explored the idea of neurodiversity in entrepreneurs. They developed a Taoist concept of yin and yang to illustrate the double-edged influence that ADHD has across the entrepreneurial lifecycle in the *Dueling Banjos* model (Lerner, Hunt, & Verheul, 2017).

This model offered a pioneering framework for understanding entrepreneurship through the lens of ADHD and neurodiversity. Central to the model were 19 research propositions, which examined how ADHD-related traits, such as impulsivity, hyperfocus, distractibility, and high energy, could alternately support or hinder entrepreneurial performance.

These propositions were not isolated claims; they systematically built toward the development of a seven-stage entrepreneurial lifecycle. Each stage reflected a distinct set of challenges and behaviors, ranging from opportunity identification to innovation and renewal. The 19 propositions served to map how ADHD influenced each of these stages, offering a nuanced view of entrepreneurial fit over time.

The seven stages: Interest, Opportunity Identification, Nascent Behavior, Resource Acquisition, Resource Coordination, Value Capture, and Innovation and Renewal, emerged directly from the authors' effort to organize the propositions into a coherent, longitudinal framework (Fig. 1.7).

Figure 1.7 The Seven Stages of Entrepreneurship

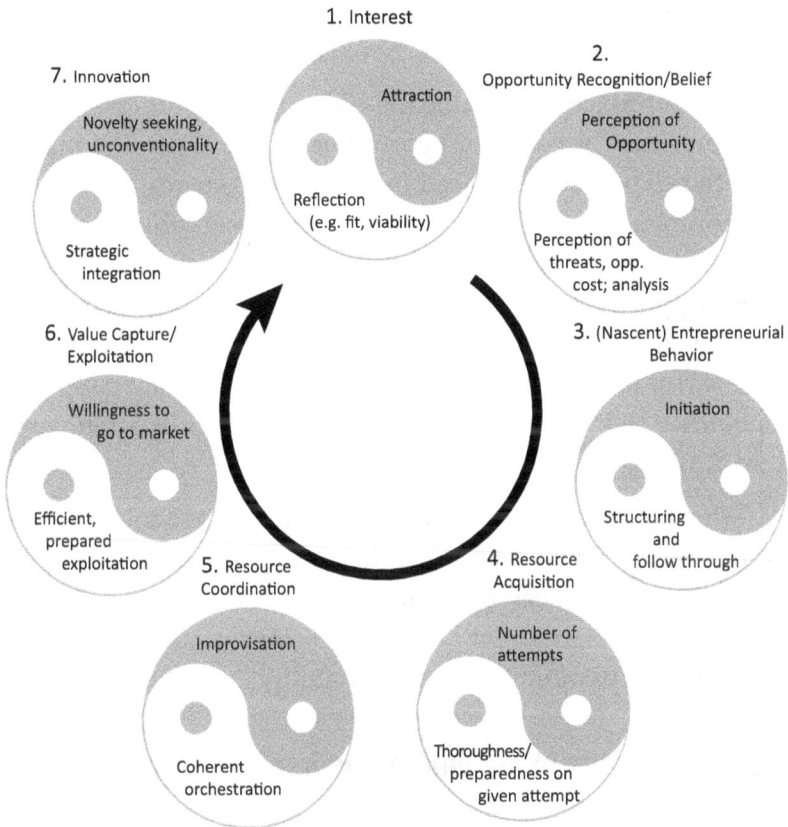

1. Interest
Attraction
Reflection (e.g. fit, viability)

2. Opportunity Recognition/Belief
Perception of Opportunity
Perception of threats, opp. cost; analysis

7. Innovation
Novelty seeking, unconventionality
Strategic integration

3. (Nascent) Entrepreneurial Behavior
Initiation
Structuring and follow through

6. Value Capture/ Exploitation
Willingness to go to market
Efficient, prepared exploitation

4. Resource Acquisition
Number of attempts
Thoroughness/ preparedness on given attempt

5. Resource Coordination
Improvisation
Coherent orchestration

(Lerner, Hunt & Verheul, 2017)

Yin and Yang:

The *Dueling Banjos* model was designed to reflect how individual traits interact dynamically with shifting entrepreneurial demands. The Taoist-inspired duality (yin and yang) shows how the same trait can either be an asset or a liability, depending on context. For example, ADHD-related traits may drive opportunity recognition and creative idea generation in early venture stages (yang / positive), but hinder resource management and operational execution in later stages (yin / negative). Though focused on ADHD, the framework invited broader application to other forms of neurodiversity, such as autism or dyslexia, which may also align differently with each stage of entrepreneurship.

This approach is valuable not only for neurodiverse entrepreneurs but also for neurotypical ones. By following how the 19 propositions lead into the seven stages, entrepreneurs gain a deeper understanding of when their strengths are likely to be most impactful and where they may need support. The model encourages better team design, strategic delegation, and stage-appropriate leadership. It is a powerful tool for improving entrepreneurial outcomes, enhancing resilience, and fostering inclusive innovation across all cognitive profiles.

When aligned thoughtfully, both neurodivergent and neurotypical experiences can enhance entrepreneurship effectiveness. This can be achieved by identifying and anticipating the different hats their journey requires and by thoughtfully planning their sustainability engagement.

1.3.4 Core Traits of the Entrepreneurship Spectrum

The following is a summary of the six core neurological traits that make up the Entrepreneurship Spectrum and how they have a positive or negative impact on enterprise development (Lerner, Hunt, & Verheul, 2017). Learning these traits equips entrepreneurs to harness their natural tendencies while strategically managing limitations. This helps them create a pathway to business success and meaningful, sustainable impact.

1. **Impulsivity and action orientation (Positive trait):**
   - Entrepreneurs often face extreme uncertainty and must make decisions without complete information.

An impulsive or bold action orientation may lead to quicker decision-making and faster market entry.

- Universally, this trait can help entrepreneurs overcome analysis paralysis and act decisively, which is crucial during early-stage venture creation.

2. **Hyperactivity and high energy (Positive trait):**

- High energy levels are essential for handling the exhaustive demands of starting and growing a business.

- All entrepreneurs can benefit from sustained enthusiasm and stamina, especially in fast-paced or competitive industries.

3. **Creativity and divergent thinking (Positive trait):**

- Disinhibition and risk-taking can lead to novel connections and ideas, fueling innovation and non-traditional approaches to problems.

- Entrepreneurs who embrace unconventional thinking are better equipped to disrupt industries and capture new markets.

4. **Distractibility and sensation-seeking (Negative but useful in moderation):**

- Though often seen as negative, mild distractibility can lead to serendipitous discoveries and openness to new opportunities.

- Entrepreneurs benefit from staying alert to emerging trends and enjoy the excitement of pivoting strategies when necessary.

5. **Disorganization and inconsistency (Negative trait):**

- These traits can hinder scaling and long-term operations, making routine tasks and stakeholder communication difficult.

- Recognizing these weaknesses allows entrepreneurs to build complementary teams or structures to compensate (e.g., delegating execution to Chief Operating Officer [COO] roles).

6. **Sensationalism and overconfidence (Mixed trait):**

- Overhyping ideas may mislead others or overlook feasibility, but can also serve as powerful vision-casting when tempered.

- All entrepreneurs must balance bold storytelling with grounded execution to secure buy-in while delivering results.

1.3.5 Self-Assessment Tool for Entrepreneurs

The following is a self-assessment tool based on Lerner, Hunt, and Verheul's work and shared with their permission. The tool helps all entrepreneurs identify their strengths and weaknesses across the seven stages of entrepreneurship development, from the initial idea to innovating within an established enterprise.

It then uses a Strengths, Weaknesses, Opportunities, and Threats (SWOT) analysis to help one plan how to engage with sustainability opportunities. It shows where one can take the lead and become a changemaker within an enterprise. To use it, simply imagine yourself in an entrepreneurial role, either with a business idea you're exploring or within an enterprise you're currently involved in. Let's see how you can do this using three steps.

Step 1: Imagine yourself going through the entrepreneurship journey and using the different skills listed

On the following neurodiverse entrepreneurship assessment, rate yourself on a scale of one to five based on how well you perform or enjoy each skill (Table 1.3). Once you complete the assessment, add up your total points in each stage. This will help to identify the stages of entrepreneurship you excel in. For help interpreting the skills and stages, refer to the appendix at the end of this section (Table 1.5).

Table 1.3 Entrepreneurship Assessment

Skill	Weak 1	Developing 2	Average 3	Strong 4	Excellent 5
1. Interest					
Natural curiosity					
"Can do" attitude					
Problem solver, sees "big picture"					
Business experience					
Creative, "thinks outside the box"					
2. Opportunity identification					
Able to make decisions					
Patient					
Practical minded					
Research-oriented					
Detailed, analytical					
3. Nascent entrepreneurial behavior					
Action-oriented					
Convincing communicator: "seller"					
Team builder, includes others					

(*Continued*)

Skill	Weak 1	Developing 2	Average 3	Strong 4	Excellent 5
Organized, keeps track of things					
Planner: looks ahead, timeline, goals					
Prioritizes and organizes different activities					
Finds and evaluates relevant information					
4. Resource acquisition					
Visionary: sees opportunity					
Clear communicator, negotiator					
Administrative, arranges actions					
Enjoys numbers, budgets, and spreadsheets					
Reliable, follows through					
5. Resource coordination					
Creates policy and procedures					
Sets and enforces standards					
Creative problem solver					
Good at improvising when necessary					
Prepared, has a "plan B"					
6. Value Capture: Strategy					
Comfortable with uncertainty					

Skill	Weak 1	Developing 2	Average 3	Strong 4	Excellent 5
Innovative and intuitive					
Prepared, calculative					
Efficient					
Able to "stay the course"					
7. Innovation and renewal					
Willing to change					
Cautious					
Structured					
Strategic					
Visionary, seeks opportunities					

Overall:

Skill	Weak 1	Developing 2	Average 3	Strong 4	Excellent 5
Prioritizes and organizes different activities.					
Finds and evaluates relevant information.					

(Adapted from Lerner, Hunt, & Verheul, 2017).

Step 2: Review the outcomes of the assessment

Think back to the work you completed on the BMC in Section 1.1 and your new thoughts on sustainability after looking at the three frameworks in Section 1.2. Where do you see your own neurodiversity playing out? What strengths do you bring that can help an enterprise become more sustainable? Where are the weaknesses?

Looking at the strengths, where do you see action points or opportunities emerging? Looking at the weaknesses, where do you see threats or setbacks? Note your findings in a SWOT of your assessment results as shown in Table 1.4.

Table 1.4 SWOT assessment

Strengths	Weaknesses
Opportunities	**Threats**

Step 3: Lastly, review the threats you identified

Think about how you can prevent them or transform them into an opportunity. Do you need partners with different skills? Skill-building classes? A mentor? Make a short implementation plan based on your entrepreneurship skills and your own neurodiversity strengths.

- Satoshi Tajiri, the autistic creator of *Pokémon*, turned his childhood obsession with bug collecting and arcade games into a $100+ billion global franchise that encourages exploration, connection, and creativity, reflecting his unique way of seeing the world.

- Richard Branson started his first business at age 16—despite struggling in school due to ADHD. He credits his impulsiveness and creativity with launching the Virgin Group, now spanning airlines, music, media, and even space travel!

TIPS

- Balance your traits with your team. If you're high on creativity but low on organization, surround yourself with people who thrive on structure to strengthen your enterprise.

- Take the self-assessment honestly. Use it as a planning tool to build your sustainability strategy based on what you do best—and where you need support.

POINTS TO REMEMBER

- **Different minds build stronger enterprises.** Whether one is neurodivergent or neurotypical, understanding how one thinks helps one contribute to sustainability in their own way, through creativity, planning, empathy, or structure.

- **Neurodiversity is a strategic advantage.** Entrepreneurs with autism, ADHD, or dyslexia may have deep, specialized strengths like systems thinking or bold innovation. These traits can drive sustainability solutions, especially when balanced with team support in weaker areas.

- **Self-awareness fuels sustainability leadership.** Using tools like the Entrepreneurship Spectrum and SWOT analysis helps all entrepreneurs, regardless of thinking style, identify where they can lead sustainability efforts and where collaboration is key.

ACTIVITY

Balancing the spectrum: Discuss an example of a business scenario where impulsivity is helpful and one where it could harm progress. How can an entrepreneur mitigate the downside without losing the upside?

Team design: Imagine you scored low on "organized, keeps track of things" but high on "visionary, sees opportunity." What complementary roles or partners would you bring onto your team, and how would you motivate them?

Table 1.5 — Appendix of quick-reference definitions for each self-assessment skill

Skill term	Brief definition (what to look for in yourself)
Natural curiosity	You regularly ask questions, explore unfamiliar topics, and enjoy learning simply for the sake of discovery.
"Can-do" attitude	A tendency to see challenges as solvable and to approach tasks with confidence and optimism.
Interest	
Problem solver/ sees the "big picture"	Connects details to overarching goals, diagnoses root causes, and generates workable solutions.
Business experience	Prior involvement in operating, managing, or launching a venture that gives you practical know-how.
Creative / "thinks outside the box"	Generates novel ideas, combines concepts in new ways, and is comfortable deviating from tradition.
Opportunity Identification	
Able to make decisions	Weighs options efficiently and commits to a choice without excessive delay or second-guessing.
Patient	Willing to wait for information, results, or market adoption without losing focus or motivation.
Practical minded	Prefers realistic, workable approaches over abstract or overly idealistic plans.
Research-oriented	Enjoys gathering data, consulting multiple sources, and verifying facts before acting.
Detailed, analytical	Notices small discrepancies, uses logic and data to draw conclusions, and documents findings thoroughly.
Nascent Entrepreneurial Behavior	
Action-oriented	Quickly moves from planning to doing; takes concrete steps rather than over-deliberating.

(Continued)

Skill term	Brief definition (what to look for in yourself)
Convincing communicator/ "seller"	Persuades others through clear, engaging language and compelling evidence or stories.
Team builder/ includes others	Creates a collaborative atmosphere, delegates meaningfully, and fosters a sense of belonging.
Organized/ keeps track of things	Maintains orderly files, schedules, and systems so that tasks, resources, and deadlines are visible.
Planner (timeline, goals)	Sets specific milestones, assigns deadlines, and maps activities to larger objectives.
Prioritizes and organizes different activities	Ranks tasks by importance and urgency, allocating attention and resources accordingly.
Finds and evaluates relevant information	Locates credible data, compares sources, and extracts insights that inform decisions.
Resource acquisition	
Visionary/ sees opportunity	Spots unmet needs or emerging trends and imagines ventures or solutions before others do.
Clear communicator, negotiator	Expresses ideas plainly, listens actively, and reaches agreements that satisfy multiple parties.
Administrative/ arranges actions	Sets up structures, schedules, and workflows that coordinate people and resources smoothly.
Enjoys numbers, budgets and spreadsheets	Comfortable analyzing financial data, creating budgets, and using spreadsheet tools.
Reliable/ follows through	Delivers on promises consistently and meets commitments without repeated reminders.
Resource Coordination	
Creates policy and procedures	Formalizes processes in written guidelines to ensure consistency and accountability.
Sets and enforces standards	Defines quality or performance benchmarks and monitors adherence across the team.
Creative problem solver	Produces inventive fixes when standard methods fail or constraints are tight.
Good at improvising when necessary	Adapts on the fly, using available resources to handle unexpected situations.
Prepared/ has a "plan B"	Anticipates possible setbacks and outlines alternative courses of action in advance.

Skill term	Brief definition (what to look for in yourself)
Value Capture—Strategy	
Comfortable with uncertainty	Makes decisions and proceeds despite incomplete information or ambiguous outcomes.
Innovative and intuitive	Generates original ideas and trusts well-honed instincts when data are limited.
Prepared, calculating	Ensures that plans move methodically, assessing risks and returns before committing resources.
Efficient	Completes tasks using the least time, effort, or cost without sacrificing quality.
Able to "stay the course"	Remains committed to a strategy long enough for it to bear fruit, resisting impulsive pivots.
Innovation and renewal	
Willing to change	Open to revising methods, products, or goals when new evidence or environments demand it.
Cautious	Proceeds carefully, checking assumptions, and limiting exposure to unnecessary risk.
Structured	Prefers clear frameworks, routines, and hierarchies to guide work and decision-making.
Strategic	Aligns short-term actions with long-term objectives, weighing competitive positioning.
Visionary, seeks opportunities	Continuously scans for new possibilities to innovate, reposition, or expand the venture.
Overall	
Prioritizes and organizes different activities	Sorts tasks by importance and urgency, then sequences them into a clear schedule so time, people, and resources are used efficiently.
Finds and evaluates relevant information	Quickly locates credible data or sources, judges their reliability and usefulness, and extracts key insights to guide decisions.

1.4 Alphabet Soup: The SDGs and the BMC

It is often said that entrepreneurs, not politicians or governments, will lead us to a more just and sustainable future through their innovation, creativity, and agility. This is a lot of responsibility for the entrepreneur who is set on trying to meet customer needs and solve problems while generating revenue. It can be overwhelming. Where to begin and what to do are common questions faced by entrepreneurs and professionals curious about helping with sustainable development.

Sustainability frameworks from Section 1.2 help to identify places where sustainability can be built into the supply chain, community relations, and employees, but they do not address specific actions. The Sustainable Development Goals (SDGs), developed and evolving over the past 40 years, give specific actions, meaning, measurement, and accountability to the broad idea of sustainability.

1.4.1 Origin of the MDGs and SDGs

The notion of SDGs originated in the 1990s when there was a growing awareness of the need for a global sustainability plan, as evidence of environmental degradation, growing inequalities, and abuses of unfettered industrialization became more obvious (United Nations, 1992). There was also an awareness of the new millennium, the year 2000 arriving soon, with people thinking about what the next century would look like. Global summits were held and ideas shared.

The first global conversation about sustainability took place in 1992, at the Rio Earth Summit held in Brazil and hosted by the United Nations Conference on the Human Environment (UNCHE) (United Nations, 1992). The UNCHE had spent the past 20 years studying and defining sustainable development. This summit marked the beginning of global discussions on sustainable development, emphasizing the need for environmental protection and economic development. Attended by more than 178 countries, it gave leaders and organizations a place to meet, talk, share impacts, and insights.

The success of this summit led to the organization of the 2000 Millennium Summit in New York, the largest gathering of heads of state and governments of all time (United Nations, 2000). Here, the eight Millennium Development Goals (MDGs) emerged, quantifiable actions focused on reducing extreme poverty, to be achieved by all countries by the year 2015 (Fig. 1.8).

Figure 1.8 The Millennium Development Goals

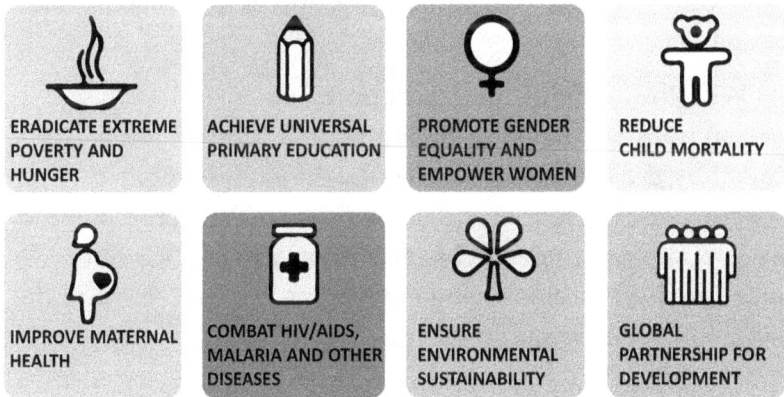

ERADICATE EXTREME POVERTY AND HUNGER

ACHIEVE UNIVERSAL PRIMARY EDUCATION

PROMOTE GENDER EQUALITY AND EMPOWER WOMEN

REDUCE CHILD MORTALITY

IMPROVE MATERNAL HEALTH

COMBAT HIV/AIDS, MALARIA AND OTHER DISEASES

ENSURE ENVIRONMENTAL SUSTAINABILITY

GLOBAL PARTNERSHIP FOR DEVELOPMENT

(MDG Monitor, 2025)

MDGs were as follows:

1. Eradicate extreme poverty and hunger
2. Achieve universal primary education
3. Promote gender equality and empower women
4. Reduce child mortality
5. Improve maternal health
6. Combat HIV/ AIDS, malaria, and other diseases

7. Ensure environmental sustainability

8. Establish a global partnership for development

The MDGs created actions and initiatives, building a new demand for socially focused enterprises that measured success in poverty reduction, rather than revenue generated. This led to the emergence of the social enterprise as a valued entity, an organization that can do good for others, while managing a balanced budget and creating an impact for stakeholders. Many were non-profit organizations that sourced funding from government, grants, and foundations. They operated in the same space as private enterprises, providing jobs and transforming resources to meet customer needs.

With the 2015 deadline fast approaching, and MDGs not on track to be met, in 2012, a second Rio Summit was called by the United Nations (UN), the Rio +20 (United Nations, 2012). Here, it was acknowledged that an economic development plan needed to accompany the MDGs with more goals to meet growing environmental concerns and the need for an economic structure.

Less developed nations were suffering the effects of climate change, spurred on by more developed nations with cars, factories, airplanes, and many carbon-producing activities. Less developed nations did not have the resources to manage the new climate-driven droughts, sea rise, floods, and natural disasters they were facing. They banded together, asking for help and resources. In addition, it was recognized that industry and civil society had a role in contributing to sustainable development. Incentives and goals were needed to create places for all actors; thus 17 Sustainable Development Goals and the term green economy emerged.

By 2015, the 17 new SDGs were defined and agreed upon with the objective of meeting urgent social, economic, and environmental challenges facing the world (United Nations, 2015) (Fig. 1.9).

Figure 1.9 Sustainable Development Goals

(United Nations, 2015)

SDGs included the original eight goals, plus nine new ones focused on the environment, energy, and enterprise. 193 member states endorsed the SDGs, committing to meet these new goals by 2030 with a multifaceted coalition of civil society, private and public enterprises, church groups, community organizations, and government agencies. The 17 SDGs are as follows:

1. **No Poverty:** End poverty in all its forms everywhere.
2. **Zero Hunger:** End hunger, achieve food security, improve nutrition, and promote sustainable agriculture.
3. **Good Health and Well-being:** Ensure healthy lives and promote well-being for all at all ages.

4. **Quality Education:** Ensure inclusive and equitable quality education and promote lifelong learning opportunities for all.

5. **Gender Equality:** Achieve gender equality and empower all women and girls.

6. **Clean Water and Sanitation:** Ensure availability and sustainable management of water and sanitation for all.

7. **Affordable and Clean Energy:** Ensure access to affordable, reliable, sustainable, and modern energy for all.

8. **Decent Work and Economic Growth:** Promote sustained, inclusive, and sustainable economic growth, full and productive employment, and decent work for all.

9. **Industry, Innovation and Infrastructure:** Build resilient infrastructure, promote inclusive and sustainable industrialization, and foster innovation.

10. **Reduced Inequality:** Reduce inequality within and among countries.

11. **Sustainable Cities and Communities:** Make cities and human settlements inclusive, safe, resilient, and sustainable.

12. **Responsible Consumption and Production:** Ensure sustainable consumption and production patterns.

13. **Climate Action:** Take urgent action to combat climate change and its impacts.

14. **Life Below Water:** Conserve and sustainably use the oceans, seas, and marine resources for sustainable development.

15. **Life on Land:** Protect, restore, and promote sustainable use of terrestrial ecosystems, manage forests sustainably, combat desertification, and halt biodiversity loss.

16. **Peace, Justice and Strong Institutions:** Promote peaceful and inclusive societies, provide access to justice for all, and build effective, accountable institutions.

17. **Partnerships for the Goals:** Strengthen the means of implementation and revitalize the global partnership for sustainable development.

Again, the world is not on track to meet these goals, with setbacks from the COVID pandemic and an escalation of wars and climate-related disasters. The United Nations Development Program (UNDP), which manages the goals, reported in 2025 that goal acquisition was at a 35-year low with growing inequality and global turmoil, making the sluggish progress seem even more difficult to turn around (UNDP, 2025).

This takes us back to the opening statement of this unit, where more responsibility is being put on the industry, with its agility, innovation, and creativity, to find a better way forward. This is a favorable time for entrepreneurs to be thinking about sustainability because it ties in with the larger global agenda of meeting SDGs.

1.4.2 How the BMC Supports Entrepreneurs in Meeting SDGs

For entrepreneurs who want to seize opportunities to help the world meet its goals while creating good for others and growing markets, the Business Model Canvas (BMC) is a good place to start. Using the BMC, places where the SDGs can be applied emerge. This creates positive action steps towards realizing the goals; it also helps expand into new markets and build stronger customer, supplier, and community relations.

When the SDGs become design constraints inside the BMC, they reveal unmet needs, lower long-run costs, and differentiate the brand. Entrepreneurs who treat these constraints as innovation briefs often discover new revenue lines and stronger impact narratives that the market will pay for. Table 1.6 presents an example of how SDGs can be addressed in different parts of the BMC, with new innovations and opportunities arising.

Table 1.6 **The SDGs Applied to the BMC**

BMC component	Relevant SDGs	Opportunities for business	Winning combinations (SDGs)
Customer Segments	1, 4, 10	Target underserved markets with inclusive products/ services.	Solar kits for off-grid communities (1, 7, 10)
Value Propositions	3, 7, 12	Offer sustainable, health-conscious, or circular solutions.	Biodegradable packaging for organic food (3, 12)
Channels	9, 11	Use digital and sustainable logistics to broaden access.	E-learning platforms in rural areas (4, 9)
Customer Relationships	5, 16, 17	Build ethical, inclusive, transparent relationships.	Women entrepreneur networks (5, 17)
Revenue Streams	1, 7, 8	Create inclusive economic models and recurring revenue from sustainable services.	Pay-as-you-go clean energy (1, 7, 8)
Key Resources	5, 6, 8, 15	Invest in sustainable materials and fair labor.	Sustainable textiles and fair labor (8, 12, 15)
Key Partnerships	13, 17	Partner with NGOs, governments, and ethical suppliers.	Public-private clean water project (6, 17)
Key Activities	2, 3, 9, 13	Innovate with sustainability and social impact in operations.	Climate-smart agtech (2, 9, 13)
Cost Structure	12, 13	Reduce waste and emissions to cut long-term costs.	Circular manufacturing (9, 12)

HIGHLIGHTS

- The Millennium Development Goals (MDGs) were the first global sustainability targets, launched in 2000, and aimed to reduce extreme poverty by 2015.

- With the SDG progress stalling, the UN is increasingly looking to enterprises, not just governments, to carry the load. Entrepreneurs with bold ideas and agile models are being called upon to do what diplomacy can't: invent our way to a more just, sustainable future.

- The 4 Ps of Sustainability guide responsible business. People, Planet, Profit, and Purpose help businesses make decisions that balance social, environmental, and economic impact.

- The Dueling Banjos method maps entrepreneurial growth. This reflective tool outlines seven stages of entrepreneurship, helping individuals assess strengths and areas for development.

- Even small enterprises can align with the UN's Sustainable Development Goals. Local businesses like lemonade stands can support global goals such as decent work, reduced inequality, and responsible consumption.

TIPS

- Start with your BMC. Look at each component and identify where a specific SDG aligns—this reveals new impact-driven business opportunities.

- Don't aim to address all 17 SDGs at once. Choose 2–3 that most closely match your mission, operations, or customer needs to focus your impact.

> **POINTS TO REMEMBER**
> - The SDGs provide measurable, actionable goals for making sustainability tangible across sectors—including entrepreneurship.
> - Entrepreneurs can help fill the gap left by governments by using innovation and agility to meet global challenges.
> - Treating SDGs as design constraints in your business model can lead to innovation, market differentiation, and new revenue streams.

1.4.3 Exercise

Applying the Sustainable Development Goals to the BMC transforms the way a business creates, delivers, and captures value. It helps identify opportunities for impact, risk mitigation, market advantage, and alignment with stakeholder values.

Look at how the SDGs intersect with each of your BMC components and where you can find specific opportunities and winning combinations. Add at least three SDGs to your BMC and explain how you will build them into your enterprise and the value they will be creating.

> **ACTIVITY**
>
> How can an entrepreneur leverage the Business Model Canvas to prioritize and integrate at least three SDGs in ways that create both social impact and competitive advantage? Provide real or hypothetical examples to illustrate your ideas.

Table 1.7	Enterprises using BMC-based sustainability strategies		
Real-world company	Key SDGs	Canvas integration	Competitive edge
M-KOPA (East Africa)	(7) Affordable & Clean Energy, (1) No Poverty, (10) Reduced Inequality	• *Value Proposition & Revenue Streams:* pay-as-you-go solar and smartphones. • *Customer Segments:* low-income, off-grid living with no utilities such as electricity or water. • *Key Partnerships:* Safaricom/ M-Pesa for mobile-based money transfer, payments, and micro-financing service.	1 million+ households electrified and 2.1 Mt CO_2 avoided; an effective and integrated data-driven banking and credit pipeline that rivals can't match (M-KOPA, n.d.)
Patagonia	(12) Responsible Consumption, (13) Climate Action, (15) Life on Land	• *Key Resources:* regenerative-organic cotton, recycled polyester. • *Key Activities:* take-back old, used garments to repair and (sometimes) resell them. • *Value Proposition:* "buy less, buy better."	Premium pricing plus cult-level loyalty; product returns < 1% in outdoor-apparel average (Patagonia, n.d.)
Interface Carpets	(9) Industry Innovation, (12) Responsible Consumption, (13) Climate Action	• *Cost Structure & Key Activities:* ReEntry take-back loop*, carbon-negative tiles. • *Channels:* university procurement contracts with embodied-carbon specifications.	Wins long-term flooring contracts and positions as first mover in carbon-neutral interiors (Interface, n.d.).

Note: A "ReEntry take-back loop" allows businesses to extend the lifespan of materials and products, divert waste from landfills, and potentially reduce production costs. This is done by recovering used products from consumers, bringing them back into the production process, and repurposing them to recapture value. This process is also known as "reverse logistics."

In this chapter, we explored the foundations of sustainability, not as a buzzword or rigid checklist, but as a flexible, creative mindset that can transform any enterprise, from a simple lemonade stand to a multinational business. Using the Business Model Canvas as a foundational tool, we learned how to integrate sustainability into every segment of an enterprise: from sourcing materials and choosing community partners to shaping marketing strategies and managing financial flows.

Next, we were introduced to three powerful sustainability frameworks, the Four Ps, Four Pillars, and Four Lenses, which serve as essential tools for navigating sustainability in a strategic and meaningful way. Through a neurodiverse entrepreneurship self-assessment, we reflected on our personal strengths and challenges, recognizing how different ways of thinking can support sustainable leadership.

We also examined the SDGs to identify measurable, actionable targets that align our enterprises with global needs. These goals helped us see where our businesses can generate meaningful impact while also uncovering new opportunities for growth and innovation.

By the end of the chapter, we are now equipped with the language, tools, and mindset needed to begin reshaping our enterprises, regardless of size or stage, to thrive economically, socially, and environmentally. This chapter calls on us, as current or future entrepreneurs, to be bold, curious, and inclusive in our pursuit of both purpose and profit.

Chapter Summary

- The Business Model Canvas is a practical, creative platform for building sustainability into any business.

- The Four Ps (People, Planet, Profit, Purpose), Four Pillars (Institutions, Consumers, Producers, Government), and Four Lenses (Resources, Health, Policy, Exchange) offer diverse frameworks for thinking about sustainability.

- Every entrepreneur is unique—understanding one's strengths through the entrepreneurship spectrum helps build better teams and smarter strategies.

- The UN's 17 Sustainable Development Goals provide a globally supported blueprint for actionable, measurable change—and a competitive advantage for value-driven enterprises.

- Sustainability starts small, but scales fast—with the right mindset, tools, and intention, any business can help build a better future.

QUIZ

1. **What is the main purpose of using a lemonade stand to teach sustainability concepts?**
   a. It's an example of a large, global company.
   b. It avoids the need for financial planning.
   c. It simplifies the application of sustainability principles to business.
   d. It focuses only on customer service.

2. **What part of the Business Model Canvas includes the activities employees perform to deliver the product?**
   a. Key Resources
   b. Key Partnerships
   c. Key Activities
   d. Customer Relationships

3. **What benefit does partnering directly with an organic lemon producer provide?**
   a. Makes pricing more difficult to control
   b. Increases distributor markups
   c. Builds a reliable supply chain and strengthens the brand story
   d. Reduces product uniqueness

4. **Which of the following is *not* one of the original three Ps of the Triple Bottom Line?**
   a. People
   b. Planet
   c. Policy
   d. Profit

5. In the Four-P model, the fourth P stands for
   _____.
   a. Prosperity
   b. Possibility
   c. Patience
   d. Purpose

6. According to Doane (2001), by how much did the
   eco-ethical product category grow in 2001?
   a. 45%
   b. 19%
   c. 10%, it shrank.
   d. 0%, it stayed the same.

7. How many Sustainable Development Goals were
   adopted by the UN in 2015?
   a. 8
   b. 10
   c. 15
   d. 17

8. What key shift occurred between the MDGs and the
   SDGs?
   a. The MDGs focused more on climate change than
      the SDGs.
   b. The SDGs replaced governments with private
      companies.
   c. The SDGs expanded to include economic and
      environmental goals alongside poverty reduction.
   d. The SDGs eliminated the need for global
      partnerships.

9. **How can entrepreneurs use the BMC to engage with the SDGs?**

   a. By using it to apply for grants from the UN
   b. By treating SDGs as innovation briefs within each business component
   c. By only focusing on environmental goals
   d. By outsourcing all sustainability efforts

10. **Which pair of neurological traits is identified as generally *positive* for early-stage venture creation?**

    a. Disorganization and overconfidence
    b. Impulsivity and action orientation
    c. Distractibility and sensation-seeking
    d. Hyperactivity and disorganization

Answer Key

1 – c	2 – c	3 – c	4 – c	5 – d
6 – b	7 – d	8 – c	9 – b	10 – b

CHAPTER 2

Customers and Channels

Key Learning Objectives

- Integrate sustainability as a strategic lens, pulling from concepts of Suma Qamana.
- Map customers and design solutions to align customer needs with enterprise value.
- Discover scalable growth found in micro-customer segments that can form new markets.
- Case Study: Grove Collaborative—a company that mastered customer connection and sustainable delivery.

Chapter One introduced sustainability frameworks and the SDGs, creating a common focus that demonstrated the growing need for entrepreneurs to seek and implement new sustainability solutions. In Chapter Two, we look at concrete methods through which sustainability can be realized in enterprises, specifically in the emotional, creative side of the BMC, where relationships are built.

As entrepreneurs strive to meet the challenges of climate change, inequality, and market volatility, a new language of sustainability is emerging, one that goes beyond carbon footprints and compliance. This is a language rooted in wisdom, traditions, ecological systems, and cooperative economics. In this chapter, we look at ways the Suma Qamana sustainability paradigm is used with the Right-Side Connections of the BMC, focusing on customer segments, customer relations, and channels (Fig. 2.1).

Collaborating with customers, keeping them included, informed, and giving them ways to participate in sustainability efforts creates a loyal, dedicated client base. Such a client base can evangelize brands and expand their reach to new customer areas.

Figure 2.1 Focus on Right-Side Connections

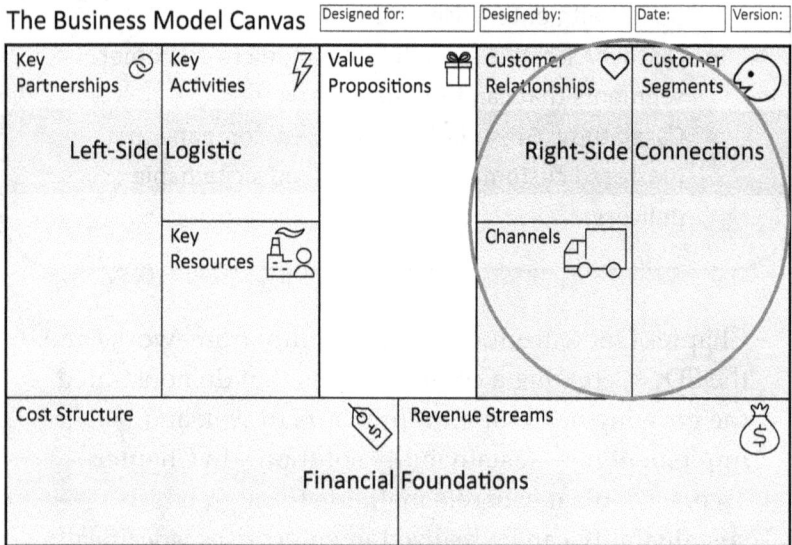

The Business Model Canvas

Key Partnerships	Key Activities	Value Propositions	Customer Relationships	Customer Segments
Left-Side Logistic			Right-Side Connections	
	Key Resources		Channels	
Cost Structure		Revenue Streams		
		Financial Foundations		

(Adapted from the Strategyzer BMC Model, 2025)

In all, four powerful sustainability paradigms, Suma Qamana, Circles of Sustainability, Permaculture, and the Solidarity Economy, offer a comprehensive framework for all areas of the BMC, building businesses that are not only profitable but also regenerative, inclusive, and resilient. This chapter begins with Suma Qamana. Using the Suma Qamana framework with right-side connections, consumer relations are strengthened and expanded.

2.1 Suma Qamana: Indigenous Wisdom

Rooted in Andean indigenous knowledge, Suma Qamana means "living well" in the Quechua language (Fernández, 2009). Living well means living in harmony with oneself, others, and nature. It is the opposite of the Western model of "living better" through competition and accumulation.

Suma Qamana addresses sustainability from a humanistic, place-based perspective. It emphasizes equilibrium, mutual care, and interdependence (Choquehuanca Céspedes, 2023). The Andean nations of Bolivia and Ecuador adopted Suma Qamana ideologies into their constitutions in 2008 and 2009, creating a collective understanding of development, where the good life (living well) is intertwined with the well-being of the community and the environment.

The four core values of Suma Qamana, *Ruray: Doing, Munay: Love, Yachay: Knowledge, and Ushay: Power,* are often presented as a cross, the *Chakrana,* with each side balancing the other (Fig. 2.2).

Figure 2.2	Suma Qamana Chakrana, Symbolizing Balance

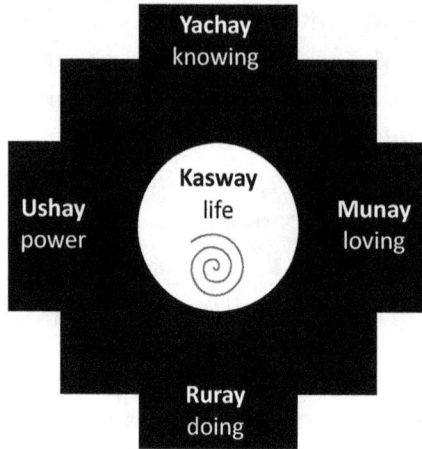

(Stenn, 2025)

Kasway, or life, shown at the center of the *Chakrana*, is presented as a spiral, which is different from the Western linear way of viewing time. With time as a spiral, it becomes dimensional and personally connected. The future is forever becoming the present, moving on to be the past. With *Kasway*, life moves through us instead of us moving along its timeline. It connects us directly to our past ancestors and future to-be family. This makes decision-making more personal and inclusive. We can pull knowledge from our ancestors while also thinking of how our decisions impact our future generations.

Under Suma Qamana, the earth is given the same protections as a human, which means people damaging the earth can face criminal charges. This creates importance, requiring transparency and accountability, for enterprises' environmental impacts. Suma Qamana also requires extensive community representation and collective decision-making, giving voices and leadership power to the marginalized. This has resulted in the emergence of new resilient economies as impoverished, marginalized people are brought into the mainstream with their indigenous ways being valued and followed.

Among Bolivia's Aymara and Quechua people, indigenous ways include a deeper connection to places, seasons, spirituality, and ceremony, amplifying *Munay* (love). Researchers found this indigenous *Munay* connection to be key in building the trust and resilience needed to get through economically challenging times (Stenn, 2022).

Increased regulation by Suma Qamana slowed down industrial growth, making it more costly, while improving the quality and value of what was created. This shift led to a new mindset allowing enterprises to check their use of (and benefit from) products generated from the earth's resources (Artaraz, Calestani, & Trueba, 2021). Overall, Suma Qamana expanded people's access to enterprise and generated a more mindful approach towards resource use while building income and opening new markets.

In entrepreneurship, Suma Qamana inspires businesses to think deeply about the future, value emotional engagement, be thoughtful about resource use, and seek equitable exchange (Stenn, 2019). It encourages founders to ask, "Does our business improve life for all, employees, customers, communities, and the earth?" This may seem a bit altruistic and off topic for an enterprise, but when a community's needs are met and employees feel cared for with resources used in a balanced way, more meaningful production, creativity, and innovation ensue with everyone benefiting, especially the enterprises (Stenn, 2014).

Suma Qamana values can be applied to enterprises to uncover new areas of connection and growth, which strengthen relationships, improve products, and build sales (Table 2.1).

Table 2.1	Application of Suma Qamana principles in enterprise

Term	Definition	How it is applied to an enterprise
Yachay, Knowledge	Deep understanding and wisdom. Recognizes interconnectedness and values diverse worldviews.	• Encourages supply chain transparency and ethical sourcing • Enhances strategic planning with systems thinking • Builds resilience through continuous learning and adaptation
Munay, Love	Emotional, spiritual, and relational well-being. Emphasizes love, willpower, intuition, and balance.	• Builds a positive workplace culture and strong morale • Encourages employee and customer loyalty through celebration and gratitude • Fosters community through empathy and connection
Ruray, Doing	Inspired action and creation. Encourages productivity, innovation, and embracing failure as part of learning.	• Fuels experimentation and creativity in product/ service development • Supports inclusive policies and governance • Embraces opposites (e.g., failure and success) to create stronger systems
Ushay, Power	Dynamic energy, decision-making, and transformation. Reflective use of power and influence in relationships.	• Strengthens stakeholder negotiations and supply chains • Promotes ethical leadership and decision-making • Encourages transparent and mutual value exchange

2.1.1 Suma Qamana in Action: Sustainable Development in Intag, Ecuador

The principles of Suma Qamana are key in understanding customers, but also in looking at one's enterprise as a balanced whole. In Ecuador's Intag Valley, rural indigenous communities became a powerful example of how Sumak Kawsay, the Ecuadorian version of Suma Qamana: Living Well, can guide sustainable development.

Rather than measuring progress by immediate gain or foreign investment, the people of Intag redefined development through the principles of Sumak Kawsay, focused on community health *(Munay)*, environmental harmony and clean water *(Yachay)*, local self-determination *(Ushay)*, and action *(Ruray)*. This led to more balanced, long-term solutions that turned communities and their assets into multiple, sustainable enterprises.

The community wins in safeguarding biodiversity:

The Intag Valley region is a vast cloud forest and biodiversity hotspot home to 15,000 people and a significant portion of the world's plant species with high levels of bird, mammal, and amphibian diversity, including endangered frog species (Zorilla, 2014). It is also a region rich in copper, which is buried deep under the tropical jungles and rivers. In the 1990s, the Ecuadorian government opened the region to mining. This triggered a decades-long struggle between local communities and international mining companies, backed at times by state institutions. Communities feared mining would bring deforestation, water contamination with heavy metals and harmful chemicals, biodiversity loss, and forced displacement.

In 2008, Ecuador adopted a new constitution based on the principles of Sumak Kawsay, which recognized the "rights of nature." Using these new protections, Intag residents, led by women like Cenaida Gauchagmida, organized to oppose mining projects, not simply to reject economic activity, but to choose a different development path, one rooted in Sumak Kawsay (Harvey, 2023). Their approach focused on regenerative, community-based enterprises, including:

- Shade-grown coffee cooperatives that protect forest biodiversity while providing fair income to farmers.

- Ecotourism initiatives that welcome visitors to experience the region's rich biodiversity and local culture without harming the land.

- Agroecological farming and forest conservation programs, many supported by women-led organizations and youth groups.

The communities achieved a major legal victory in 2023 when Ecuador's Constitutional Court upheld the rights of nature and community consent, halting a mining project in Intag due to threats to ecosystems and human well-being (Deleny, 2024). This ruling marked a significant win for both the rights of nature (enshrined in Ecuador's 2008 Constitution) and Sumak Kawsay as a lived political and legal framework.

Sumak Kawsay gave Intag a framework in which to organize, envision, and act on economic development alternatives that made sense for the community and environment. By rejecting short-term resource extraction in favor of long-term ecological and social well-being, Intag demonstrated how Sumak Kawsay can help in the development of practical, grassroots models of sustainable development. Their example offers a real-world path toward a more just and balanced relationship between humans, nature, and economic development.

2.1.2 The Sustainable Leadership Pyramid

Looking at contemporary sustainability practices, the Sustainable Leadership Pyramid (Fig. 2.3) has some of the elements that Suma Qamana addresses, presented in an organizational framework. The Pyramid highlights the 23 practices necessary to support sustainable development and cohesion within an enterprise. (Bergsteiner, 2020).

Figure 2.3 **The Sustainable Leadership Pyramid**

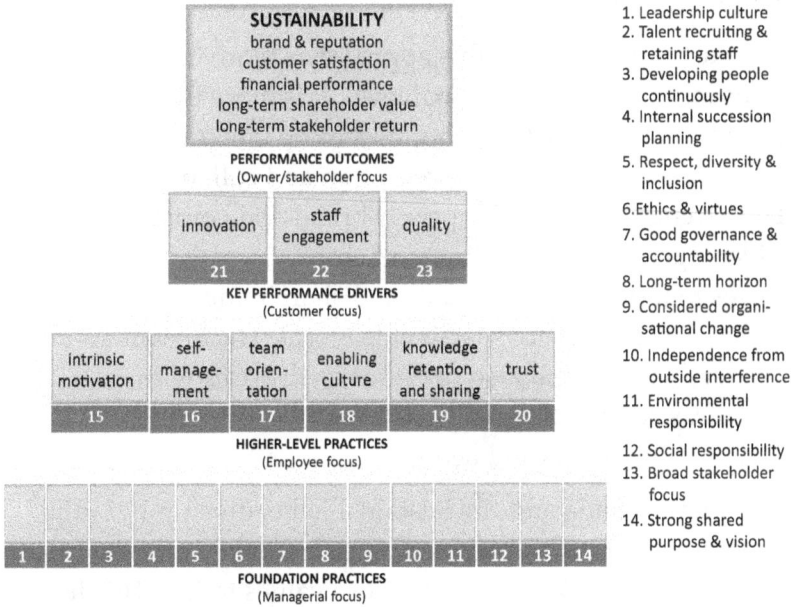

(John, 2025)

The elements in the Sustainable Leadership Pyramid use a honeybee philosophy of leadership, with a more collaborative, building approach (Avery & Bergsteiner, 2010). This is similar to how a beehive operates, with many different bee types working together in complex ways, performing multiple jobs, including pollination and producing an abundance of resources.

This contrasts with the more common locust leadership approach, where efficiency and speed are valued. Such an approach results in over-harvested resources and bare fields, similar to the massive destruction that locust swarms cause. Organizational honey bee behavior leads to more sustainable and profitable long-term results, while locust behavior can bring short-term profit but ultimately diminish the organization. The 23 practices of the pyramid drive genuinely sustainable leadership.

Like Suma Qamana, this approach is more inwardly focused, at the organizational level. It is more than a triple bottom line approach and builds a more integrated, cohesive employee-management coordination and collaboration. This strengthens the enterprise's brand and competitive advantage, creates customer and employee satisfaction, drives long-term performance and shareholder value, and makes for a more sustainable world. The Sustainable Leadership Pyramid also provides enterprises with the infrastructure, language, and metrics for setting sustainability goals and actions.

Suma Qamana and the Sustainable Leadership Pyramid foster transparent and aligned organizational values, empowering workers to bring those values to life. This leads to a more integrated and creative organization. Such an environment of integrated creativity becomes contagious, especially when consumers are invited to participate, highlighting the role of Right-side Connectors. Section 2.2 will explore this dynamic in greater detail.

FUN FACTS

- The shape used to represent the four principles of Suma Qamana is the *Chakrana*, or Andean Cross, a symbol in Andean cosmology, which the Western world calls the Southern Cross constellation.

- The *Chakrana* represents the balance between opposites and the interconnectedness of all life. Its symbolism in Suma Qamana reflects the holistic, relational nature of this sustainability model.

- The Suma Qamana framework intentionally embraces opposites (e.g., wealth and scarcity, tradition and innovation) as necessary to maintain harmony and balance. This is referred to as *qhari-warmi*, male-female (Stenn, 2018).

TIPS

- Use the Suma Qamana principles to engage underserved customer segments by recognizing and including their lived experiences.

- Celebrate customers and community milestones to build emotional connection and strengthen brand loyalty. *Munay* in action!

POINTS TO REMEMBER

- Suma Qamana focuses on harmony with self, others, and nature as a foundation for sustainable living and business.

- Each of the four principles, *Munay, Yachay, Ushay, and Ruray*, plays a distinct role in sustainable enterprise, influencing how businesses relate to people and resources.

- "Ruray" is the driver. It ensures that ideas of love, knowledge, and power are translated into meaningful, practical action.

DISCUSSION QUESTIONS

- In what ways might applying Suma Qamana challenge traditional business strategies focused on growth and competition?

- How can small businesses integrate *Munay* (love and health) into their customer relationships without compromising efficiency or professionalism?

2.2 Customer Mapping: Build Value + Relieve Pain

Customer mapping is the process of defining customer segments by matching their needs to enterprise values. Using a customer-centric approach, entrepreneurs shift their mindset from selling features to delivering benefits, building stronger customer connections.

In today's marketplace, successful ventures are not built by simply having a good product or service; they are built by deeply understanding and serving the needs, desires, and values of specific customer segments. This section offers entrepreneurs a hands-on roadmap for building value-driven, customer-centered, and scalable enterprises.

The Business Model Canvas provides three areas in which to connect with and understand customers (Osterwalder & Pigneur, 2010):

1. **Channels:** How the customer receives a good or service.
2. **Customer Relationship:** How the customer is included in an enterprise, good, or service.
3. **Customer Segments:** Who, specifically, the customer is: demographically and psychographically.

Depending on the Customer Segment, Channels, and Customer Relationships can change.

Let's understand how these components create a sustainability connection between the customer and the enterprise.

2.2.1 Role of "Channels" and "Customer Relationships" in Building Value and Relieving Pain

Customers are presented as "segments" in the BMC because they are unique individuals, with specific characteristics, needs, and pains that, when understood on a more individual level, go deeper and help to form enduring relations.

Strategyzer, the company behind the BMC, developed Value Mapping as a shared thinking method to align customer needs and pains with the benefits and properties of the product/ service (Value Proposition) (Osterwalder, Pigneur, Bernarda, & Smith, 2014). The premise is that customers seek goods or services that serve a purpose for them, whether to relieve a pain by fixing something that is a problem or produce a gain by achieving a benefit for themselves.

A customer's decision to engage with a product or service depends on the cost—whether in time, money, or both—and the perceived value it offers. The commitment of the customer to continue to engage with the product or service is based on the relationship they feel towards the enterprise and the value the product or service continues to bring to them.

Attracting and maintaining customers and building long-term relationships are key to developing sustainable enterprises. Often, enterprises miss the mark with customer connections because they are too focused on their goods or services' production or features, and not focused enough on the specific customer needs. It is easy to become enamored with sustainability work, engaging in principles of Suma Qamana, building radical connections with the community, and gaining internal organizational support. However, customers may initially not see, understand, or value this work. If customers are valuing this work, it may be for reasons different than your own.

For example, one might not know if a customer is buying a product because of its social mission or because of its ability to perform. One may ask, are organic carrots desirable to a customer because they taste good, are more nutritious and safe, or because they support healthier environments through their farming methods? Knowing customer motivation towards buying sustainable products enables the enterprise to form a more solid relationship with its customers. Thereafter, inviting customers to get involved with sustainability efforts can turn customers into valuable brand advocates. In this way, engaging in sustainability practices with an eye towards Right-Side Connections (Customer Segments, Customer Relationships, and Channels) strengthens the overall BMC.

2.2.2 The Value Proposition Canvas

The Value Proposition Canvas (VPC) takes a deep look at the alignment of the Customer Segment and the Value Proposition. The Value Proposition is the overall definition of a product or service, including its unique selling points and competitive advantage. It reflects an enterprise's sustainability efforts and, like a kaleidoscope, shifts depending on which Customer Segment is looking at it, from which angle.

The VPC, as illustrated in Figure 2.4, creates a way to match customer needs and pains to product pain relievers and gain creators, aligning the kaleidoscope to best appeal to that particular customer. Looking at one's product or service from the customer perspective creates new ways to develop and present it, finding the right fit.

Figure 2.4 **Value Proposition Canvas**

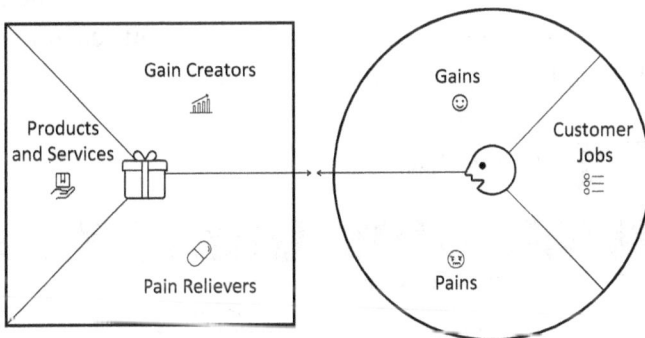

Gain Creators

Products and Services

Pain Relievers

Gains

Customer Jobs

Pains

(Strategyzer, n.d.)

The VPC provides an uncomplicated space to find customer-centric ways to express your product or service in a way that speaks directly to your customer. This helps to find out if your idea makes a real difference for a real person. As the customer changes, so does the value you bring to them, so a single enterprise has multiple VPCs. Here is how a VPC is built:

Step 1: Customer Profile

Who are you really serving? Whether you're serving students, families, community members, or global consumers, every customer is trying to accomplish something. These are their "Customer Jobs," as represented on the right side of the VPC (Fig. 2.4).

Customer jobs can be functional, supportive, social, or personal (Table 2.2). Functional and supportive jobs are more outward-focused and value getting things done, while social and personal jobs are more inward-focused with an emotional value. Job importance changes with customers based on their situation.

Sometimes multiple jobs can be accomplished at once, with a product or service filling both a task and an emotional job. Sustainability practices often appeal to both the task and emotional side of a Customer Job. When choosing which job to address, focus on what really matters to your customer — what keeps them up at night or helps them feel fulfilled.

Table 2.2	Customer Jobs	
Focus	**Customer Jobs**	**Examples**
Outward	Functional Jobs: basic tasks	Commuting, cooking, shopping, paying bills
Outward	Supporting Jobs: background tasks	Evaluating products, maintaining tools, helping others, learning

(Continued)

Focus	Customer Jobs	Examples
Internal	Social Jobs: image or perception	Looking professional, feeling accepted, fitting in
Internal	Personal Jobs: emotional	Feeling secure, proud, relaxed, unique

Step 2A: Pain Relievers

What is the problem? Once a Customer Job is selected, the pains associated with it need to be explored. Pain is something that frustrates, annoys, or limits a customer. It comes in different forms and is measured by intensity (how painful it is) and frequency (how often it happens). The following are some basic pain points and definitions:

- Undesired outcomes: bad results, poor experiences
- Problems or characteristics: lack of time, money, or energy
- Obstacles: barriers that slow them down
- Risks: worries about failure or harm

The best match for a good or service is one that addresses multiple Customer Jobs and resolves frequent, intense pain.

Example:

An example of this would be a 28-year-old intern who is walking to an important job interview when their shoe breaks again (Undesired Outcome). They need a new shoe (Functional Job) that looks good (Supporting Job), and they need it now (high intensity). This tends to happen often for this individual (high frequency).

If they were to find a strongly made, fashionable shoe that is guaranteed to last, right now, they would be a very loyal and grateful customer. Unless your enterprise is a good quality shoe store located exactly at the place where the person's shoe broke, you might not get that immediate sale and resolve that pain.

However, you can identify that customer as a customer niche or a specific category. A customer profile could be made of a customer who walks a lot and needs good-looking, reliable, professional shoes that hold up. They can be appealed to through social media marketing, retail, e-commerce, or other means. Understanding customer pain in relation to their specific job needs enables an enterprise to effectively connect products and services to specific customers, thus speaking their language.

Step 2B: Gain Creators

Customer Jobs can be addressed from a pain (needs-based) or gain (wants-based) perspective. The path chosen depends on the Customer Job. The Gain Creators stage emphasizes growing the positive. Gains are the outcomes a customer wants. They are measured by relevance, how important it is to them, and impact, how much it helps. The following are some basic gains and definitions:

- Required: must-haves
- Expected: standard features
- Desired: nice-to-haves
- Unexpected: delightful surprises

The best match for a good or service is one that addresses multiple Customer Jobs and creates relevant and impactful gains.

Example:

An example in this case could be a 35-year-old parent who wants to earn an MBA (to gain education, prestige, and new career opportunities) but does not have the time or money to do so. A Gain Creator could be an online learning program with financing. The program would meet the customer's wants by providing the required education degree, expected online accessibility, and desired financing. Something unexpected could be a bonus scholarship offered.

Each of these examples is from a very singular customer segment, a customer from a specific demographic, age, and place in their career. Building a customer segment-focused VPC lets one directly and accurately address the pains and gains of that individual, winning them on board as a new client. Working in this manner of deeply understanding the individual customer and gaining targeted wins lets enterprises build stronger and longer-lasting customer relationships.

Delivering what matters through a VPC Fit:

If you look carefully at the VPC (Fig. 2.4), the customer on the right has an arrow going towards the products and services on the left, and the products and services have an arrow going towards the customers on the right. This is a reminder that customer mapping happens from both sides, the customer perspective, but also from the good or service.

Once one knows their customer, it's time to look more closely at the goods and services. Pain Relievers reduce or remove a specific pain your customer has. For example, a product or service could save time, lower costs, or reduce anxiety. Gain Creators help customers achieve their desired outcomes. Maybe a product or service makes life easier, more fun, or more meaningful.

Products and services often have many pain relievers and gain creators. The key is to accurately match these to the needs and pains the customer has, taking the customer-centric focus first—avoiding the common mistakes of value mapping. Common mistakes are being too vague, broad, or abstract. The key is to focus on solving real, specific problems for each customer.

A VPC Fit happens when the value map (what is offered) directly addresses the customer profile (what they need). A "fit" is when your value is matched to customer needs and wants. An enterprise does not have to be everything to everyone. It just needs to deliver real value to the right people. From the customer's perspective, fit means your offering solves an important problem for them or helps them get a job done better than before.

Introducing the Five-Stage Design-Thinking Cycle:

In the context of bridging the VPC and your product or service—finding your fit, the design-thinking cycle offers a powerful five-stage framework: Empathize, Define, Ideate, Prototype, and Test (Dam, 2025).

Stage 1: First, Empathize roots the process in a deep understanding of your customer's needs, pains, and gains— precisely the inputs on the Canvas's customer segment side.

Stage 2: Next, Define helps you frame those needs as a clear, human-centered problem, guiding your value proposition to address them directly.

Stage 3: During Ideate, you generate creative ways your product or service could be structured, mapping to the value map side of the Canvas, including products and services, pain relievers, and gain creators.

Stage 4: Then, Prototype enables you to quickly materialize and visualize parts of your product or service for the customer, aligning proposed solutions with elements of the value map.

Stage 5: Finally, the Test validates whether your value proposition resonates with real customers, allowing you to refine the Canvas and the product. This iterative, non-linear cycle ensures that both the VPC and the design of your offering evolve in close alignment with customer realities, creating a tight fit (Dam, 2025).

In sustainability work, an enterprise is not just trying to do good; it is trying to solve the right problem for the right people in the right way. That means understanding the customer deeply. The VPC helps one avoid assumptions while testing ideas and designing products and services that connect. The five-stage framework creates a place to verify solutions. Together, these practices create a strong foundation for long-term social, environmental, and financial value. Sustainability starts with empathy. To be successful, know your customer, design with care, and keep checking for fit.

2.2.3 Customer Mapping in Action: "Who Gives a Crap" Found the Right Fit

Let's explore how a company can build a customer-centric approach to toilet paper. "Who Gives a Crap (WGAC)" used the power of customer mapping, aligning customer needs and pains with the values of the enterprise, to grow from a crowd-sourced start-up in 2012 to a $52 million eco-friendly enterprise with 18% annual growth and global sales (Tissue Online, 2024).

Instead of focusing on features like "softness" or "quilted comfort," WGAC designed its customer relationships around benefits like environmental sustainability, humor, convenience, and global sanitation support. Thus, they built deep connections with ethically minded, eco-conscious consumers.

Listening closely with Slack and Daasity:

Using tools such as Slack and Daasity, WGAC determined their core customer segment, which included socially conscious, millennial, and Gen Z consumers who wanted everyday products to reflect their values of sustainability, health, and equity. These segments were concerned with convenience and transparency, and enjoyed a quirky brand identity with humor (Sentence, 2020).

Slack gave WGAC a live channel for customer feedback across teams. Staff members regularly shared and reviewed real-time customer messages, reactions, and suggestions, ensuring that customer sentiment is integrated into decisions around product development, messaging, and service (Cain, 2022).

Daasity, an e-commerce analytics platform, offered WGAC a more data-driven approach, enabling WGAC to analyze customer behavior, sales trends, and retention patterns. Daasity helped WGAC to identify key customer segments and their purchasing behavior, track which messages or campaigns resonate most, and understand pain points related to shipping, pricing, and product use. This integration of qualitative (Slack) and quantitative (Daasity) tools enhanced WGAC's ability to perform precise customer mapping and build loyalty through responsiveness.

Turning customers into advocates:

Understanding customer needs allowed WGAC to frame its value proposition not just around the product, but around the emotional and social value customers experience by participating in a mission-driven purchase. WGAC used direct-sales Channels, selling primarily through its Direct-to-Consumer (D2C) online platform. Here, it offered subscriptions for recurring deliveries, thus eliminating friction and supporting customer convenience.

In its Customer Relationships, WGAC engaged customers with a cheeky brand voice, transparent impact reporting, and humorous updates via email and social media. Its tone built relatability, while its mission built trust, turning toilet paper customers into lifelong brand advocates.

Through customer mapping and a values-driven approach, WGAC scaled globally while staying closely connected to customer motivation. Their use of Slack and Daasity ensured a feedback loop that continuously aligned operations with customer desires, helping them build value, relieve pain, and maintain a highly loyal customer base.

FUN FACTS

- Strategyzer's Value Proposition Canvas was downloaded more than one million times within its first year online, making it one of the fastest-adopted business-design tools ever (Strategyzer, n.d.).

- The Business Model Canvas was born via a large-scale kickstarter-style campaign, which included 470 corporate "co-creators" in 45 countries who, in 2008 to 2009, paid to try out and give feedback on early prototypes of the BMC and VPC. What emerged was the version being used today. (Osterwalder & Pigneur, 2010).

- In CB Insights' 2024 analysis of 400 startup post-mortems, 42% of founders said their venture failed because there was "no market need"—precisely the pitfall customer mapping is designed to prevent (TST Technology, 2024).

TIPS

- When mapping pains and gains, interview at least three customers from each micro-segment to avoid designing for a single outlier.
- Revisit your Value Proposition Canvas every quarter; rapid iterations keep customer "Fit" aligned with shifting market conditions.

POINTS TO REMEMBER

- A true "Fit" exists only when a product's top pain relievers or gain creators match a customer's most intense pains or most desired gains.
- The five-step design-thinking cycle is iterative; teams should expect to loop back from *test* to *ideate* repeatedly.
- Embedding sustainability in the value proposition can create both functional benefits (cost, durability) and emotional gains (impact, pride).

2.2.4 The Value Proposition Canvas Activity

Let's make it real. Follow these steps to build your own VPC:

1. Print out your VPC or grab a large sheet of paper.
2. Get some sticky notes (post-its or tape and note paper).
3. Identify one Customer Segment. The exercise in Section 2.2.5, *Identifying Your Target Audience (The Avatar)*, provides guidance on creating customer avatars, icons, or figures—visual representations of a typical customer. Think about your customer in this segment. Ask yourself open-ended questions about jobs, pains, and gains they may have or want.

4. Create 12 sticky notes for each job, pain, and gain. Post them on the Customer Profile part of the VPC. Take a photo.

5. Remove the sticky notes. Number and rank them by importance. Take a second photo of your ranked responses.

6. Pause and reflect. Ask, did you make common mistakes such as being too general or confusing yourself with your customer?

7. Verify your hunches with real customers. Ask at least 20 people in your customer group about their needs and gains in relation to your product or service. Asking "why" helps to dig deeper into each job. For example, ask, "Why does it matter?" When they respond, ask "Why?" again. Continue the process for 3 more times for a total of 5 "why" drill downs. This helps to really dig deep into people's rationale and assumptions, creating a better understanding.

8. Repeat the exercise again for steps three to five, this time looking at a specific product or service (offering).

Often, enterprises have multiple offerings. Each offering can have its own VPC and customer base. It is not unusual to have dozens of very specific customer profiles linked to specific products and services within a single enterprise. Ask what your product or service does. Identify 12 gain creators and 12 pain relievers. Rank these in order of importance.

Compare the findings of your product or service to the pains and gains of your customer. Look where there are matches and where there are not. For instance, are there things your customer needs that you can further address? Or features you have that are not so important to the customer. See how you can better align your value proposition to your customer. Reflect on your findings. Think about who your top five customer types are and what their specific gains and pains are.

DISCUSSION QUESTIONS

- How might you adjust your pain-relief or gain-creation strategy when expanding from an early-adopter niche to a mainstream segment?

- In what ways could a company accidentally undermine sustainability gains while scaling, and how could customer mapping help prevent that?

2.2.5 Exercise: Identifying Your Target Audience (The Avatar)

Create your customer "avatar" icon or figure representing a particular person. Here's how:

Step 1: Your Avatar's Demographic

1. Where do they live?
2. What's their name?
3. What do they look like? (Height, weight, hair, clothing, shoes, etc.)
4. How old are they?
5. What do they do for a living?
6. What do they do for fun?
7. What are their political views?
8. Where do they go on vacation?
9. What kind of personality do they have? (Fiery, friendly, uptight, panicky, reserved, shy, etc.)

Step 2: Your Avatar's Needs/ Problems

1. What's their biggest desire? For example, you're a nutritionist and their biggest desire is to lose weight healthily.

2. What's their biggest problem? For example, they have a family of five to feed and a very busy job—there's little time for healthy meals.

3. How can you help them right now? For example, you could give them a free meal plan for a week, so that they know you really know your stuff, and then you can help more in the future.

Step 3: Where to Find Your Avatar

1. What websites/ blogs do they read?
2. What forums do they visit?
3. What pages do they "like" on Facebook and social media?
4. What're they googling for information on?
5. Do they listen to podcasts/ watch YouTube videos? (If so, on what?)
6. What events do they attend?
7. Is it easy to find their contact information, and will they find it acceptable to be called/ emailed?

Step 4: Visual

Create a visual image of your avatar. What do they look like? You can use a magazine, photos, or drawings.

2.3 Building Sustainability

While many enterprises desire to be more sustainable, they often struggle with implementation due to a lack of expertise, resources, or a clear understanding of how to integrate sustainability into their core operations (Elkington, 2020).

Here is the first step in overcoming those challenges, starting with the customer. Using powerful paradigms such as Suma Qamana, new connections are formed between customers and enterprises, thus increasing the enterprise's long-term impact. Section 2.1 took a deep dive into the concept of Suma Qamana and showed how it changes the way one envisions the enterprise and government by building more connections, intention, and love into an enterprise.

Section 2.2 demonstrated how to take a deep look at the customer, empathizing with who they are, and how they understand products and services based on their own pains and gains. Viewing an enterprise through the eyes of the customer enables a product or service's value propositions to better align with customer pains and gains.

In this section, we see how Suma Qamana concepts are applied to the BMC Customer Relationships, Customer Segments, and Channels. This creates concrete new ways to implement sustainability concepts into an enterprise, along with strengthening customer connections and expanding customer categories.

Applying a Suma Qamana concept to a BMC section is a three-step process that involves imagination and creativity. It can be done alone, but is often best done with a small group of three to seven stakeholders. Stakeholders include partners, employees, and customers—someone with a vested interest in the business. Having multiple viewpoints encourages more out-of-the-box thinking and brings new ideas to the table.

Step 1: Brainstorm current applications

Start with Suma Qamana and brainstorm the ways it is currently expressed in an enterprise. For example:

- Where does *Yachay* (knowledge) already exist? Perhaps it is in the enterprises' recipes, formulas, designs, and technology.

- Where is *Munay* (love, or celebrations, and care for others)? Perhaps it is in the annual meeting awards ceremony, health care benefits, or personal days off.

- Where is *Ushay* (power)? Perhaps it is in the management structure, customer feedback loops, or seniority.

- *Ruray* (doing) is usually easy to find. For instance, it may be the production process, the doing, that most enterprises are very good at.

When the ideas of Suma Qamana are applied to everyday operations, they become easier to understand and expand upon.

Step 2: Applying Suma Qamana

Look at the BMC customer areas studied and mapped out in Section 2.2 with the new insight into the customer experience, pains, and gains. Adjust this mapping with input from your brainstorming team. Then, individually think of how Suma Qamana ideas can be expanded to improve the overall customer experience and build sustainability in the enterprise.

Share ideas and add them to the BMC. Table 2.3 is an example of applying Suma Qamana thinking to the lemonade stand at the farmers' market. Note how multiple aspects of Suma Qamana can address the same area.

Table 2.3	Applying Suma Qamana thinking to customer-focused BMC elements	

BMC element	Suma Qamana principle	How it builds sustainability at a lemonade stand
Customer Relationships	Munay (Love & Health)	• Build heartfelt, joyful experiences with customers. • Offer a free sample with a smile. • Remember returning customers' names. • Celebrate "Lemonade Loyalty Days" with small treats or thank-you notes. • Create a sense of belonging and emotional engagement.
	Ruray (Doing)	• Actively co-create the customer experience. Let kids decorate cups or help stir the lemonade. • Invite feedback on flavors. • These small actions empower participation and deepen connection.
Customer Segments	Yachay (Knowledge/ Resources)	• Recognize diverse customer needs. Offer traditional, sugar-free, and herbal lemonade for health-conscious shoppers, children, and elders. • Learn from your community to meet everyone's needs meaningfully.
	Ruray (Doing)	• Take the initiative to include underserved segments. Create a "pay-what-you-can" jar or offer student discounts. • Innovate new flavors based on community suggestions. These actions turn inclusivity into practice.

BMC element	Suma Qamana principle	How it builds sustainability at a lemonade stand
Channels	*Ushay* (Power/ Exchange)	• Share power with your customers by using ethical, local ingredients and telling their story. • Use refillable cups or compostable packaging. • Sell through word-of-mouth, hand-decorated signs, or a shared stand with other vendors.
	Ruray (Doing)	• Experiment with new ways of delivery, like a "flavor of the day" wheel customers can spin. • Offer a texting list for flavor updates. • These hands-on ideas activate imagination and make delivery systems engaging and memorable.

Step 3: Aligning Suma Qamana with SDGs

Enter the SDGs. To further integrate sustainability into core operations, match Suma Qamana actions to the Sustainable Development Goals. Next, think about what other goals can be addressed with a few more Suma Qamana-SDG-inspired actions (outlined in Table 2.4).

Tying in the SDG language with an enterprise helps to connect to a larger community of sustainability innovators, build clear messaging to customers, and teach consumers to learn and engage with the SDGs. The United Nations' SDG Academy is a good resource for people wanting to learn and do more with the SDGs (SDG Academy, 2025).

Table 2.4	Broadening sustainability with SDGs and Suma Qamana-insipired actions			
BMC element	Suma Qamana principle	How it builds sustainability (as seen in Table 2.3)	Relevant SDGs	New goal-based actions (Inspired by SDGs and Suma Qamana)
Customer Relationships	*Munay* (Love & Health)	• Build heartfelt, joyful experiences with customers. • Offer a free sample with a smile. • Remember returning customers' names. • Celebrate "Lemonade Loyalty Days" with small treats or thank-you notes. • Create a sense of belonging and emotional engagement.	SDG 3: Good Health & Well-being SDG 11: Sustainable Cities & Communities	• Start a "Kindness Jar" where customers leave notes for the next visitor. • Host community lemonade story-sharing days. • Offer fruit-infused lemonade that promotes wellness and hydration.

BMC element	Suma Qamana principle	How it builds sustainability (as seen in Table 2.3)	Relevant SDGs	New goal-based actions (Inspired by SDGs and Suma Qamana)
Customer Relationships	*Ruray* (Doing)	• Actively co-create the customer experience. Let kids decorate cups or help stir the lemonade. • Invite feedback on flavors.	SDG 4: Quality Education SDG 10: Reduced Inequalities	• Conduct a mini-workshop on how to make lemonade from scratch. • Display kids' art on the stand ("Lemonade Gallery"). • Rotate stand management with youth volunteers from diverse backgrounds.
Customer Segments	*Yachay* (Knowledge)	• Recognize diverse customer needs. Offer traditional, sugar-free, and herbal lemonade for health-conscious shoppers, children, and elders. • Learn from your community to meet everyone's needs meaningfully.	SDG 2: Zero Hunger SDG 3: Good Health & Well-being SDG 10: Reduced Inequalities	• Include locally-grown herbs (mint, hibiscus) for new health-focused options. • Offer allergy-friendly alternatives. • Create a "Lemonade for All" menu with visual symbols for ingredients.

(Continued)

BMC element	Suma Qamana principle	How it builds sustainability (as seen in Table 2.3)	Relevant SDGs	New goal-based actions (Inspired by SDGs and Suma Qamana)
Customer Segments	*Ruray* (Doing)	• Take the initiative to include underserved segments. Create a "pay-what-you-can" jar or offer student discounts. • Innovate new flavors based on community suggestions.	SDG 1: No Poverty SDG 5: Gender Equality SDG 12: Responsible Consumption	• Partner with local shelters or food banks for "Community Lemonade Fridays." • Add a "Flavor by Grandma" series featuring elder-recommended recipes. • Run lemonade labs with youth groups for social innovation.
Channels	*Ushay* (Power, Exchange)	• Share power with your customers by using ethical, local ingredients and telling their story. • Use refillable cups or compostable packaging. • Sell through word-of-mouth, hand-decorated signs, or a shared stand with other vendors.	SDG 12: Responsible Consumption SDG 13: Climate Action SDG 8: Decent Work & Economic Growth	• Set up a "zero waste" zone with upcycled tableware. • Highlight your local lemon supplier on the stand with photos or stories. • Collaborate with other kid vendors for shared exposure and support.

BMC element	Suma Qamana principle	How it builds sustainability (as seen in Table 2.3)	Relevant SDGs	New goal-based actions (Inspired by SDGs and Suma Qamana)
Channels	*Ruray* (Doing)	• Experiment with new ways of delivery, like a "flavor of the day" wheel that customers can spin. • Offer a texting list for flavor updates.	SDG 9: Industry, Innovation & Infrastructure SDG 17: Partnerships for the Goals	• Use Quick Response (QR) codes for digital punch cards or sustainability tips. • Include solar-powered juicers to demonstrate renewable energy. • Collaborate with a local farm to run a pop-up lemonade stand during harvest days.

2.3.1 How Suma Qamana Principles and Customer Mapping Helped Siklus Adapt to a New Sales Environment and Stay Sustainable

Siklus is an Indonesian retail startup founded in April 2020 with a $2.2 million investment grant. It provided refill options for fast-moving consumer goods (FMCGs), personal care, and home products aimed at addressing plastic-waste challenges in Jakarta. The company offered a sustainable alternative to single-use packaging through refillable containers (Kurniawan & Sunitiyoso, 2024).

By 2022, the company had a successful refill subscription model. They picked up used personal care, food, and cleaning supply containers from customers in Jakarta, refilled them with products from the FMCG manufacturers' facilities, and delivered them back to the customer, all within one day. Customers saved money in the process, often paying 20% less than new retail product costs, and manufacturers enjoyed more sales with less investment into costly single-use containers. Annual sales were at $368,000, and the business was successfully expanding the number of products it was offering.

From setback to strategy:

In 2023, a new regulation from Indonesia's National Agency of Drug and Food Control (BPOM), or *Badan Pengawas Obat dan Makanan,* restricted Siklus from selling personal care products via refill due to concerns about hygiene and skin-contact products, as Siklus staff simply refilled and redelivered used customer containers. This led to a 58% drop in revenue and forced Siklus to redesign its business model.

The company used design thinking and the Business Model Canvas to adapt, focusing heavily on customer insights and inadvertently engaging in Suma Qamana ideas. They surveyed 100 of their current customers and conducted in-depth interviews with three managers and nine customers to learn what the next approach should be.

As a result, three main customer types, or personas, emerged, each with unique pains and gains. Listed below are the personas that guided Siklus' redesign of its business model to meet real customer needs in the face of regulatory changes:

- Ideal Iqbal represented young, single males aged 18 to 25 who were motivated by environmental concerns and aimed to reduce plastic waste. While Iqbal was budget-conscious, he valued sustainable practices and was concerned about contamination from manual refill methods.

- Active Amanda was a single woman aged 18 to 25 who shopped more frequently and was driven by both affordability and ethical consumption. She was highly engaged in sustainable practices and looked for diverse product offerings and clear evidence that her purchasing choices had a positive environmental impact.

- Natural Nikita was a young married mother aged 26 to 35 who prioritized convenience and time-saving when shopping for personal and home care products. Nikita was environmentally aware but had limited time for errands. She valued the ability to access safe, hygienic products from home.

A business model built on shared responsibility:

Based on this data, the solution that Siklus chose in response to regulatory challenges was to adopt a "Return from Home" business model. This approach allowed customers to order products in special washable, refillable containers such as aluminum bottles and have them delivered to their homes. When empty, Siklus picked up, cleaned, and reused the containers.

This revised model continued to reduce single-use plastic waste while maintaining convenience and affordability for the customer and the manufacturer. It also created a new source of revenue for Skilus as they became distributors and cleaners of washable, reusable containers.

Siklus's transition to a "Return from Home" model reflects the principles of Suma Qamana, emphasizing harmony, shared responsibility, and care. By applying *Yachay* (knowledge), the company deeply understood customer needs through interviews and surveys. Through *Munay* (love and care), Siklus prioritized customer well-being and environmental stewardship, offering safe, convenient, and sustainable packaging solutions.

Ushay (power) was expressed by involving customers in feedback and giving them agency in shaping the system, while *Ruray* (action) guided the practical implementation of a circular, waste-reducing business model. This values-driven approach allowed Siklus to meet new regulations while staying true to its mission of collective well-being and sustainability.

FUN FACTS

In Bolivia and Peru, children with their families often run real-life lemonade-style stands. They sell homemade drinks like *chicha morada* or *refrescos*, integrating local ingredients and community values. Such approaches make these micro-businesses natural examples of Suma Qamana in action (Stenn, 2018).

TIPS

A simple lemonade stand can embody complex sustainability practices, from inclusive pricing to compostable packaging, making it a great teaching tool.

POINTS TO REMEMBER

- Sustainability is not just environmental; it also includes social inclusion, community engagement, and ethical practices.

- Applying values like love (*Munay*), doing (*Ruray*), and knowledge (*Yachay*) can help embed sustainability in everyday business decisions.

> **DISCUSSION QUESTIONS**
> - How can small businesses like a lemonade stand influence larger systems of sustainability through their everyday actions?
> - What other Suma Qamana values might be applied to a different BMC element, like Key Partnerships or Revenue Streams?

2.4 Case Study: Grove Collaborative

Grove Collaborative's Struggle to Scale—How a Mission-Driven Startup Battled Investor Skepticism

Introduction:

Grove Collaborative began in 2012 as *ePantry*, a D2C subscription service for eco-friendly home goods. Its founder, Stuart Landesberg, had long dreamed of leading a sustainability-focused company like Seventh Generation. With just a 200-square-foot storage unit in San Francisco and a passion for responsible consumption, Landesberg launched ePantry.

The goal was to deliver products from brands like Mrs. Meyers, Method, and Toms of Maine directly to eco-conscious consumers. The company became a certified B Corp and donated a portion of sales to rainforest preservation efforts.

Despite gaining traction with customers and offering a convenient model for sustainable living, ePantry struggled to secure growth capital. Between 2012 and 2016, Landesberg faced 173 investor rejections, even as he proved market demand and operational capacity. He stood at a crossroads, with strong customer support, but no investor buy-in.

The Challenge:

While ePantry had proven its business model in terms of consumer interest, it failed to resonate with investors. The main challenge was a disconnect between the company's sustainability-focused value proposition and what investors wanted to see: scalable growth, strong return on investment (ROI), and market differentiation.

Investors didn't find the company name compelling or clear, and many did not understand the long-term economic value of a mission-driven company. Additionally, high operational costs, including pre-purchasing inventory, made cash flow tight. Although Landesberg offered a socially conscious product, he lacked the messaging and financial clarity that could attract capital.

This challenge highlights the importance of understanding different customer segments; in this case, the "customer" was not just the consumer but also the investor. This case is an illustration of misalignment between product-market fit and investor-market fit, a key lesson in business model design.

The Solution:

Landesberg acted on the feedback he received from investors and made two bold changes:

- **Rebranding the company:** He changed the name from ePantry to Grove Collaborative, a name that better reflected the company's mission and natural ethos. The new branding helped communicate the company's identity more clearly and aligned more effectively with both customers and potential investors.

- **Creating a proprietary product line:** Grove began producing its own line of low-waste, eco-friendly cleaning and personal care products. These products were marketed through multiple channels, including D2C subscriptions, retail partnerships (e.g., Target, Walmart), and e-commerce platforms like Amazon.

This strategy, known as consolidated diversification, allowed the company to streamline offerings under a mission-aligned brand while reaching multiple customer segments through targeted channels. It also improved margins, scalability, and investor appeal by building intellectual property and brand equity.

The Impact:

The results of these strategic pivots were impressive:

- Within two years, Grove Collaborative was ranked #37 on the Inc. 5000 list of fastest-growing U.S. companies (2018).
- By 2021, Grove had over 1,000 employees.
- In 2022, Grove merged with Virgin Group Acquisition Corp. II and went public at a valuation of $1.5 billion.
- The company continues to operate under the Grove name, selling both proprietary and curated eco-friendly goods.

The transformation helped align the company's social mission with economic performance, making it a model for mission-driven growth.

Conclusion:

Grove Collaborative's journey is a compelling example of how understanding your audience, whether they are consumers or investors, can make or break a business. By repositioning its brand and rethinking its product strategy, Grove overcame early challenges and became a major player in the sustainable goods industry. Its success story teaches aspiring entrepreneurs how to leverage the BMC and sustainability frameworks not only to create value but also to communicate that value effectively to all stakeholders.

Discussion Questions:

- What was Grove's original value proposition, and why did it appeal to customers but not to investors?
- How might ePantry have approached investors differently to better align with their interests?
- In what ways did Grove's rebranding support both customer engagement and investor confidence?
- Which SDGs does Grove Collaborative align with, and how can these be used as leverage points in impact investing?

Activity:

Use the Business Model Canvas to map Grove Collaborative as it existed in 2015 and then again, after its transformation in 2020. Highlight changes in value proposition, customer segments, channels, and revenue streams. Create a new customer map using investors as the primary customer segment. Show how that changes the way Grove Collaborative is understood.

In Chapter Two, we explored how sustainability moved from abstract ideals to practical, customer-centered enterprise practices. We began with the Suma Qamana framework, rooted in Andean wisdom, which emphasized harmony, care, and balance across four core values: *Yachay* (knowledge), *Munay* (love), *Ruray* (doing), and *Ushay* (power). These principles were shown to enhance enterprise operations by deepening relationships with customers, building inclusive workplace cultures, and promoting ethical leadership.

We studied how the Value Proposition Canvas was a powerful tool for aligning customer needs with enterprise offerings. By understanding functional, emotional, and social customer jobs, alongside their pains and gains, entrepreneurs could create products and services that truly resonated. It was stressed that success came from developing a strong "Fit" between what customers value and what enterprises offer.

The chapter also offered concrete methods for integrating sustainability into the Business Model Canvas through customer relationships, segments, and channels. Through a playful example of a lemonade stand, we saw how Suma Qamana values and SDG goals can work together to expand impact, diversify markets, and build stronger, more inclusive businesses.

By focusing on empathy, co-creation, and intentional design, we learned that sustainable business is not only possible but also more profitable, resilient, and meaningful when built around the needs of people and the planet!

Chapter Summary

- Suma Qamana is a sustainability paradigm rooted in the Andean values, *Yachay, Munay, Ruray*, and *Ushay*, which guides enterprises toward more ethical, balanced, and community-centered business practices.

- The Value Proposition Canvas is a tool for identifying customer jobs, pains, and gains to develop offerings that are meaningfully aligned with real customer needs.

- Suma Qamana values can be practically applied to the Business Model Canvas areas of Customer Relationships, Segments, and Channels to integrate sustainability and deepen customer connection.

- Applying customer mapping, rebranding, and sustainability values helped Grove Collaborative scale and attract investment despite early funding challenges.

QUIZ

1. **What does the Quechua term Suma Qamana mean?**
   a. Constant improvement
   b. Competitive growth
   c. Living well in harmony with people and nature
   d. Innovation through enterprise

2. **Which of the following best describes how *Munay* applies to customer relationships?**
   a. Increasing transaction speed to boost revenue
   b. Using data analytics to segment customer groups
   c. Building emotional connections through celebration and respect
   d. Offering discounts based on customer loyalty

3. **In the Suma Qamana framework, which principle represents the element of action that drives the others forward?**
   a. *Yachay*
   b. *Ushay*
   c. *Munay*
   d. *Ruray*

4. **Which two sections of the Business Model Canvas focus most directly on understanding and serving customers?**
   a. Key Partners and Key Activities
   b. Channels and Customer Relationships
   c. Revenue Streams and Cost Structure
   d. Value Proposition and Key Resources

5. In the Value Proposition Canvas, "Pains" are best described as:

    a. Features that delight the customer unexpectedly
    b. Emotional benefits customers hope to feel
    c. Frustrations, obstacles, or risks that hinder customers from completing a job
    d. External market factors outside the firm's control

6. According to the chapter, a true "Fit" occurs when:

    a. The enterprise can satisfy every possible customer segment simultaneously.
    b. Customer Jobs exactly match the firm's revenue goals.
    c. The offering's pain relievers and gain creators address the customer's most intense pains or desired gains
    d. The firm's sustainability goals are publicly certified by a third party

7. Why do many enterprises struggle to become more sustainable?

    a. They are not interested in sustainability.
    b. They have too many resources to manage.
    c. They lack expertise, resources, or understanding.
    d. Sustainability is not a business concern.

8. In the lemonade stand example, how is the principle of *Ruray* (doing) applied in customer relationships?

    a. By using only organic lemons
    b. By inviting feedback and participation in activities
    c. By reducing product prices
    d. By advertising widely online

9. What is one way the lemonade stand builds sustainability through *Yachay* (knowledge)?

   a. Offering diverse lemonade types based on customer needs
   b. Using plastic cups to save money
   c. Offering free samples to everyone
   d. Avoiding feedback from customers

10. Which value of Suma Qamana is associated with systems thinking and continuous learning?

   a. *Munay*
   b. *Ushay*
   c. *Yachay*
   d. *Ruray*

Answer Key

1 – c	2 – c	3 – d	4 – b	5 – c
6 – c	7 – c	8 – b	9 – a	10 – c

CHAPTER 3

Operations and Infrastructure

Key Learning Objectives

- Understanding permaculture as a model of abundance.
- Empowering and creating value for employees.
- Analyzing supply chains from a values-based perspective while expanding markets with win-win collaborations.
- Exploring sustainable development in the coffee industry through direct trade supply chains and long-term partnerships with the help of the Equal Exchange case study.

Moving along the BMC, we shift from the Right-side Connections, customer side of things (Chapter Two) to Left-Side Logistics, operations, and infrastructure (Fig. 3.1). Here, we take a deep dive into Key Activities, Key Resources, and Key Partners, touching on topics such as sourcing, operations, energy, employee management, and ally development.

Figure 3.1 Left-Side Logistics

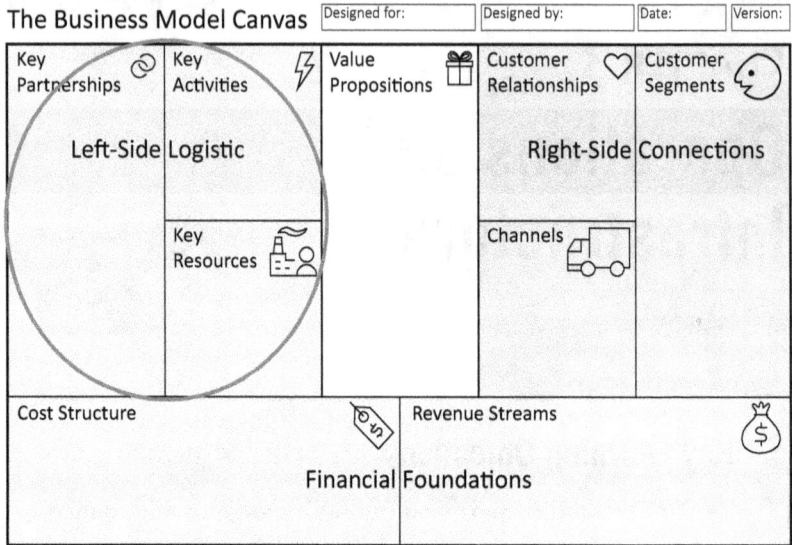

The Business Model Canvas

Key Partnerships	Key Activities	Value Propositions	Customer Relationships	Customer Segments

Left-Side Logistic

Right-Side Connections

Key Resources

Channels

Cost Structure | Revenue Streams

Financial Foundations

(Adapted from the Strategyzer BMC Model, 2025)

Left-Side Logistics focuses on how things are made, by whom, with what, and who helps.

As an entrepreneur, Logistics is where the most power lies and the greatest impact for sustainability can take place. Operations offer more independence from consumer whims and demand (pains and gains), giving an entrepreneur the freedom to engage in new technologies, work with suppliers of choice, appreciate the workforce, and build innovation, resulting in a more robust Value Proposition.

However, knowing how and where to make these changes is difficult. A nature-based model, such as Permaculture, shows how symbiotic relationships and a mindset of abundance create many new approaches to logistics. Exploring operations from a permaculture perspective increases possibilities, reduces risk, engages the community, and expands and strengthens the Value Proposition.

3.1 Permaculture as Abundance

Permaculture originated in Australia in the 1970s as a model of permanent agriculture and culture. Here, balanced nature systems supported each other in production and growth within human-designed environments (Holmgren, 2002). Pioneered by Bill Mollison and David Holmgren, permaculture initially focused on creating regenerative agriculture and building systems focused on care of the earth, care of people, and a redistribution of surplus. Over time, it has been applied to different types of systems, including entrepreneurship and economic development.

Permaculture is based on three core tenets:

1. Each component of the system carries out various functions.
2. Each preferred system is maintained by multiple components.
3. Everything in the system is interrelated to everything else.

Applied to entrepreneurship, permaculture is about seeking and forming win-win relationships for sourcing and transforming products, employing others, and working with organizations and communities in a spirit of goodwill, trust, and abundance (Stenn, 2017). It sounds idealistic and "pie-in-the-sky," but it is actually good business practice.

3.1.1 Permaculture and Strategic Management

Figure 3.2 compares Permaculture and Strategic Management practices, showing the similarities and compatibilities of the two practices. Incorporating permaculture models into an enterprise aligns organizational practices with ecological and social systems, creating a transformative approach to sustainability. The Spiral Integration model in the figure below harmonizes permaculture ethics, care for the earth, care for people, and fair share, with strategic management processes (Akhtar, Lodhi, & Khan, 2015).

Figure 3.2 *Permaculture* **principles and** *Strategic Management* **practices aligned with Spiral Integration**

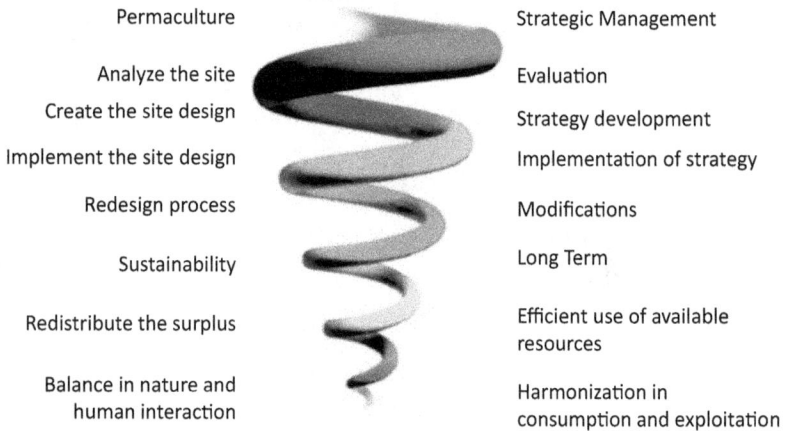

Permaculture	Strategic Management
Analyze the site	Evaluation
Create the site design	Strategy development
Implement the site design	Implementation of strategy
Redesign process	Modifications
Sustainability	Long Term
Redistribute the surplus	Efficient use of available resources
Balance in nature and human interaction	Harmonization in consumption and exploitation

(Akhtar, Lodhi, & Khan, 2015)

The Spiral Integration emphasizes a dynamic, connected approach involving continuous analysis, development, implementation, and revision. This ensures businesses maintain equilibrium among stakeholder capacities, resources, and demands. By placing permaculture's ecological and social considerations into strategic planning, organizations can move beyond traditional economic metrics to build long-term sustainability, becoming "Regenpreneurs" (regenerative entrepreneurs).

Such management models are key elements for enterprise development. It is the management of resources and outcomes that makes an enterprise viable. Permaculture also offers innovative management models rooted in nature concepts to facilitate sustainable enterprise development. These models focus on the importance of shifting from conventional hierarchical structures to models that prioritize long-term objectives, intrinsic motivation, emergent coordination, and collective wisdom (Vitari & David, 2017).

They encourage organizations to adapt to socio-ecological realities, promoting resilience and sustainability. By adopting permaculture-inspired management practices, businesses can innovate in ways that are ecologically sustainable, socially responsible, and economically viable.

3.1.2 The Apple Tree Analogy: Three Ways Permaculture Supports Sustainability

To best imagine permaculture in an applied entrepreneurship environment, think of an apple tree. If an apple tree's purpose is to procreate: to create a seed that would grow into a seedling and ensure the survival of the species, then it only needs to produce a single apple with a single seed. That would be the most efficient way to use limited resources with a targeted outcome. It would also be the riskiest because if anything happened to the seedling, it would be a total loss for the tree. Like enterprises, nature does not like risks, though, counter to enterprises, it works with a sense of abundance.

Using this analogy, let's explore the following three ways in which permaculture supports sustainability.

1. **Symbiotic relationships:**

    A symbiotic relationship is a close and long-term interaction between two different species. Apple trees produce scores of apples with multiple seeds inside, surrounded by delicious fruit. Animals (and humans) consume the apples, scattering the seeds away from the tree so they do not grow, competing for space and nutrients. This is an exchange.

The tree gives animals sustenance, and the animals distribute the tree's seeds. There are other exchanges here. Apple flowers need to be fertilized for seeds and fruit to grow. So, the tree offers pollen and nectar to bees in exchange for pollinating the flowers. The tree has no formal relationship with bees or animals, yet they work together in a mutually beneficial way, helping each other to meet their needs by providing essential sustenance and services.

These exchanges are not efficient. The tree produces more apples than the animals can eat, and not every flower turns into an apple. There is excess. At the same time, there is reduced risk. By overproducing flowers and fruit, the tree protects itself from damage, such as a late frost or a lower yield. It also builds a stronger relationship with bees and apple-eating animals as these partners begin to rely on the tree for its goods, and the tree relies on them for their services. Permaculture looks at where symbiotic relationships can be formed. Practitioners ask, where do intersections exist between one enterprise's resources and another's services?

2. Community sharing:

Like any enterprise, an apple tree needs energy. The apple tree also uses multiple means of exchange and partnerships for its energy production. It makes leaves that absorb energy from the sun through photosynthesis, creating food for itself. The sun is a passive partner. It provides energy, which the tree absorbs, though the sun receives nothing in exchange for the energy given. That is OK. Not every relationship in permaculture is an even exchange; this is where abundance and generosity come into play.

In the fall, the tree drops its leaves, which are composted by worms and microbes into nutrients for the tree, absorbed through its roots. In exchange, the worms and microbes get sustenance and shelter from the decomposing materials while the tree gets energy from their waste. Relationships are formed with community partners who use each other's excess for their own benefit. Permaculture looks at community and how one organization's waste can become resources for another. Practitioners ask: What waste am I producing that someone else may be able to use?

3. Connected models:

Lastly, a tree, like an enterprise, needs a healthy, renewable environment so resources are not depleted. An example is a tree's relationship with rain production. Clouds produce rain, which washes nutrients down through the soil to the tree's roots. In turn, the tree absorbs the water through its roots, eliminating it as vapor through its leaves via transpiration, returning it to the clouds. The clouds hold the moisture until it turns to rain, and the cycle begins again. This cyclical model ensures the clouds have water and the tree has rain.

Spiral, cyclical models, or closed loop production, take place in permaculture as formal exchanges with specific, predictable outcomes. Permaculture looks at resources and tracks their lifecycle and regeneration. Practitioners ask: What am I using that can be reused again, and who can help with this? All processes are interconnected and influence each other with their outcomes.

Nature is resilient. It works in systems of redundancy with multiple partners (Akhtar, Lodhi & Shah Kahn, 2017). In this way, an apple tree can withstand a short drought, early frost, hurricane winds, or other unforeseen disasters. Even with broken branches, torn-off leaves, or frozen flowers, the tree has multiple resources to keep going. The earth can feed it, new leaves can be made, and systems started up again.

Nature is not efficient. If it were, the apple tree would be a single branch with a single apple, using the least amount of resources to achieve its goals (procreation). If anything happened to the branch or the apple, the tree would fail. Having multiple systems working on similar tasks creates options, abundance, reduced risk, and builds resilience. Through its inefficiency, nature grows sustainability.

The lessons learned from permaculture, the value of symbiotic relationships, community sharing, and cyclical models can be applied to enterprises to build strength, reduce risk, and grow resilience (Table 3.1).

Table 3.1	Expanding sustainability practices through permaculture lessons

Permaculture principle	Definition	Enterprise application
Symbiotic Relationships	Long-term, mutually beneficial exchanges between two or more distinct entities.	• Identify and cultivate partnerships where one organization's resources align with another's services. • Seek intersections that enable collaborative value creation and reduce risk.
Community Sharing	The use of community networks and resource exchange, where one party's excess can benefit another, without always requiring equal return.	• Share surplus materials, information, or services. • Convert "waste" into value by identifying community partners who can benefit from or repurpose enterprise by-products.

Permaculture principle	Definition	Enterprise application
Cyclical Models	Closed-loop systems where outputs are reused or regenerated within the system, promoting continuous renewal and sustainability.	• Track resource use, seek regenerative practices, and design operations to minimize depletion. • Establish systems where inputs and outputs are balanced and reused where possible.

FUN FACTS

• Permaculture practices do not just benefit enterprises; they improve farming too. Permaculture farms can yield up to 200% more calories per acre than conventional monoculture farms. This is because permaculture systems mimic natural ecosystems, utilizing vertical space, multiple crop layers, and perennial crops. Permaculture practices create abundance in community and production. (Ferguson & Lovell, 2014).

• Permaculture-related circular economy practices, like repair, reuse, and remanufacturing, can cut CO_2 emissions by 48% by 2030 and save businesses up to $630 billion annually in material costs. These regenerative strategies boost enterprise profits by lowering inputs, creating new revenue streams, and building customer loyalty (Ellen MacArthur Foundation, 2015).

TIPS

• When analyzing an enterprise's waste, ask: *Can someone else use this as a resource?* This mindset fosters community sharing.

• When designing enterprise operations, ask: *Where can I form symbiotic relationships that benefit both my business and others?*

> ### POINTS TO REMEMBER
>
> - In nature, permaculture practices emphasize abundance over efficiency, prioritizing the creation of regenerative systems that restore and enhance natural resources.
>
> - In business, permaculture introduces a nature-based systems thinking approach, guiding organizations to build resilience and sustainability through interconnected and adaptive design.
>
> - The three main permaculture principles, symbiotic relationships, community sharing, and cyclical models, help reduce risk and increase sustainability.

> ### DISCUSSION QUESTIONS
>
> - How might adopting a permaculture approach change the way a business views its supply chain and waste management practices?
>
> - In what ways does shifting from hierarchical structures to permaculture-based management models impact employee motivation and organizational sustainability?

3.2 The Human Resources Function

The Human Resources (HR) function is one of the key components of sustainable enterprise operations. A committed, engaged workforce brings strength and stability to an organization, creating less employee turnover with more cooperation and synergy. Permaculture-based thinking affects Key Activities, surrounding HR functions, in the Business Model Canvas by introducing nature-based, regenerative practices. Let's see how this happens.

Permaculture is all about cycles, redundancy, and abundance. This differs from linear efficiency-driven enterprise models. Working with abundant, interconnected systems rather than efficient, linear models allows enterprises to become adaptive, resilient, and inclusive, especially in how they manage people and operations (HR). Matching human behavior with ecological principles strengthens workforce ethics and purpose while creating new alignment with Sustainable Development Goals.

The following are five permaculture-inspired management practices that can improve the HR function, morale, and resource use, as illustrated in Figure 3.3.

Figure 3.3 Permaculture principles applied to Key Activities

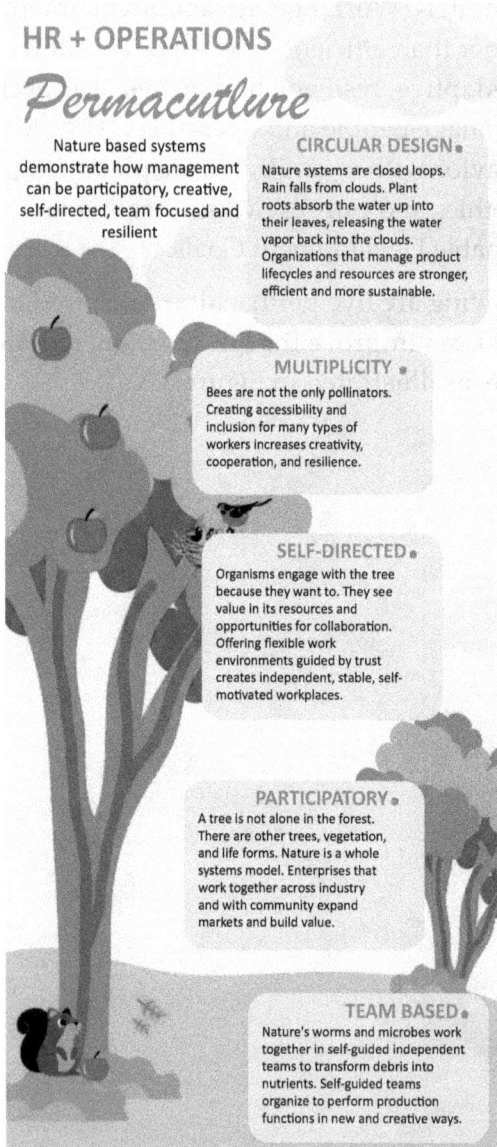

HR + OPERATIONS
Permacutlure

Nature based systems demonstrate how management can be participatory, creative, self-directed, team focused and resilient

CIRCULAR DESIGN.
Nature systems are closed loops. Rain falls from clouds. Plant roots absorb the water up into their leaves, releasing the water vapor back into the clouds. Organizations that manage product lifecycles and resources are stronger, efficient and more sustainable.

MULTIPLICITY.
Bees are not the only pollinators. Creating accessibility and inclusion for many types of workers increases creativity, cooperation, and resilience.

SELF-DIRECTED.
Organisms engage with the tree because they want to. They see value in its resources and opportunities for collaboration. Offering flexible work environments guided by trust creates independent, stable, self-motivated workplaces.

PARTICIPATORY.
A tree is not alone in the forest. There are other trees, vegetation, and life forms. Nature is a whole systems model. Enterprises that work together across industry and with community expand markets and build value.

TEAM BASED.
Nature's worms and microbes work together in self-guided independent teams to transform debris into nutrients. Self-guided teams organize to perform production functions in new and creative ways.

Permaculture principles applied to Key Activities create new nature-inspired ways to engage and value employees while improving operations and meeting SDGs.

3.2.1 Circular Design

Circular design is about creating closed-loop models that follow the lifecycle of a product from production to disposal. When loops are not closed, resources are lost. The key to building sustainability is to recognize where the production loop can be closed to improve an organization's efficiency and value.

Nature systems are closed loops. For example, rain falls from clouds and onto the earth. Plant roots absorb the water from the earth and transfer it up to their leaves. The water is then released back into the atmosphere as vapor via transpiration. The release of water vapor helps form clouds, which eventually leads to more rainfall. The water is in a closed loop: it falls, is processed and transformed, and then returns to be used again.

Enterprises have an incredible influence through their buying power. Mimicking this process in enterprises involves clever thinking, innovation, and partnerships. Conducting an inventory of resources and inputs used by an organization is the first step in identifying closed-loop opportunities. A closed loop begins with the origin of a product and continues through six question steps as outlined in Table 3.2.

Table 3.2	The Circular Design questioning model		
Step	**Focus**	**Guiding questions and prompts**	**Typical data to note**
1. Product	Pick an everyday item	• What single item will you trace? (e.g., paperclip, pen, stapler)	Product name and SKU

(Continued)

Step	Focus	Guiding questions and prompts	Typical data to note
2. Material origin	Where do the raw materials come from?	• What natural resources form the item? • Where, on earth, were they extracted? • Which companies carried out mining/harvesting and refining?	Ore type, mine location, refinery site, primary processors
3. Transport	Follow every physical move	• Route from mine/field → refinery → component maker → assembler → distributor → retailer → your office • Modes used (truck, rail, ship, plane, car) plus energy and carbon at each leg	Mileage, fuel type, carriers, distribution hubs
4. Packaging	Trace materials and movement of the package	• What materials (paper, plastic, ink, glue) enclose the product? • Where were those materials sourced and processed? • How was packaging transported and in what quantities?	Paper grade/forest source, resin type, print shop, secondary packaging

Step	Focus	Guiding questions and prompts	Typical data to note
5. People	Map the human hands involved	• Who mined, milled, molded, drove, packed, sold, repaired machines? • What are their working conditions and communities? • How does each step affect livelihoods and well-being?	Labor locations, workforce size, wage context, safety/environment notes
6. Planet	Sum up the environmental impacts	• Energy sources for mining, smelting, manufacturing, transport, and retail • By-products (tailings, emissions, wastewater) • Land-use changes (deforestation, habitat loss) • Company sustainability policies and metrics	Total energy mix, Greenhouse Gas (GHG) estimates, waste streams, and environmental certifications

Following these steps builds a Circular Thinking mindset.

Let's apply this model by using the following steps to understand the sustainable logistics opportunities that production presents:

Step 1

The first step is to choose a product to study. An easy place to start is with office products, for example, a paperclip. This is a familiar, everyday product that most offices use.

Step 2

Here, we determine material origin. Think of what the paperclip was made of, starting with the part of Earth the materials originated from. How was that metal mined, transformed, where, and by whom?

Step 3

The next step is transportation. Think about where that production traveled. Were mined metals transported to a processing facility that turned them into wire? Did a different company buy that wire to bend it into clips? Were finished products sent to a distribution center? Were they then transported to a store for your purchase? Did you drive to the store to get them and bring them to the office? Each step in the transportation process is a use of energy resources and carbon production.

Step 4

Step four is packaging. How was the item packaged? Were the paperclips in a bulk pack of cardboard boxes wrapped in plastic? Where did that paper come from? The plastic? Think of steps two and three again, for the packaging. What resources were used for it, starting at the earth level? Think of the trees, oil, the inks used for printing on the paperclip boxes, and the adhesives used.

Step 5

Here, we look at people. Going back through steps two, three, and four, explore where the people are in this story. Think of every hand that touched each part of this production, the miners, factory workers, timber harvesters, paper mill employees, drivers, sales staff, and mechanics who keep the factory machines working. Every hand that touches the paperclip, its production and distribution, belongs to a living human being with hopes, dreams, families, and loved ones. Think about how the purchase you are making affects the environment they work in.

Step 6

The final step is the planet. Think of how this entire cycle is impacting the planet in different ways. What are the byproducts or additional resources needed for paperclip production? For example, where is the heat coming from to melt minerals into metal? How are the trees being harvested for the paper in the boxes? What is the energy model used by the manufacturer you are purchasing the final product from?

A closed-loop model is only fully closed if all parts of the model are examined and accounted for, and it is only as strong as its weakest link. Knowing the origin, production, and impact of materials an enterprise consumes creates an opportunity to make more informed, impactful choices that benefit others while still meeting enterprise needs.

Thinking this deeply about a single item can feel overwhelming and time-consuming. Today's Artificial Intelligence (AI) and advanced data search systems make closed-loop solutions easy to find. Tools like the Circular Design Decision Tree make it easier to choose the right solution for your enterprise (Fig. 3.4).

Figure 3.4 A Circular Design Decision Tree for selecting sustainability-minded suppliers

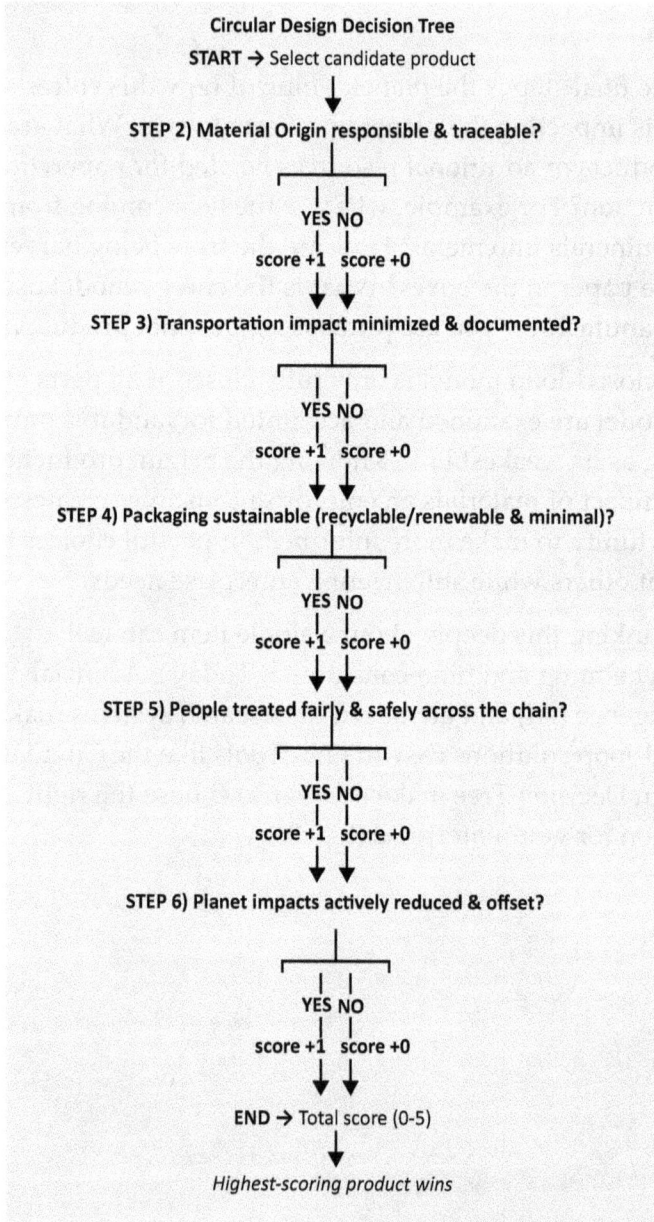

Circular Design Decision Tree

START → Select candidate product

↓

STEP 2) Material Origin responsible & traceable?

YES — score +1   NO — score +0

STEP 3) Transportation impact minimized & documented?

YES — score +1   NO — score +0

STEP 4) Packaging sustainable (recyclable/renewable & minimal)?

YES — score +1   NO — score +0

STEP 5) People treated fairly & safely across the chain?

YES — score +1   NO — score +0

STEP 6) Planet impacts actively reduced & offset?

YES — score +1   NO — score +0

END → Total score (0-5)

Highest-scoring product wins

The following is an example of using Circular Design thinking tools to find a supplier for sustainably produced paperclips. A simple online search for "sustainably produced paper clips" uncovers many options. These are the top three:

- Before Breakfast paper company in London, England, is a specialist in using sustainably-sourced materials to create "stationery that inspires everyday tasks and creativity in the workspace," including recycled paper and paperclips (Before Breakfast, 2025).

- Midori P-Clips offers paper clips made of eco-friendly, durable fiber paper in the form of little animals. Further research reveals that Midori was a Japanese stationery brand founded in 1950, which became Designphil in 2007, a company with strong corporate social responsibility (CSR) principles and a commitment to sustainable development (Designphil Inc., 2025).

- ACCO Brands, in the U.S., made recycled metal paperclips packed in recycled paper boxes. ACCO is a $1.67 billion company founded in 1893, based out of Illinois, with a strong commitment to global partnerships and community connections (ACCO Brands Corporation, 2025).

The six-step circular design decision tree model (Fig. 3.4) identifies which product fills which step to help with the purchasing decision for that material. Scores can be increased for steps that an enterprise may emphasize more than others. If there is insufficient information, suppliers can be contacted and questioned, or steps can be skipped.

There are many eco-ethical, mindfully created options for products when one takes the time to look for them. The benefit of the circular design, closed loop mindset is that when one finds another enterprise working with the same values, a synergy forms with shared missions and matching goals. Often, product scale, cost, and customization can be negotiated with more effective connections made.

The relationship an organization has with like-minded suppliers strengthens their mission, helps employees feel good about what they are supporting, and creates energy, value, and income for all businesses working for good. While it may seem a bit cumbersome and time-consuming to scrutinize all aspects of one's production this way, it soon becomes an automatic habit or mindset. One also finds that as they seek out sustainability-minded enterprises and closed-loop systems, they find allies who can make recommendations for other suppliers. Suddenly, one is in a whole new eco-verse.

3.2.2 Circular Design in Action: The Ocean Cleanup's Closed-Loop Approach

Using permaculture-inspired, closed-loop approaches to sustainable logistics is not just for for-profit enterprises. Non-profit organizations and government agencies also benefit from applying sustainable principles to their operations. The Ocean Cleanup, founded in 2013 by Dutch engineer Boyan Slat, is a nonprofit organization headquartered in the Netherlands with operations in 10 countries. Its mission is to develop and deploy technologies to remove plastic pollution from oceans and intercept waste flowing through rivers before it enters marine environments.

The Ocean Cleanup's goal is to clean the Great Pacific Garbage Patch (GPGP) and remove 90% of floating ocean plastic by 2040. As of June 2025, Ocean Cleanup had removed 64 million pounds of marine trash worldwide. In July 2025, it began partnering with Amazon Web Services, Inc. (AWS), to use AI to better identify and predict the movement and location of the GPGP (The Ocean Cleanup, 2025).

The Ocean Cleanup exemplifies a profitable Non-Governmental Organization (NGO) that embeds circular design thinking across its entire operation, from sourcing waste materials, iterative technological development, optimized logistics, and transparent supply chains to product creation and community partnerships. Its closed-loop mindset has enabled real environmental impact while generating revenue to sustain the mission. The Ocean Cleanup follows the circular design decision tree in the following way.

Step 1: Product

The Ocean Cleanup transforms recovered ocean plastics into consumer products, most notably, designer sunglasses made from certified Great Pacific Garbage Patch material, sold at $234 each. By early 2022, the sold-out run of 21,000 sunglasses became a revenue stream that supports its cleanup mission. Engaging with Key Partnerships, the Ocean Cleanup also provides plastic materials to enterprises better equipped to transform waste into new products, such as truck bed liners and limited-edition record albums by the band Coldplay (The Ocean Cleanup, 2025).

Step 2: Material origin

The Ocean Cleanup sources plastic waste directly from the ocean and rivers, specifically targeting the floating fraction of plastics larger than 15 mm. They partner with other organizations that sort and transform the waste into usable materials using a certified Chain-of-Custody material origin standard developed with DNV GL, guaranteeing the material to be 100% ocean-harvested plastics. (The Ocean Cleanup, 2025)

Step 3: Transportation

Collected plastic enters sorting and recycling chains optimized to reduce transport emissions. Data-driven route planning and lifecycle assessments guide logistics decisions, ensuring a lower carbon footprint per ton of extracted plastic (van Giezena & Wiegmans, 2019).

Step 4: Packaging

Product packaging is deliberately minimal and made from recycled or recyclable materials such as large nets and bins. The intention is to keep all material flows within a closed loop wherever possible.

Step 5: People

The Ocean Cleanup collaborates globally, employing and working alongside hundreds of local staff in river cleanup deployments (e.g., Indonesia, Malaysia, Guatemala, United States) and partnering with recycling firms. In the U.S., a dedicated nonprofit branch, American Friends of The Ocean Cleanup (AFTOC), raises funds and supports alignment with the mission.

Step 6: Planet impact

Operating as a closed-loop entity, the Ocean Cleanup aims to clean up 90% of ocean plastic by 2040, while simultaneously intercepting river-borne inputs from the world's most polluted rivers, targeting 1,000 rivers that release 80% of river-based ocean pollution. Independent impact assessments ensure that cleanups do not inadvertently harm marine life or produce carbon cycling (Egger et al., 2025).

3.2.3 Exercise

Discuss how to use a Circular Design Decision Tree (Table 3.3).

Table 3.3	Actions and tools for a Circular Design Decision Tree

Action	Tools and Methods
Define criteria	Agree on what counts as a "YES" for each step (e.g., third-party certification, published GHG data, fair-trade audit, FSC-certified packaging, etc.).
Collect evidence	Use CSR reports, supplier disclosures, life-cycle databases, interviews, or field visits to answer each YES/NO question.
Traverse the tree	For every candidate item, walk the branches in order, and add one point for each YES.
Compare scores	Rank all items by total points; if tied, apply a tie-breaker such as lowest cradle-to-gate carbon intensity.
Document rationale	Keep a short grid showing answers and evidence for transparency and future audits.

Extensions

- Weighting: If your stakeholders view some steps as more critical (e.g., People or Planet), assign weights (e.g., Material Origin = 1 pt, Planet = 2 pts) and adjust the decision rule to "highest weighted score."

- Use this template as a living framework: refine the YES/ NO definitions and weightings to match the priorities of your process, partner NGO, or procurement policy.

3.2.4 Multiplicity

Bees are not the only pollinators. Nature has multiple systems and players for accomplishing the same task. Using the apple tree model, flowers are not just pollinated by bees, but also by butterflies, other insects, animals, and the wind. If something were to happen to the bees, the tree could still be pollinated. Multiplicity and redundancy are sustainability traits favored by nature.

Mimicking nature on the organizational level and creating accessibility and inclusion for many types of workers increases creativity, cooperation, and resilience. Workers can vary in their education, background, age, ethnicity, gender identity, neurodiversity, and abilities. Permaculture-inspired management in multiplicity can be seen in diversity, equity, and inclusion (DEI) functions.

The Pew Center research shows that employees favor diverse workplaces, with 65% of U.S. adults feeling like it is a good thing for organizations to focus on (Minkin, 2025). In addition, greater workplace multiplicity creates happier and more productive organizations rife with innovation, top talent from many sectors, multiple perspectives, and more innovative, out-of-the-box thinking with expanded production and marketing opportunities. In fact, ethnically diverse companies were found to be 35% more likely to have higher financial returns than the national industry median (Hunt, Layton & Prince, 2015).

Multiplicity does not just happen. Just like with Circular Design, an intention to pursue and value multiplicity needs to be set and a multiplicity mindset developed. An enterprise can look at the makeup of its local community, specific market segments, personal connections or experiences, or skills it wishes to foster, and people in these different areas to create workplaces that are inviting to the group the enterprise wishes to welcome. Looking towards the Key Partnerships part of the BMC connects enterprises with organizations that can help with workplace integration of different workforce types.

Example:

The German software company SAP hosts the "Autism at Work" program, holding regional summits to link people on the autism spectrum with workplaces while educating both on how to best work together. "Autism means I am different; not less," explained Dr. Temple Grandin, an author, researcher, and autistic advocate (Autism at Work, 2019).

Investment firms, banks, and big data companies recognize the ability that people with autism are able to see patterns that neurotypical people often miss, making them an important asset for organizations (Adams, 2020). Programs such as Autism at Work and other support and advocacy groups help enterprises to find and engage more diverse talent from all walks of life.

Unlike bees and butterflies, people often need to be taught to work together so that diverse needs are met and communication is supported. Butterflies and bees both pollinate flowers, but do so differently. Including cross-training, where people learn each other's ways of doing things, helps build resiliency, enhance adaptability, expand institutional memory, and ensure systems remain in operation.

HIGHLIGHTS

People on the autism spectrum often excel at spotting complex patterns that neurotypical individuals may overlook—a talent now prized by investment firms, banks, and big-data companies seeking analytical advantage (Adams, 2020).

3.2.5 Self-Directed

Permaculture is about letting nature systems self-direct and make their own choices to try out new things and see what is best. Self-direction includes being flexible, seeking opportunity, and leaving room for others. Returning to the apple tree example, it is not mandated that bees and butterflies pollinate flowers; they do it on their own. Bees and butterflies are autonomous and make their own choices about which flowers, trees, or plants to visit. At the same time, other insects and animals can also participate in pollination. There are no restrictions on flower access. Competition exists, but is passive; there is enough for all. Nature works in systems of abundance. The motivation for pollinators to visit the apple tree flowers is based on location and reward, the pollen and nectar.

Pollinators are self-motivated, operating autonomously, creating a harmonious relationship with the tree. In the workplace, permaculture-inspired management favors employee self-regulation and self-motivation. This empowers workers to create schedules and reward-based tasks that best meet their own and the organization's goals—emphasizing employee-driven purpose and internal awards. This approach pays off.

"Highly motivated employees are more likely to volunteer to help out when someone needs help; they are highly collaborative and cheer their fellow coworkers on," explained leadership coach and trainer Jennifer Recla (Schooley, 2024). Organisms engage with the tree because they want to. They see value in its resources and opportunities for collaboration. Offering flexible work environments guided by trust creates independent, stable, self-motivated workplaces.

3.2.6 Participatory

A tree is not alone in the forest. There are other trees, vegetation, and life forms. Nature is a "whole systems model." This whole systems model reflects the permaculture value of the intelligence of the whole. While a single apple tree has been the focus of our understanding of applied permaculture principles, it is important to remember the tree is part of a larger ecosystem, which includes fields, forests, and built environments.

Taking a whole systems approach enables multiple perspectives and options to emerge through participatory, iterative processes. New and diverse perspectives create opportunities for enterprises to strengthen, improve, or expand their approaches. Building participation and democracy in the HR function opens the use of tools such as consent-based decision-making, feedback loops, self-guided projects, shared leadership, equity, and inclusion, giving all stakeholders a voice. This mindset also opens enterprises to working with other organizations, turning competition into collaboration and creating additional Key Partnerships.

3.2.7 Team-Based

The self-directed, participatory worker mindset leads to the next permaculture-inspired management principle, Teams. Using the apple tree example, nature's worms and microbes work together in self-guided, independent teams to transform debris such as leaves and compost into rich nutrients. Symbiotic relationships form without a central command or leadership. Resources and tasks are distributed based on knowledge, skill, and need, not hierarchy.

In nature, fungi are not better than worms or voles; they are coexisting organisms working together to complete similar goals (decomposition). Examining teams from the permaculture perspective creates self-guided groups that perform production functions in new and creative ways. An upside-down management structure emerges, where the base comes first, with employee-organized tasks communicated down to management.

Similar to the other nature-based systems studied, non-hierarchical team-based methods need to be intentionally built and nurtured to function. Enterprises can encourage team-based development through peer-to-peer decision-making, transparent communication, and rotating facilitation roles to harness collective intelligence.

Applying permaculture principles to the HR function shifts traditional top-down management policies toward collaborative, empowered, individually driven, sustainable models. It gives enterprises a new way to look at the resources they consume and creates opportunities to form meaningful partnerships outside of the enterprise for added strength and reach. Permaculture principles emphasize collaboration, knowledge sharing, redundancy, and teams performing independent functions.

TIPS

- Trace just one item. Kick-start circular design by mapping the six-step journey of a simple object—say, a paperclip—to uncover immediate opportunities to close resource loops.

- Trust drives motivation. Offer employees autonomy in schedules and task design; highly motivated workers naturally collaborate and step in to help colleagues (Schooley, 2024).

POINTS TO REMEMBER

- Participatory, whole-systems thinking transforms competition into collaboration by giving every stakeholder a voice and building strong external partnerships that amplify impact.

- Multiplicity—cultivating diverse, redundant talent streams—boosts creativity, resilience, and market reach.

- Shifting from linear, efficiency-driven models to regenerative, closed-loop systems makes enterprises more adaptive and inclusive.

DISCUSSION QUESTIONS

- How might your organization adapt the six-step circular design model to a product or service other than office supplies, and what data would you need first?

- When introducing consent-based, participatory decision-making, what practical steps or tools could your organization use to involve all stakeholders effectively while maintaining operational efficiency?

3.3 Supply Chains

The supply chain can be thought of as the backbone of an enterprise. It is the source of materials that make up the goods or services sold. As with the Circular Design model in Section 3.2, the supply chain is another area where an enterprise has tremendous power in affecting sustainability outcomes for itself and others.

An enterprise has full control over the supply chain choices it makes and the products and services it offers. Using the same permaculture-inspired, Circular Design questioning applied to suppliers, on one's own enterprise products and services, is a game-changer. Adding self-analysis brings in all the operations represented by Key Resources in the BMC. Here, internal processes are examined, including energy use, materials transformation processes, and the lifecycle of the goods or services produced.

Taking a holistic, full lifecycle view of a product examines the environmental and social impacts of the good or service produced from the sourcing of raw materials to the final product disposal. The following five pillars for supply chain transparency identify areas for engagement, innovation, and improvement for stronger sustainability practices (Table 3.4).

Table 3.4 **The Five Pillars of Supply Chain Transparency**

Pillar	Key Resources Factor
1. Green design and operations	Eco-friendly product design, clean inputs, low-carbon logistics, and clear end-of-life plans.
2. End-to-end transparency	Openly disclosing provenance, labor conditions, and emissions, backed by blockchain/ Radio-Frequency Identification (RFID) audit trails.
3. Circularity	Designing products and reverse-logistics loops so materials are recovered, remade, or resold rather than discarded.
4. Cross-stakeholder collaboration	Brands, competitors, and suppliers sharing data and unified codes of conduct (e.g., Fashion Revolution model).
5. Digital enablement and common standards	AI, Internet of Things (IoT), advanced analytics, and cloud Enterprise Resource Planning (ERP) to monitor, predict, and report against globally recognized benchmarks (UN Global Compact, Environmental, Social, and Governance frameworks).

For a fully sustainable supply chain, sustainability practices need to be followed both by the enterprise and its suppliers and contractors. If suppliers and contractors cannot demonstrate five-pillar supply chain transparency, the enterprise can work with them to improve practices or find different, more aligned partners. Ultimately, an enterprise is responsible for its entire supply chain, and the supply chains of the subcontractors and suppliers it chooses to work with.

3.3.1 First Pillar

Green Design and Operations are mainstream concepts now, with many options available in sustainably produced materials from mushroom-grown packing molds to upcycled fashion, organic clothing, and renewable energy sources. Green design can be retroactive, where current production is re-examined and modified, or it can be implemented from the start for new ventures or product lines. Any place is a good place to start.

3.3.2 Second Pillar

End-to-end transparency is requested by savvy customers for all the processes in enterprises' sustainability claims, and enterprises need to know their sustainability claims are valid. Digital technology brings new ways to connect directly with supply chains, providing end-to-end transparency.

Transparency tools include the use of RFID tags to track the exact movement of goods, video-informed proof of labor conditions, data-backed emissions information, and real-time contact with producers via social media and online communications. Shared information about production processes helps to build customer commitment and trust in the brand, and better oversight.

A quick study of the fashion industry, where brands outsource almost all production, demonstrates the importance of the Circularity and Cross-Stakeholder Collaboration pillars of supply chain transparency.

3.3.3 Third Pillar

Circularity creates responsibility for the production process, including the production, repurposing, or disposal of waste, whether it's material scraps, by-products, or products at the end of their lifecycle. The fashion industry is one of the world's largest polluters as measured by Circularity. Well-known global brands create fashion designs that are contracted out overseas for production. This is where supply chains break down with little transparency and accountability, and harm takes place (Lundberg & Devoy, 2022). From toxic farming methods of cotton and natural fibers, to energy-heavy synthetic fiber production, to labor exploitation and landfill mountains made of fast fashion throw-aways, the fashion industry's harms span the entire supply chain and the globe (European Parliament, 2020).

Negative consequences of non-circular supply chains include farmer suicides, deaths of factory workers in fires and preventable accidents, and environmental degradation. This leads to increasing consumer and government pressure on fashion brands to be more sustainable and transparent about their sourcing and production. Ultimately, a lack of Circularity in fast fashion's supply chains affects the whole industry, the planet, and millions of people globally.

Building Circularity requires systemic change: cutting over-production, paying living wages, investing in safe chemistry and circular design, and enforcing transparency and accountability at every tier. A permaculture sustainability mindset can help build Circularity transparency. This includes using reverse-logistics loops, so materials are recovered, remade, or resold rather than discarded.

Circularity follows the product from the landfill back to the factory workers, fabric mills, and farmers' fields, looking at all places where material transformations were made. Exposing the full supply chain is the first step to finding weaknesses and fixing them.

3.3.4 Fourth Pillar

The Cross-Stakeholder Collaboration pillar of supply chain transparency focuses on the relationship enterprises have with suppliers and contractors. A permaculture mindset expands the idea of stakeholders to include the community and competitors. By getting to know stakeholders in a more holistic way, insights into their needs and resource usage arise, fostering greater trust and commitment. This is where circular design loops can be explored with creative solutions to waste with material re-use and repurposing.

The cross-stakeholder approach enables growth, labor, and economic challenges to be discussed with more open solutions developing. Bringing in Chapter Two's Suma Qamana model creates places for friendships to form *(Munay)* with data, knowledge *(Yachay)*, and resources *(Ushay)* being shared.

Example:

Continuing with the fashion industry example, weak Cross-Stakeholder Collaboration left brands vulnerable. Contractors often subcontracted out jobs, making accountability and oversight of labor and production conditions difficult. There was no clear connection between the farmers and the fabrics they grew fiber for, energy use was unaccounted for, and fast fashion lifecycles and disposal were not measured.

As a result of growing consumer and government regulatory backlash, industry members banded together, creating the Fashion Revolution Model as a way for brands to be more sustainable (Fashion Revolution, 2024). By working together, competitors explored universal methods of supply chain transparency and greater sustainability. Sharing the burden lightened the load, benefiting all of them.

The resulting Fashion Revolution Model was a closed-loop model that captured the social, ecological impact of fashion production, including farming, water use, carbon production, synthetics, labor and working conditions, waste, and product life cycles. Brands were assessed based on the fashion industry transparency index, with results published in global reports.

"What Fuels Fashion?" was a 2024 global fashion transparency index report that ranked 250 of the world's biggest apparel companies on how openly they disclosed, and advanced, decarbonization of their operations and supply chains. The 2024 assessment found that, though there is more consumer awareness and demand for sustainable fashion, the sector is still struggling to make meaningful change.

According to the report, large, well-known clothing brands produce massive amounts of garments, numbering in the millions of units per year. The majority of the clothing is disposed of after just seven to ten wears, with 66% of it going to landfills and much of it being incinerated (Lundberg & Devoy, 2022). The synthetic fibers used in many garments are most toxic when incinerated.

Taking steps towards change:

Brands can help their outsourced producers improve their sustainability practices by introducing them to Circular

Design permaculture ways of thinking and helping them to transition to more sustainable production. Taking the permaculture mindset and connecting with producers in more direct, authentic ways enables closer relationships to grow, meaningful production to be developed, and long-lasting, sustainable fashion to emerge. Circularity makes visible the full Circular Design.

Many producers, industry, and non-profit organizations support Circularity and Cross-Stakeholder Collaboration through guidelines, memberships, assessments, and certifications. Some of these include fair trade, which focuses on the producer and community experience, organic methodologies which manage inputs in agriculture, and B-corps which look at whole organization processes including labor, internal structures, and energy use.

Certifications and memberships in these organizations build collaboration and best practices for resource acquisition, production, and scaling. Reaching out to and collaborating with stakeholders builds stronger, more resilient enterprises.

POINTS TO REMEMBER

- Responsibility is shared: An enterprise is answerable for its own supply chain *and* that of its chosen suppliers and subcontractors.

- Circularity is action-oriented: Reverse-logistics loops recover, remake, or resell materials instead of discarding them.

- Collaboration multiplies impact: Competitors that share data and standards (e.g., Fashion Revolution) lighten the sustainability workload for everyone.

3.3.5 Fifth Pillar

The fifth pillar is Digital Enablement and Common Standards. Digital Enablement makes space for technology to assist and manage the transaction for greater sustainability. Technologies such as AI provide new ways to build and streamline complicated processes such as warehousing and rapid shipping while minimizing carbon footprints. Blockchain processes accurately track complex supply chains, making sure farmers and subcontracted factory workers are seen and counted.

IoT (Internet of Things) is made up of devices and platforms that connect and communicate seamlessly, allowing for more efficient and accurate automation communicated over the internet. ERP (Enterprise Resource Planning) systems are software platforms that integrate and manage a company's core business processes, such as finance, human resources, sales, and supply chain, into one unified system with a shared database. Combining IoT with ERP effectively automates core business processes, enhancing overall efficiency and supporting better decision-making.

Building on the concept of Stakeholder Collaboration (see Pillar 4, Table 3.4), Common Standards focus on organizations and certifications that define and regulate sustainability practices. These standards establish measurable benchmarks that not only improve enterprise accountability but also drive the creation of new sustainability goals (Common Standards).

Example:

An example of Common Standards in action is the United Nations Global Compact. The Compact offers a voluntary, principles-based framework for enterprises to follow to operate responsibly, report transparently, and actively collaborate for a more inclusive, equitable, and sustainable global economy.

Common standards are present in Environmental, Social, and Governance (ESG) performance frameworks. These frameworks give enterprises guidelines, metrics, and criteria for valuing and measuring sustainability, making it easier for investors, regulators, and other stakeholders to compare performance across enterprises and industries and for enterprises to make better-informed decisions.

Applying the five pillars of supply chain transparency to the farmers' market lemonade stand example shows how even the most basic enterprises can develop, measure, and grow sustainability in their production. The following chart matches production-focused sustainability actions to the SDGs (Table 3.5). This chart suggests how a farmers' market lemonade stand could engage with the Five Pillars of Supply Chain Transparency to advance the seven SDGs. A healthy, interconnected, transparent supply chain is a competitive advantage that sets examples for others, creates positive messaging, and increases enterprise value.

Table 3.5	Five Pillars of Supply Chain Transparency applied to a lemonade stand	
Pillar	**Sustainable supply chains at the farmers' market lemonade stand**	**Key SDGs advanced**
1. Green design and operations	• Source organic lemons and fair-trade sugar locally. • Offer reusable-jar deposit options or certified-compostable cups and paper straws. • Sweeten with local honey; run a small solar panel to power the cooler and Point of Sale (POS) processing equipment.	(12) Responsible Consumption and Production: Cuts waste and non-renewable inputs. (13) Climate Action: Lowers GHG with local sourcing and solar power. (7) Affordable and Clean Energy: On-site solar generation.

(Continued)

Pillar	Sustainable supply chains at the farmers' market lemonade stand	Key SDGs advanced
2. End-to-end transparency	• Chalkboard and QR code list every supplier, distance travelled, and farming practices. • Weekly social-media stories from lemon orchards and apiaries. • Ingredient cost/ impact breakdown on the menu.	(12) Responsible Consumption and Production: Public reporting on sustainable practices. (8) Decent Work and Economic Growth: Highlights decent work in the supply chain. (16) Peace, Justice and Strong Institutions: Access to information and accountability.
3. Circularity	• Collect rinds for compost or a local soap-maker's essential oil extraction. • Discount for customers returning jars. • Use ice-melt greywater to irrigate mint/ basil planters for specialty flavors.	(12) Responsible Consumption and Production: Substantially reduce waste via prevention, reduction, recycling, and reuse. (15) Life on Land: Supports soil health through composting.
4. Cross-stakeholder collaboration	• Shared produce deliveries with neighboring vendors; shared refrigerated trucks. • Sit on market "zero-waste" committees and co-develop cup-return stations. • Donate unsold lemonade to the market café for baked goods glaze.	(17) Partnerships for the Goals: Multi-stakeholder cooperation. (12): Shared waste-reduction infrastructure. (13): Joint logistics lower emissions through coordinated freight and warehousing activities.

Pillar	Sustainable supply chains at the farmers' market lemonade stand	Key SDGs advanced
5. Digital enablement and common standards	• Cloud POS tracks sales, inventory, and waste; exports data for carbon-per-cup metric. • Display market sustainability scorecard aligned to local ESG standards. • IoT cooler sensor feeds a live dashboard providing safe, energy-efficient storage.	(9) Industry, Innovation and Infrastructure: Digital tools for efficiency. (12): Data-driven Resource Management. (13): Quantifying and Cutting Emissions.

FUN FACTS

• Mushroom magic: Some enterprises now replace petroleum-based foam with mushroom-grown packing molds, material literally "grown" from mycelium that fits products like a custom glove, protecting them in shipping (Hunter, 2023)

• Cooler runoff to herb garden: In the lemonade-stand example, melted ice water is captured as grey water to irrigate on-site mint and basil planters, closing a tiny but clever circular loop.

TIPS

• Start anywhere: Green design can be introduced retroactively to existing lines or baked into new ventures. Any step forward counts.

• Track what matters: Simple technologies like RFID tags or QR-coded menus quickly add end-to-end transparency without massive budgets.

> **DISCUSSION QUESTIONS**
>
> - How might Digital Enablement (Pillar 5) help small or micro-enterprises overcome resource constraints when pursuing transparent, sustainable supply chains?
>
> - In industries with long, multi-tier supply chains (e.g., electronics or food), what incentives or policy mechanisms could motivate suppliers at the lowest tiers, such as raw-material extractors or smallholder farmers, to adopt the five pillars of supply-chain transparency?

3.4 Case Study: Equal Exchange

Brewing a Just Cup: How Equal Exchange Disrupted Global Coffee Trade

Introduction:

Equal Exchange is a pioneering U.S.-based worker-owned cooperative that launched in 1986 with the goal of revolutionizing global trade by establishing ethical and transparent supply chains. Founded by Jonathan Rosenthal, Michael Rozyne, and Rink Dickinson, former managers of a New England food co-op, the enterprise was born from a desire to expose the hidden labor behind food products and redistribute value to smallholder farmers.

| Figure 3.5 | The Equal Exchange Fairly Traded Cooperative |

(Equal Exchange, 2025)

Their first import was roasted Nicaraguan coffee beans during a U.S. embargo. With an initial $100,000 raised from friends and family, the trio bet on a vision where fairness, transparency, and community development replaced profit-maximizing commodity trade.

The Challenge:

At the time of Equal Exchange's founding, global agricultural supply chains were opaque and exploitative. Farmers were treated as anonymous commodity suppliers, earning a tiny fraction of a product's retail value, often under 2% for coffee. Multinational corporations controlled distribution, consumers were unaware of production conditions, and small-scale producers faced market volatility and institutional neglect. The three founders questioned:

Could trade be honest, empowering, and transparent, serving both farmers and consumers?

Furthermore, they faced immediate legal and logistical challenges. The U.S. embargo on Nicaragua made direct trade nearly impossible. Infrastructure in rural Latin America was poor, relationships with producers were unestablished, and no precedent for fair trade or direct sourcing existed. They were navigating legal barriers, logistical uncertainty, and an untested business model.

The Solution:

Equal Exchange circumvented the embargo by working with a Dutch partner who roasted and shipped the coffee, allowing them to receive the product legally. Once launched, they introduced a direct trade model, eliminating intermediaries and working directly with small farmers. They called their suppliers Producer Partners, building long-term relationships and paying above-market prices.

Each purchase was coupled with social investments: road repairs, schools, teacher training, and production upgrades. Inspired by the co-op model, they helped farmers organize into cooperatives, creating shared ownership and collective decision-making. This structure enabled bulk selling, direct contracting, and democratic governance, which they termed the Alternative Trade Economy. Back home, they engaged ethically motivated consumers, "Citizen Consumers," and later partnered with church groups through an Interfaith Program that distributed coffee via 10,000 congregations.

| Figure 3.6 | Equal Exchange |

(Equal Exchange, 2025)

Over the years, Equal Exchange developed and refined the Alternative Trade Economy, a collaborative production model that linked producers, consumers, and trade partners.

They also pioneered organic certification, shade-grown cultivation, and regenerative farming, before any of these were mainstream. Later, they expanded into cocoa, chocolate, nuts, bananas, and dried fruit using the same model.

The Impact:

By 1989, Equal Exchange broke even; by 1991, sales reached $1 million. In 2005, they operated the largest worker-owned coffee roasting facility in the U.S. They redefined ethical consumption, influenced global fair trade policies, and established a template for values-driven enterprise.

Equal Exchange built deep supply chain partnerships, transformed marginalized producers into empowered co-op members, and created a loyal base of socially conscious consumers. Despite a consolidating marketplace and the mainstreaming of fair trade, Equal Exchange remained independent, transparent, and mission-aligned—scaling both impact and profits.

Conclusion:

Equal Exchange's journey illustrates how ethical supply chains can thrive in a capitalist marketplace. Their model prioritized values over volume, yet achieved scale through partnerships, storytelling, and relentless advocacy. As the marketplace evolves, with technologies like blockchain and B-Corp certification, Equal Exchange must decide how to maintain authenticity while continuing to grow.

Discussion Questions:

- What are the trade-offs between scaling a values-based enterprise and staying true to its founding mission?
- How do cooperative structures enhance or limit a business's ability to respond to market demands?
- What mechanisms ensure transparency and trust as a company like Equal Exchange grows?
- Should Equal Exchange pursue new technologies (e.g., blockchain) or remain focused on personal relationships?

Activity:

Research a fair trade product you use regularly. Trace its supply chain. Who produces it? Who distributes it? How transparent is that process? Compare it to Equal Exchange's model.

In Chapter Three, we explored the operational heart of our enterprises through the lens of permaculture, shifting our focus from customers to infrastructure and sustainability. We examined Key Activities, Key Resources, and Key Partnerships in the BMC, uncovering how our choices in sourcing, production, energy, and human resources can generate abundance and reduce risk. Permaculture, a system based on natural cycles and mutual benefit, shows us how to build regenerative operations through symbiotic relationships, community sharing, and cyclical models.

We learned that by thinking like nature, embracing redundancy, cooperation, and inefficiency, we create resilient, adaptable businesses. The apple tree analogy helped us to visualize how overproduction (abundance) and diverse partnerships actually make systems stronger. We are encouraged to ask ourselves: Who can use our waste? Where can we form win-win partnerships?

Applying permaculture to our HR practices, we're challenged to redesign management with five key principles: Circular Design, Multiplicity, Self-Direction, Participation, and Team-Based Work. Through these principles, we engage employees as co-creators, welcome diversity, and build inclusive, motivating workplaces. The Circular Design Decision Tree helped us trace the lifecycle of even simple items like paperclips: tracking origin, transport, packaging, people, and planetary impact, to make more sustainable choices. Tools like this support us in shifting from linear to closed-loop systems.

We also analyzed supply chains through five pillars of transparency: Green Design, End-to-End Transparency, Circularity, Cross-Stakeholder Collaboration, and Digital Enablement. These gave us a roadmap to ensure that our operations, and those of our suppliers, uphold sustainability at every stage.

The chapter closed with the case study of Equal Exchange, a pioneering social enterprise that reshaped the coffee trade by working directly with small farmers. Their story reminds us of the power we hold to align our enterprises with justice, fairness, and ecological responsibility. By using permaculture principles and strategic management together, we can build ventures that are not only competitive and profitable but also deeply regenerative for our people, our communities, and our planet.

Chapter Summary

- As a model for sustainable operations, permaculture promotes abundance, resilience, and sustainability through symbiotic relationships, community sharing, and cyclical models. Applying these principles helps businesses reduce risk, build value, and form win-win partnerships with suppliers, workers, and the community.

- Nature-based HR practices include Circular Design, Multiplicity or diversity in offerings and methods, Self-Direction, Participation, and Team-Based Work. These foster inclusive, motivated, and regenerative workplaces aligned with SDGs.

- The six-step Circular Design model traces a product's lifecycle from raw material to disposal. This helps businesses identify sustainability gaps, reduce waste, and form strong, values-aligned partnerships.

- Sustainable supply chains are built on Green Design, End-to-End Transparency, Circularity, Cross-Stakeholder Collaboration, and Digital Enablement—where AI continues to play a larger and larger role. These pillars create accountability, reduce environmental harm, and provide a roadmap for ethical operations.

QUIZ

1. Which permaculture-inspired HR practice focuses on creating closed-loop product life cycles?

   a. Circular Design
   b. Self-Directed
   c. Multiplicity
   d. Team-Based

2. According to the Pew Research Center, what proportion of U.S. adults say it is a good thing for organizations to focus on diversity?

   a. 35 %
   b. 50 %
   c. 65 %
   d. 85 %

3. Which permaculture-inspired principle emphasizes employee autonomy, flexible scheduling, and reward-based tasks?

   a. Circular Design
   b. Participatory
   c. Multiplicity
   d. Self-Directed

4. What is the foundational ecological model applied in Chapter Three to rethink business operations?

   a. Lean management
   b. Permaculture
   c. Hierarchical control
   d. Agile

5. Which three concepts form the core ethics of permaculture?
   a. Productivity, efficiency, growth
   b. Equity, ecology, economy
   c. Care for earth, people, and surplus
   d. Input, output, impact

6. In permaculture-inspired management, what is the significance of "multiplicity"?
   a. Promotes elite recruitment
   b. Reduces competition
   c. Builds inclusive, redundant systems
   d. Focuses on cost-cutting

7. How does the concept of "community sharing" relate to enterprise waste?
   a. Encourages regulatory compliance
   b. Converts waste into shared value
   c. Mandates landfill usage
   d. Prioritizes automation

8. What kind of relationship is emphasized by permaculture's "symbiotic relationships"?
   a. Short-term supply contracts
   b. Top-down governance
   c. Mutual, informal exchanges
   d. Strict performance incentives

9. According to Chapter Three, what practice supports long-term sustainability by tracking material use and regeneration?

    a. Self-directed work
    b. Cyclical models
    c. Lean thinking
    d. Flat hierarchies

10. What management principle in permaculture emphasizes autonomous, purpose-driven work?

    a. Team-based
    b. Circular Design
    c. Self-Directed
    d. Participatory

Answer Key

1 – a	2 – c	3 – d	4 – b	5 – c
6 – c	7 – b	8 – c	9 – b	10 – c

CHAPTER 4

Financials

Key Learning Objectives

- Understand Solidarity Economy as a collaborative distribution framework.
- Expand the idea of exchange beyond the dollar.
- Create access and growth through diversified revenue.
- Explore how Green Mountain Power put energy into the hands of the community, made a profit, and connected with community solar.

The foundation of any enterprise lies in its financials, specifically, the Cost Structure and Revenue Streams sections of the Business Model Canvas (Fig. 4.1). The Cost Structure refers to how an organization pays for its goods and services, while Revenue Streams describe how it generates value and income. Together, these two components form the financial backbone of the BMC. Like an accounting system, they must be strong and balanced to support the enterprise and the rest of the business model.

Figure 4.1	The Financial Foundations

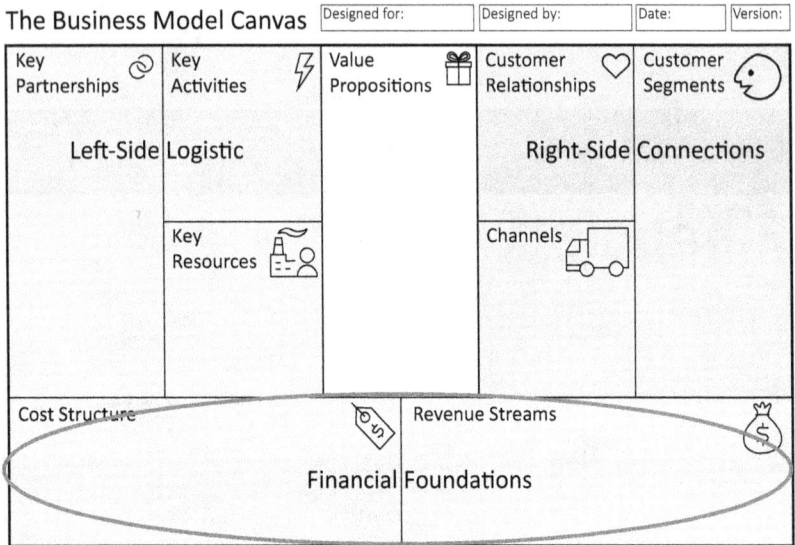

The Business Model Canvas

| Designed for: | Designed by: | Date: | Version: |

Key Partnerships	Key Activities	Value Propositions	Customer Relationships	Customer Segments
Left-Side	Logistic		Right-Side	Connections
	Key Resources		Channels	

Cost Structure	Revenue Streams
	Financial Foundations

(Adapted from the Strategyzer BMC Model, 2025)

The Financial Foundations of the BMC include the Cost Structure and Revenue Streams.

Enterprises that overpay for production or fail to charge adequately for their offerings will struggle to cover operating costs and may ultimately fail. On the other hand, while covering costs is necessary, it is not sufficient; generating surplus revenue is essential for growth and long-term sustainability. Enterprises that don't reinvest in growth and innovation risk falling behind.

Cost Structure and Revenue Streams are dynamic and interdependent, involving a variety of financial strategies. Fixed costs, such as rent, insurance, and salaries, must be managed carefully, while variable costs, like materials, labor, and shipping, fluctuate with the level of production or service delivery. Businesses that can draw on a diverse mix of cost and revenue strategies tend to be more resilient.

The Solidarity Economy offers a collaborative and creative approach to managing costs and generating revenue. By encouraging cooperation and innovation, the Solidarity Economy opens up new pathways to build financial strength and sustainability.

4.1 Solidarity Economy: Expanding the Means of Exchange

Solidarity Economy as a concept was first coined in at about the same time (1984) by Luis Razeto in Chile and Jean-Louis Laville in France. The effects of "neoliberal globalization" led by Thatcher in the UK and Reagan in the USA, with the displacement of manufacturing to China, were creating high unemployment in all OECD countries. In Latin America, those policies were often forced on countries with US-supported dictatorships. In many communities, initiated by women and indigenous peoples, civil society organizations, community organizations, Solidarity Economy became a rallying concept to create an alternative to the capitalist globalization. By necessity, just to survive, Solidarity economy-related initiatives were created at the grassroots all over the world. Today, Solidarity Economy (SE) is an interlocking ecosystem that de-commodifies essential resources, builds collaboration at every step, and redistributes value back to the community.

4.1.1 Evolution of the Term

Solidarity Economy became an international movement with a first international meeting in Peru in July 1997. At a second meeting held in Quebec City, Canada, in October 2001, the participants decided to continue by organizing a third meeting in 2005 in Dakar, Senegal. In a preparatory meeting in December 2002 in Dakar, the Intercontinental Network for the Promotion of Social Solidarity Economy (RIPESS) was formed. The term «social» is the French definition, meaning that ownership is social (people and not shares). At this event, the term "social" was added, recognizing the importance of people in the model, and the Intercontinental Network for the Promotion of Social and Solidarity Economy (RIPESS) was formed.

RIPESS grew as the main hub for hundreds of SE organizations and activists worldwide, including governments, regional developers, and the United Nations, with the goal of creating a more inclusive, people and planet-focused, sustainable economy. In 2023, the Social Solidarity Economy was recognized by the UN as the desired paradigm for realizing the SDGs (RIPESS Intercontinental, 2024).

Created out of necessity during a time of extreme uncertainty, violence, and chaos, SE has proven to be a resilient, flexible framework that performs across disasters, responds to change, and withstands uncertainty. Bringing the Solidarity Economy framework into the financial part of an enterprise creates new ways to access capital, mitigate costs, and grow revenue.

4.1.2 Diversification Through Solidarity Economy

In permaculture terms, a farmer monocropping their fields with only corn could be very efficient with high yields of corn, but is at risk for a total loss if a windstorm blows down the tall plants. They are working in a high-yield, high-risk environment. If they intercropped corn with other products such as beans or squash, the corn might have been lost in the windstorm, but the other crops would have survived. By diversifying production, the farmer reduced their risk and opened new markets for other goods.

Replace the corn with the US dollar, the main currency for global exchange, and a similar vulnerability arises. If something happens to the dollar or the local currency that is valued against the dollar, it is a direct hit for the enterprise. Having more than just dollars as a means of exchange, the enterprise reduces its risk while expanding sales to more markets.

Figure 4.2 **Solidarity Economy framework**

(Adapted from Miller, 2010)

The above image shows the five key enterprise sections with examples of each—moving in a circular design.

SE builds diversity in exchange across five key enterprise areas: Creation, Production, Exchange – Transfer, Consumption, and Surplus Allocation (Fig. 4.2) (Miller, 2010). This mimics the product cycle, where first an idea is formed, then developed, distributed, consumed, and transformed.

Each area of the SE brings new partners, resources, and means of exchange, expanding options for enterprises and reducing reliance on a single currency for all transactions. Having multiple exchange options and a spirit of cooperation protects enterprises from market fluctuations, currency scarcity, and devaluation, and minimizes risk (Kawano, 2010). Here is how this happens:

Creation:

Creation is about how products are developed, ensuring entrepreneurs have a place to start. It includes shared resources in space, knowledge, and investment, treating natural and cultural resources as commons, not commodities. These resources can be found in community land, such as the commons, open spaces, such as a town park that can be used for meetings, product demonstrations, and celebrations. Makerspaces and co-working shared office spaces also create accessible starting points for an enterprise.

In the spirit of SE creation, knowledge can be found through partnerships with universities and schools, in libraries and online affinity groups, or from open-source data. Investment takes place in closed-loop models where community funds are lent to community members, benefiting the community and creating more resources for all. Engagement in creation reduces raw-material costs and price volatility, builds brand authenticity around stewardship, and keeps innovation cycles fast because knowledge circulates freely.

Creation, like all parts of SE, is a two-way street where enterprises partake in creation but also look to give back to it by sharing creation resources such as space, knowledge, and investment with others.

Production:

Production is about how things are made and by whom, with the intention of creating a positive impact for workers, communities, and the planet. Production reduces risk by decentralizing work, favoring cottage industry, worker cooperatives, unions, and flexible work methods. Worker wages fund community projects. Communities occupy natural environments.

The workforce and community cannot be separated. A healthy community needs a healthy environment. In this way, the enterprise is intrinsically connected to the people and planet (workers, community, and environment) through Production. Using a SE mindset towards production creates places for cooperative governance and household and community production, building collaboration and creativity.

This results in higher labor commitment and lower turnover, flexible job-rotation that boosts cross-training, faster buy-in, speeding innovation, diversified inputs, protection from supply shocks, and loyal local supplier networks. An enterprise integrating itself into the community via SE Production finds that the community has its back when it is needed.

Exchange – Transfer:

Exchange – Transfer is about diversifying the means of exchange, moving away from US dollar mono-cropping, and bringing in other options for buying and selling goods and services. Exchange – Transfer mechanisms work two ways, reducing costs for enterprises while also building new revenue from customers who are granted more flexible access to goods and services. There are numerous Exchange – Transfer mechanisms which can be divided into two categories: flexible pricing and alternative currencies.

1. Flexible Pricing:

Flexible pricing includes sliding scale pricing, where a suggested retail price can be given, with customers being able to pay what they choose. Name your own price or Pay-What-You-Want (PWYW) pricing is another version of this method. Contrary to behavioral logic, people tend to pay what they can, with wealthier people opting to pay more than the suggested retail price (giving back) and those with less means, paying less and accessing a product that they normally would not be able to enjoy.

Studies found that while individual PWYW price paid averages tend to be slightly lower than the suggested retail price, the number of goods sold are so large that they offset the negative revenue, creating more customers, more goods sold, and an increase in overall earnings (Gerpott, 2016).

2. Alternative Currencies:

Alternative currencies include Time Banks, where time is traded instead of currency, so someone may be providing a service that benefits goods sold. Barter Clubs enable goods to be exchanged via trade, with trade values being accumulated and exchanged amongst members in a trade banking system.

Community Currencies keep revenue circulating in local communities, encouraging local buying. Donations and gifting are also ways to engage in exchange – transfer, with the value of donations being a tax write-off and gifts generating social currency and customer loyalty within the community.

SE's Exchange – Transfer with flexible pricing and alternative currency approaches takes place on both the consumer and the industry side. Mapping an enterprise's value chain identifies places where SE Exchange – Transfer can take place. Enterprises can be both receivers and creators of SE Exchange – Transfer. Benefits include opening of new customer segments, revenue maintained even in low-cash environments, more predictable sales, reduced marketing costs with increased "word of mouth" sales, stronger relations with the community, and fewer leakages of value out of the region.

Consumption:

Consumption focuses on what goes into goods and services and how they are used by both the enterprise and the consumer. It favors shared ownership and collaboration, ethical purchasing using circular thinking about product lifecycles, and turns buyers into members.

Consumption looks at reducing material use through sustainable packaging and promoting the "right to repair or refill." This enables customers to use products longer, fix them with less waste, and encourage reuse and shared access. Examples include buyer cooperatives where members pay a fee to purchase items in bulk at discounted prices, reducing packaging and shipping costs, lending libraries that allow tools and materials to be borrowed and returned, and certifications such as Fairtrade, Organic, FSC, and B-Corp that verify the social and environmental benefits of products.

Consumption also includes Community Sponsored Agriculture (CSA), where production costs are paid up front through membership dues and consumer collaboration. Here, through customer assemblies or digital forums, customers give feedback and suggestions. Enterprises benefit from SE Consumption by having up-front cash flow through membership fees, members becoming brand evangelists and participants in product development, rapid feedback loops from customers, lower risk of product misfit, and steady sales through bulk orders.

Surplus Allocation:

Surplus Allocation is the place where abundance is shared. It is where waste is repurposed, unused resources are donated, and revenue is reinvested. It is about deciding together what happens to the extra value created.

Surplus Allocation takes place in the form of dividends shared with co-op members, profit sharing offered to producers, or patronage rebates given to customers. It may also include a gifting of surplus to communities, a percentage of sales invested for environmental causes, participatory budgeting where together costs are evaluated, member-controlled financing with credit unions and cooperative banks formed, cycling material surplus back into production, and an overall drive towards reciprocity—a way of giving back.

Engaging in SE Surplus Allocation methods creates in-house venture capital funding for new initiatives so founders can launch faster without conventional investors. It creates affordable capital where interest payments circulate back to members instead of leaving the region, and it cuts disposal costs and opens secondary revenue streams.

Engaging in SE methods creates many diverse, inclusive ways to manage the finances of an enterprise, balancing costs and revenue. It helps to grow customer loyalty, participation, and strengthen community connections for further growth, shared risk, and increased resilience.

TIPS

- Map your value chain to spot where flexible pricing or alternative currencies such as time banks, barter clubs, and community currencies can cut costs or open new revenue streams.

- Share creation resources, such as makerspaces, open-source knowledge, or community investment banking, to keep innovation cycles fast and raw-material costs low.

POINTS TO REMEMBER

- Solidarity Economy diversifies exchange through Creation, Production, Exchange – Transfer, Consumption, and Surplus Allocation, reducing reliance on a single currency.

- Flexible pricing models like sliding scale and Pay-What-You-Want (PWYW) can widen access for customers while maintaining or increasing total revenue.

- Engaging in SE methods builds resilience, strengthens community ties, and balances costs with revenue growth.

- How could an enterprise in your community incorporate alternative currencies or flexible pricing to reduce risk and expand its customer base?

- SE emphasizes Surplus Allocation, sharing, or reinvesting extra value. What concrete actions could a local enterprise take to practice surplus allocation (e.g., participatory budgeting, profit-sharing, cycling material surplus back into production), and what potential obstacles might arise when putting these actions into practice?

4.2 Cost Structure: Strategic Purchasing

Applying the SE framework to the Cost Structure of the BMC creates many ways to strengthen and expand solid, sustainable supply chains. However, a chain is only as strong as its weakest link. If an enterprise is following sustainability principles to build resilience and innovation, and its suppliers are not, that leaves a vulnerability to the enterprise.

The principles of SE focus on collaborating to create a better good for all. This creates a place for enterprises to interact with and assist suppliers (including producers and contractors) in building good practices in their organizations. In turn, this opens new ways for collaboration and exchange, creating win-win outcomes for all.

These are a few of the best practices for sustainability in the Cost Structure that enterprises have successfully used to grow their businesses:

- Everlane is a clothing company that builds transparency where suppliers, materials, and costs are shared in all stages of production. Thus, it grows accountability, customer trust, and loyalty, while setting an example for other companies (Everlane, n.d.).

- Dean's Beans Organic Coffee Company is a direct buy roaster that knows and shares supplier stories, celebrating their traditions and cultures while building better brand relations with consumers (Dean's Beans, n.d.).

- Ten Thousand Villages holds suppliers to the same sustainability practices as the enterprise, ensuring all supply chains are strong and environmentally safe (Ten Thousand Villages, n.d.). Since 1946, they have been helping suppliers to become more sustainable, forming solid relationships and improving livelihoods for supplier communities and workers.

The SE framework creates many opportunities and avenues to strengthen Cost Structures. The following is a quick-reference guide that shows how each of the five Solidarity-Economy (SE) areas can feed directly into the Cost Structures, with an emphasis on sustainable purchasing and procurement (Table 4.1).

Table 4.1	Applying SE key areas to reduce and stabilize costs	
SE Area	**Sustainable-purchasing tactics**	**How does it reduce or stabilize costs**
1. Creation	• Engage in using "commons" spaces (makerspaces, public parks) for R&D and small-batch prototyping. • Use open-source designs and university partnerships for shared knowledge. • Seek community-based micro-investment or revolving funds for up-front inventory buys.	• Cuts facility rental and equipment capital expenses. • Shortens learning curves; lowers design-error waste. • Replaces high-interest debt with low- or no-interest community capital.

(Continued)

SE Area	Sustainable-purchasing tactics	How does it reduce or stabilize costs
2. Production	• Source from worker co-ops or cottage producers; negotiate long-term, values-aligned supply contracts. • Adopt flexible, community-based job rotation to cover peak orders instead of temporary-agency mark-ups. • Offer a do-it-yourself (DIY) option.	• Locks in predictable, fair pricing and reduces supplier-switching costs. • Minimizes overtime premiums and agency fees; creates shared loyalty that lowers defect rates. • Lowers production costs: the customer performs the labor.
3. Exchange – Transfer	• Set up barter, time-bank, or community-currency agreements for services such as transport, maintenance, or professional advice. • Donate unneeded materials or waste.	• Offsets cash expenses. • Can trade excess capacity or staff time. • Keeps working capital in the community. • Tax deduction lowers disposal costs.
4. Consumption	• Join or form buyer co-ops to bulk-purchase raw materials, packaging, and office supplies. • Use lending libraries and tool sharing. • Offer CSA options where customers pay up front for their product, sharing in risk. • Adopt refill- /repair-friendly component choices so inputs are reused internally (closed loops).	• Secures volume discounts and lowers per-unit shipping and packaging expenses. • Reduces capital costs in owning and maintaining equipment. • Provides zero-interest capital for production, shared risks. • Extends component life, reducing repurchase frequency and waste-handling fees.

SE Area	Sustainable-purchasing tactics	How does it reduce or stabilize costs
4. Consumption	• Seek products with sustainability certifications: organic, fair-trade, B-Corps.	• Builds customer loyalty and long-term relationships through component and refill purchasing. • Verifies the quality of the goods.
5. Surplus Allocation	• Reinvest a share of yearly savings into on-site renewable energy, waste-to-resource systems, or supplier-training grants. • Use participatory budgeting with staff and suppliers to decide where surplus goes, emphasizing projects that further shrink recurring costs. • Bank with community credit unions. • Swap extra materials. • Compost and recycle.	• Generates compounding cost reductions (ie, lower utility bills) and locks in future supply resilience. • Builds transparency and trust, often unlocking in-kind contributions from partners that reduce out-of-pocket spending. • Helps to earn interest on reserves while providing capital for cooperative lending. • Exchanges unused items for things of value, saving money. • Creates value with waste.

4.2.1 Creating a Collaborative Cost Structure

While a list of cost-saving ideas and benefits may be helpful, implementing them is the tricky part. Here are some tips on how to get started and manage a more sustainable, collaborative Cost Structure.

1. **Start big:** List the largest procurement line-items first (materials, energy, logistics, professional services). Work on them one at a time. Are there ways to approach your use of them differently?

2. **Match:** Match each item to one or more SE tactics that can lower its fixed or variable costs. For example, in Exchange – Transfer, an energy company may have carbon offset credits that an enterprise can qualify for. For Consumption, an enterprise can partner with competitors to bulk buy and share materials.

   In the SE model, competitors become collaborators. Enterprises working in the same industry with similar products know their supply and production needs better than anyone. They are in a unique position to collaborate on materials and equipment, forming buying clubs or co-ops, and then differentiate product lines and customer segments.

3. **Quantify the shift:** Create a monetary value for the action. For example, if an enterprise is trading an unused conference room to a local Time Trade group for monthly meetings and receiving social media marketing services in exchange, include the monetary value of the social media marketing services provided.

4. **Note non-financial upsides:** Include the supplier loyalty, risk hedging, and brand equity that the SE move also creates. These often translate into indirect cost avoidance and new customers. For example, the Time Trade members are grateful for the enterprise's conference room use and could favor purchasing the enterprise's goods.

5. **Loop surplus back:** Create new ways to bring additional SE investments back to the organization, creating a self-reinforcing savings cycle.

By weaving the five SE areas into purchasing decisions, an enterprise converts cost centers into collaborative value-creation nodes. This helps to shrink expenses, while also buffering against market shocks, deepening community ties, building a loyal supplier and customer base, and meeting new SDGs.

Applying these principles to the farmers' market lemonade stand example creates fun, innovative ways to expand services while reducing costs and building sustainability (Table 4.2).

Table 4.2   SE framework applied to a farmers' market lemonade stand

SE Area	Sustainable purchasing tactic	Cost Structure impact	SDGs advanced
1. Creation	• Co-design recipes and booths with other vendors (share slicers, juicers, signage templates). • Recruit a small community to crowdfund for the first bulk lemon order instead of a bank loan.	• Avoids buying specialist equipment or design services. • Replaces interest-bearing debt with zero-interest community capital.	(8) Decent Work and Growth
2. Production	• Buy organic "seconds" lemons from nearby growers and process them the same day; sign a season-long, fair-price contract. • Rotate preparation shifts with local youth organizations instead of paying temporary-agency helpers.	• "Ugly" lemons cost 30-40 % less than retail but taste the same; longer contracts keep price swings down and help producers manage cash flow. • Partnering with a local organization brings in organization members as customers, too	(12) Responsible Consumption and Production (8) Decent Work and Growth

(*Continued*)

SE Area	Sustainable purchasing tactic	Cost Structure impact	SDGs advanced
3. Exchange – Transfer	• Barter leftover lemonade pulp with a nearby jam vendor for free ice. • Use the local time bank to pay a graphic-design student for menu boards.	• Eliminates daily ice expense and reduces waste. • Creates meaningful work for a student, building their experience.	(12) Responsible Consumption and Production (17) Partnerships
4. Consumption	• Join a buyer co-op with two other stalls to bulk-order certified-compostable cups and straws. • Offer $0.25 discount for bring-your-own (BYO) cups, reducing cup use by approximately 40 %.	• Bulk order lowers unit-cup cost from $0.15 to $0.09 • BYO further shrinks the volume of supplies purchased.	(12) Responsible Consumption and Production (13) Climate Action
5. Surplus Allocation	• Re-invest 10% of profits in a solar-powered portable fridge next season. • Run a participatory vote with helpers about future surplus (i.e., distributing lemon seeds for people to plant at home).	• Solar unit cuts need for bagged ice (~$350/ season) after year 1 • Reduces waste and creates goodwill, and introduces a carbon-reducing project.	(7) Affordable and Clean Energy (13) Climate Action (15) Life on Land

HIGHLIGHTS

- Oldest fair-trade pioneer: Since 1946, Ten Thousand Villages has applied strict sustainability standards to its suppliers, ensuring producers were trained in safe production methods, paid well, and had their cultural values respected, decades before fair trade became a common term (Ten Thousand Villages, n.d.).

- Perfectly imperfect produce: Buying or gleaning organic seconds, the cosmetically ugly lemons in the farmers-market example, can cut raw-material costs by 30% to 40% while keeping taste identical (Craig, 2020).

TIPS

- Start with the big spenders: List your largest procurement line items (materials, energy, logistics, professional services) and tackle them one at a time with SE tactics.

- Quantify and celebrate the shift: When you swap resources (ie, trading an unused conference room for social-media services), record the dollar value and note the non-financial wins such as supplier loyalty, risk hedging, and brand recognition.

POINTS TO REMEMBER

- SE ≠ Charity: Each SE tactic must lower or stabilize costs while deepening community ties, producing true win-win solutions.

- Five-area toolkit: Creation, Production, Exchange – Transfer, Consumption, and Surplus Allocation all offer concrete levers for making an enterprise's Cost Structure both leaner and more resilient.

- Loop surplus back: Reinvest a slice of the savings (i.e., on-site solar, supplier training grants) to create a self-reinforcing cycle of cost reduction and innovation.

DISCUSSION QUESTIONS

- Which SE tactic would have the greatest immediate impact on your organization's cost structure, and why?

- How might turning "competitors into collaborators" (through shared bulk purchasing or equipment use) change your industry's competitive dynamics over the next five years?

4.3 Revenue Streams Multiplier

If the Cost Structure is the heart of an organization, ensuring that resources are available to turn materials into needed goods and services, then Revenue Streams are the lifeblood that keeps it all moving. Revenue Streams represent the ways an enterprise transforms its solutions to customer needs into meaningful exchanges of value. In the spirit of the Solidarity Economy, this value doesn't have to be limited to money; it can also include barter, time, shared resources, or other creative forms of exchange.

Expanding the types of Revenue Streams, adding more lifeblood, strengthens an enterprise by increasing its capacity to generate income in diverse ways, making it more profitable and resilient.

Examples:

The following are a few of the best practices for sustainability in Revenue Streams that enterprises have successfully used to grow their businesses.

- "A Place at the Table" is a pay-as-you-can restaurant that opened in Raleigh, North Carolina, in 2015. By 2020, they had served 35,238 meals with $62,000 worth of meals donated. In 2025, over 80 people volunteer for their meal every day, and they have 4.9 stars (out of 5) from over 500 Google reviews (Place at the Table, 2025).

- The Brattleboro E-Bike Lending Library provides free electric bike rentals in collaboration with non-profit organization Local Motion and the Vermont state transit office, VTrans. It is locally managed by another non-profit, VBike, along with the citizen-run Brattleboro Energy Committee, the town of Brattleboro's Sustainability Office, and Brattleboro Time Trade.

  It is housed at the Brooks Memorial Library, a public library in Brattleboro, Vermont (VBike, 2025). The Brattleboro E-Bike Lending Library's central currency is time, which is managed by the Brattleboro Time Trade time bank.

- Tilda's Kitchen and Market is a Kingston, New York business that purchases 90% local products and has 6% of its gross earnings coming from Hudson Valley Current, a local currency used for exchanging goods and services (Tilda's Kitchen and Market, 2025). Hudson Valley Current has over 450 business and individual members with 20,000 current circulations monthly and over 1.2 million since it began in 2014 (Hudson Valley Current, 2025). One current is valued at one dollar.

These three examples expand the way goods are accessed and traded, creating new markets, diversifying exchange, and creating a multiplier effect.

Figure 4.3 | **The Multiplier Effect of SE on Revenue Streams**

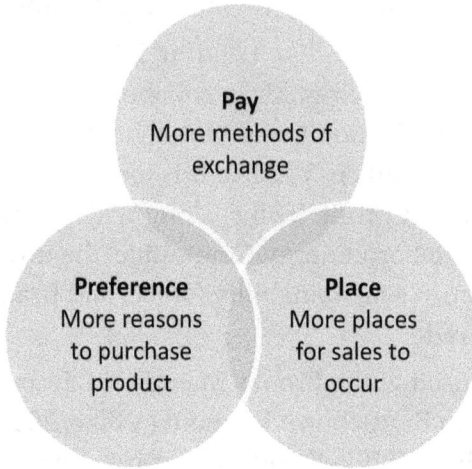

Pay
More methods of
exchange

Preference
More reasons
to purchase
product

Place
More places
for sales to
occur

The multiplier effect occurs when SE practices are applied to Revenue Streams (Fig. 4.3). SE multiplies ways customers can pay for goods and services by creating access to alternative means of exchange, including time, labor, barter, local currencies, and pay-what-you-want (PWYW) pricing.

SE multiplies the reasons customers want to buy an enterprise's products or services (preference) by connecting with causes customers find important, people customers want to support, and practices that customers want to be a part of. SE multiplies the places sales can occur, bringing products and services to new locations, including it with other initiatives, cross-promoting it with different ventures, and enlisting customers as a sales force. Together, Pay-Preference-Place, the three Ps of SE, boost total revenue while diversifying risk.

The following are examples of how the five areas of the SE framework can be applied to Revenue Streams with revenue growing outcomes (Table 4.3). These are just a few examples; using the SE framework creates limitless possibilities by presenting a new mindset and ways of experiencing exchange.

Table 4.3   Applying SE key areas to build revenue

SE key area	SE-driven revenue tactics	Revenue built and markets expanded
1. Creation	• Community-funded pre-orders or crowd-lending that convert early adopters into paying customers • Open-source or co-design licenses that let partners embed your Intellectual property (IP) in their own paid offerings (royalty stream) • Makerspace demo events that sell limited first-run editions on-site	Volume: Early capital secures inventory that is already sold. Price: Co-created products justify premium "founder-edition" pricing. Reach: Shared IP puts the offer inside partners' channels, tapping their audiences.
2. Production	• Worker- or community-owned brands that embed a fair wage story, supporting premium pricing • Micro-batch/ cottage outputs sold through pop-up markets and festivals • Revenue-sharing with local suppliers who then resell the finished good, creating a dual sales channel	Price: Values-led story sustains higher willingness to pay. Frequency: Small runs encourage "collect them all" repeat purchases. Reach: Suppliers become resellers, multiplying outlets without an extra sales force.

(Continued)

SE key area	SE-driven revenue tactics	Revenue built and markets expanded
3. Exchange – Transfer	• Pay-What-You-Want / sliding-scale menus (i.e., A Place at the Table) • Acceptance of alternative money (time-bank hours, local currency, barter credits) • Join a barter exchange and swap idle stock for trade credits	Volume: Flexible terms unlock cash-poor but motivated segments, lifting unit sales. Price: Higher-income patrons often pay more, raising average ticket value. Reach: Alternative-currency networks act as new customer pools that traditional pricing misses. Cash-flow: Trade credits spent on needed services create value from excess goods.
4. Consumption	• Membership or subscription models (CSA, buyer co-ops) with upfront dues • Refill/ repair services that upsell consumables and prolong customer lifetime value • Certified-impact labeling (fair trade, B-Corp) that opens specialty retail shelves	Cash-flow: Dues turn future sales into immediate revenue. Frequency: Refill programs create habitual, low-friction repeat buys. Channels: Certification grants access to niche stores and ethical marketplaces.
5. Surplus Allocation	• Patronage rebates that are paid out as store credit, driving return visits • Profit-share crowdfunding, where supporters earn dividends tied to future sales • Up-cycling waste into secondary products sold to new niches	Frequency: Rebates function like loyalty points, pulling customers back. Volume: Investor-customers promote and buy more to grow their own dividend. Reach: Waste-to-product lines open entirely new target segments at minimal marginal cost.

Example:

Diversifying and multiplying Revenue Streams builds the local economy. Here's a hypothetical example of how an imaginary ABC Brewery grew its customer base and brewery using barter exchange.

Barter exchange is a cashless exchange of goods and services with other barter members for credit. There are over 500 barter exchanges in North America and Latin America, and thousands worldwide (Harrison, 2025). In this example, ABC is a microbrewery and brewery that recently joined GreenTrade Exchange, a local barter club.

With a $250 membership investment, ABC was able to barter $6,000 worth of beer at retail value in exchange for barter member Carpenter Co. to build new seating in its brewery at a $1 to 1 barter credit rate, generating 6,000 barter credits.

This increased ABC's sales by 20% as more patrons could now be served. The carpenter used its 6,000 barter credits to host 12 corporate beer tasting events, pleasing its corporate customers and securing more cash contracts from corporate customers. Corporate beer tasting guests became future ABC customers, increasing ABC's cash sales.

In all, a $250 barter investment generated $49,400 in annual revenue and a bankroll of credit to use when cash flow slows or for capital improvements (Table 4.4). This is revenue that would not have happened without the barter. By opening new ways for exchange, more trade happens, risks are reduced, new relations are formed, and the economy expands.

Table 4.4	The story of ABC Brewery using SE barter to grow its business by more than 20%

SE key area	How the barter works	Revenue-Stream impact
1. Creation	ABC joins GreenTrade Exchange, a local barter club that tracks value in "Trade Credits" pegged at 1 credit = 1 USD. Annual cash fee is $250; all trades post at retail value.	Gives immediate access to 400+ member businesses (restaurants, contractors, marketers) without extra marketing spend.
2. Production	Offers: cases of seasonal beer, event-space rentals on weeknights. Needs: Brewery renovations, social-media management, locally sourced snacks.	Converts idle inventory (beer close to pull date) and underused capacity (slow-night space) into purchasing power.
3. Exchange – Transfer	Example deal: • Carpentry Co. quotes $6,000 to build reclaimed-wood booth seating. • ABC pays with 6,000 credits. • Carpentry Co. later spends those credits on 12 corporate beer tasting events (500 credits each).	Saves $6,000 cash outlay; Reclaimed wood extends the life of resources and appeals to eco-friendly customers. Booths increase brewery seating by 20%, raising weekend cash sales. Carpentry Co.'s events expose the brewery to new corporate clients.
4. Consumption	Credits earned from events flow to other members (i.e., a local print shop buys 50 cases of beer for client gifts).	Every credit redeemed for beer counts as booked revenue at full retail value, which includes the markup over wholesale.

SE key area	How the barter works	Revenue-Stream impact
5. Surplus Allocation	• 28 barter transactions • 31,400 credits earned/ spent (approximately $31,400 retail) • Net new cash customers acquired via barter events: 220 • Cash sales growth attributed to added booths: +$18,000	After one year and 28 barter transactions, the combination of cash savings and incremental cash sales produces $49,400 total economic benefit on an initial $250 membership fee. Operating cash-flow volatility drops because credits can be spent whenever cash is tight.

Applying the SE framework to the Revenue Streams of the farmers' market lemonade stand creates new ways to grow customers and sales (Table 4.5).

Table 4.5 Applying the SE framework to Revenue Streams

SE key area	SE-driven revenue tactics	Revenue and market effects	Aligned SDGs
1. Creation	• Community-funded pre-orders for a season-long Lemonade CSA. • Crowdfund a solar-powered juicer that backers get naming rights to. • Co-design "heritage" flavors with local elders and beekeepers (royalty per jar).	Volume: Upfront capital locks in demand. Reach: Backers promote the stand to their networks. Price: Premium "founder-edition" bottles.	(7) Affordable and Clean Energy (8) Decent Work and Economic Growth (12) Responsible Consumption and Production

(*Continued*)

SE key area	SE-driven revenue tactics	Revenue and market effects	Aligned SDGs
2. Production	• Source cosmetically imperfect citrus and herb scraps—upcycle waste. • Youth workers-co-op earns fair wages and ownership shares. • Micro-batch seasonal blends sold at pop-up markets and festivals.	Price: Values-led story supports a higher margin. Reach: Farmers and youth become sales ambassadors. Frequency: Collectors seek each limited batch.	(8) Decent Work and Economic Growth (12) Responsible Consumption and Production (13) Climate Action
3. Exchange – Transfer	• Pay-What-You-Can cup alongside the fixed menu. • Accept local time-bank hours and farmers-market tokens. • Barter lemonade for stall fees or surplus produce.	Volume: Flexible terms unlock cash-poor customers. Reach: Barter and token networks open new pools. Cash-flow: Reduces upfront costs.	(1) No Poverty (10) Reduced Inequalities (17) Partnerships for the Goals
4. Consumption	• Refillable mason-jar program with deposit return. • Weekly growler subscription delivered by cargo bike. • Fair-trade sugar and B-Corp story unlock ethical retail shelves.	Frequency: Jar refills create habitual repeat purchases. Cash-flow: Subscriptions convert future sales to upfront cash. Channels: Certifications open specialty shops and cafes.	(3) Good Health and Well-being (12) Responsible Consumption and Production (13) Climate Action

SE key area	SE-driven revenue tactics	Revenue and market effects	Aligned SDGs
5. Surplus Allocation	• 10% of profits fund local clean-water projects. • Compost lemon peels to nourish community gardens. • Patronage rebates paid as stand credit, boosting loyalty.	Reach: Water-project partners market the stand. Resilience: Composting cuts disposal costs and builds goodwill. Frequency: Credit rebates pull customers back.	(6) Clean Water and Sanitation (11) Sustainable Cities and Communities (12) Responsible Consumption and Production

By layering the five Solidarity-Economy areas onto Revenue Streams, an enterprise transforms from a single-channel seller into a multi-modal value creator. They become better cushioned against shocks, more attractive to mission-driven customers and employees, and positioned for steady, community-rooted growth.

FUN FACTS

There are more than 500 organized barter exchanges across North and Latin America, and thousands worldwide. This illustrates just how widespread cash-free trading networks have become (Inc., 2020).

TIPS

• Expand the three Ps: Pay, Preference, Place, to boost total revenue while diversifying risk.

• Join a barter exchange: Even a modest cash fee (i.e., ABC's $250) can unlock thousands in trade credits and new customers.

4.4 Case Study: Green Mountain Power

Powering Resilience: How Green Mountain Power Used Tesla Powerwalls to Transform Energy Storage and Grid Stability

Introduction:

Green Mountain Power (GMP), Vermont's largest electric utility, has emerged as a global leader in renewable energy innovation. Headquartered in Colchester, Vermont,

GMP serves more than 270,000 residential and commercial customers (GMP, 2023). Kristin Kelly, GMP's Director of Communications, explained, "We are the first utility in the world to earn a B Corp certification, meeting rigorous social, environmental, and accountability standards for customers" (D'Ambrosio, 2023).

Between 2017 and 2023, GMP made a bold transition from a limited pilot program to a full-scale deployment of Tesla Powerwalls across Vermont homes. This strategic decision not only provided reliable home backup power during outages but also allowed GMP to create a virtual power plant (VPP) that supported statewide grid resilience and reduced energy costs for customers.

The Challenge:

GMP faced mounting energy challenges related to grid reliability and rising peak demand costs. It also encountered the threat of extreme weather events that increasingly disrupted service. Serving a rural state with many customers located on "last mile" lines, the company needed a solution that improved grid reliability while reducing operational expenses and dependence on fossil fuels.

Last-mile lines refer to a situation where customers are located on sparsely populated roads. Getting costly service to them involves running and maintaining miles of lines through undeveloped wooded areas, resulting in a very low ROI since revenue is coming from just a few customers. The cost to serve last-mile clients is often greater than the revenue earned from them.

At the same time, customer demand for reliable, clean energy solutions was increasing. The limitations of traditional grid infrastructure made it difficult to meet peak energy needs and ensure uninterrupted service during storms and outages. In 2015, Vermonters experienced 15 power outages averaging almost 1.5 hours each and affecting over 30,000 people (Eaton, 2015). Almost half of these outages were caused by falling trees and weather-related events. GMP needed a way to modernize the grid, reduce outages, and involve customers as active energy partners.

The Solution:

In 2015, GMP partnered with Tesla to launch one of the nation's first home energy storage pilot programs. This partnership would entail GMP purchasing Tesla Powerwalls for Tesla to install and service in residential homes. Residents would be responsible for maintaining their homes and keeping the powerwalls safe. In exchange, residents would get access to the powerwall when energy outages occurred, and GMP would have access to the powerwall at all other times, reducing their reliance on expensive retail energy purchases.

The pilot was successful. By 2017, the company scaled the program leasing Tesla Powerwalls to customers for as little as $15 a month, enabling them to store solar or grid electricity for backup use during outages and peak times (Tarbi, 2023). This helped to offset GMP's purchase costs for powerwalls, while still giving customers more reliable energy access.

This innovative solution evolved into a broader strategy:

- **2017 – Pilot launch:** GMP tested the economic and operational feasibility of the Powerwall lease model.
- **2020 – Regulatory approval:** The Vermont Public Utility Commission approved GMP's request to run the Powerwall program as a regulated utility tariff, allowing broader enrollment (Green Mountain Power, 2023).
- **2023 – Cap removal:** After climate-induced events and sustained customer interest, GMP successfully

petitioned to eliminate the program's cap, which had limited installations to 500 per year. Over 2,900 customers had installed more than 4,800 batteries, with a growing waitlist into 2026 (Green Mountain Power, 2023).

The company also collaborated with commercial partners like Alias and Mount Snow to use powerwalls for reducing peak demand costs and improving energy efficiency in large-scale applications.

The Impact:

The Powerwall program has generated measurable environmental, economic, and operational benefits:

- **Reduced peak demand costs:** GMP's VPP, consisting of over 4,800 batteries and 50 megawatts of distributed storage, has saved up to $3 million annually for customers by avoiding high-cost energy purchases during peak times (Green Mountain Power, 2023).

- **Lower carbon emissions:** During one July 2018 peak demand event, stored battery energy offset 17,600 pounds of CO_2, equivalent to preventing the burning of 910 gallons of gasoline (Tarbi, 2023).

- **Positive ROI:** Customer lease payments, now $55/ month for 10 years, generate $6,600 in revenue per home, significantly offsetting battery procurement costs (D'Ambrosio, 2023).

- **Grid resilience:** During storms, batteries provide backup power, reducing outages and enhancing community safety.

These outcomes have solidified GMP's position as a trailblazer in sustainable utilities, earning national recognition from Fast Company and TIME magazine (de la Graza, 2021; Lidsky & Mokwa, 2022).

Conclusion:

Green Mountain Power's strategic embrace of distributed energy storage through Tesla Powerwalls illustrates how innovation, regulatory support, and customer partnerships can transform the utility sector. The program aligns with the United Nations Sustainable Development Goals, particularly:

- **SDG 7:** Affordable and Clean Energy
- **SDG 11:** Sustainable Cities and Communities
- **SDG 13:** Climate Action

GMP's data-driven, customer-focused approach offers a compelling model for other utilities seeking sustainable, scalable solutions to energy resilience.

Discussion Questions:

- What risks did GMP take in launching the Powerwall pilot, and how did the pilot phase help reduce them?
- How does the Powerwall program exemplify the concept of a virtual power plant?
- How did GMP balance its financials in new ways? How would you show this on their Cost Structure and Revenue Stream?
- In what ways did GMP's B Corp status influence its decision-making and stakeholder engagement?

Activity:

Reimagine GMP's Powerwall Program as a Community Energy Cooperative. Attempt to redesign this program using Solidarity Economy principles such as cooperation, equity, and community ownership. Discuss and develop a brief proposal for how the program could be managed by a local energy cooperative, ensuring access for low-income households, participatory governance, and shared environmental benefits. Highlight how your proposal builds resilience and reflects the values of a solidarity-based energy system.

In Chapter Four, we explored how financial systems grounded in the Solidarity Economy can transform enterprises into more resilient, community-rooted organizations. We began by redefining Cost Structure and Revenue Streams through the lens of SE, moving beyond conventional dollar-based transactions. We learned that the SE framework, consisting of five areas: Creation, Production, Exchange – Transfer, Consumption, and Surplus Allocation, expands access, diversifies resources, and reduces risk.

We traced the origins of SE from grassroots survival strategies in Latin America to its global recognition by the UN in 2023 as a framework aligned with the Sustainable Development Goals. Through examples and tables, we saw how enterprises could incorporate SE strategies to strengthen supply chains, lower fixed and variable costs, and create flexible, community-oriented revenue systems.

Practical applications such as Green Mountain Power's Powerwall program, ABC's barter-based brewery growth, and community-based models like "A Place at the Table" were analyzed. These case studies illustrated how SE principles, like flexible pricing, shared ownership, and participatory budgeting, can stabilize operations and build loyal, mission-aligned customer bases. Through these learnings, we can conclude that SE offers a comprehensive and proven approach for managing enterprise finances sustainably, collaboratively, and inclusively, ensuring long-term resilience and prosperity.

Chapter Summary

- Solidarity Economy is a resilient, inclusive financial framework that moves beyond dollar-based transactions by integrating shared ownership, cooperative structures, and community-based resource exchange across five areas: Creation, Production, Exchange – Transfer, Consumption, and Surplus Allocation.

- Cost Structure and Revenue Streams are dynamic, interdependent systems. Enterprises must balance fixed and variable costs with diversified and innovative revenue strategies in the BMC, including barter, time banks, and community currencies, to ensure sustainability and resilience.

- Practical SE methods like flexible pricing (e.g., Pay-What-You-Want), member-driven consumption (e.g., CSAs), and collaborative surplus reinvestment offer enterprises ways to stabilize costs, expand markets, and increase community trust and participation.

- The SE approach multiplies enterprise revenue potential by broadening payment types (Pay), customer motivation (Preference), and market access points (Place), leading to greater resilience and long-term growth, as illustrated through case examples like ABC Brewery and "A Place at the Table."

- GMP's Tesla Powerwall program demonstrates how SE-aligned financial strategies, like community partnerships, flexible leasing, and reinvestment, can create shared value, reduce energy costs, enhance grid resilience, and advance SDGs such as clean energy and climate action.

Quiz

1. Who first initiated the Solidarity Economy movement, according to the chapter?
   a. Government agencies
   b. Women and Indigenous people
   c. Multinational corporations
   d. International banks

2. Which of the following is *not* one of the five key enterprise areas that Solidarity Economy builds diversity in?
   a. Creation
   b. Consumption
   c. Marketing
   d. Surplus Allocation

3. Studies of Pay-What-You-Want (PWYW) pricing cited in the chapter found that it generally leads to which outcome?
   a. Lower average price and fewer goods sold
   b. Lower average price but a much larger number of goods sold, increasing overall earnings
   c. Higher average price with no change in volume
   d. No measurable change in revenue

4. Why is it risky for a company committed to sustainability to rely on suppliers who are not?

   a. It increases customer demand too quickly.

   b. It creates a weak link that can threaten the firm's resilience and innovation.

   c. It forces the company to pay premium prices for all inputs.

   d. It violates labor regulations in most countries.

5. Which Solidarity-Economy (SE) area explicitly encourages using barter, time banks, or community currencies to offset cash expenses?

   a. Creation

   b. Production

   c. Exchange – Transfer

   d. Surplus Allocation

6. Joining or forming a buyer co-op to bulk-purchase compostable cups and straws primarily reduces costs by:

   a. Eliminating overtime premiums for workers

   b. Securing volume discounts and lowering per-unit shipping costs

   c. Replacing interest-bearing debt with community capital

   d. Creating tax deductions for donated materials

7. What metaphor does the chapter use to describe a Revenue Stream in relation to an enterprise's Cost Structure?

   a. The heart that keeps the organization pumping

   b. The blood that flows through it

   c. The skeleton that supports it

   d. D. The brain that guides it

8. Which enterprise had served 35,238 meals with $62,000 worth of meals donated by 2020 while operating as a pay-as-you-can restaurant?
   a. Tilda's Kitchen and Market
   b. A Place at the Table
   c. ABC Brewery
   d. The Brattleboro E-Bike Lending Library

9. The Brattleboro E-Bike Lending Library's primary medium of exchange is:
   a. U.S. dollars
   b. Hudson Valley Current
   c. Time managed through the Brattleboro Time Trade time bank
   d. Barter credits from GreenTrade Exchange

10. What key risk does "monocropping" currency, like relying solely on the U.S. dollar, pose to an enterprise?
    a. It increases employee turnover.
    b. It limits innovation.
    c. It heightens vulnerability to currency devaluation.
    d. It complicates surplus allocation.

Answer Key

1 – b	2 – c	3 – b	4 – b	5 – c
6 – b	7 – b	8 – b	9 – c	10 – c

CHAPTER 5
Revisiting the Value Proposition

Key Learning Objectives

- Apply Circles of Sustainability as an impact measurement tool.
- Learn how to redefine the Value Proposition without rebuilding the enterprise.
- Understand the Blue Ocean Strategy to create value by using the Value Proposition.
- Case study: Chocolate company, Tony's Chocolonely, inspired to end child slave labor.

Sustainability is multi-layered, multi-faceted, and multi-modal. It mimics nature, can be cyclical, is dynamic, and integrates with all areas of an enterprise. A sustainability action in one area often grows new sustainability actions in other areas. It is a multiplier helping businesses to grow in new areas with strength, resilience, and stability.

After applying sustainability models to different enterprise areas, such as Suma Qamana and Customers, Permaculture and Production, and Solidarity Economy and Finances, the Value Proposition of an enterprise shifts (Fig. 5.1). The new Value Proposition is now larger and more complicated, addressing many different areas of impact, including people, community, and the natural environment.

Figure 5.1 Value Propositions

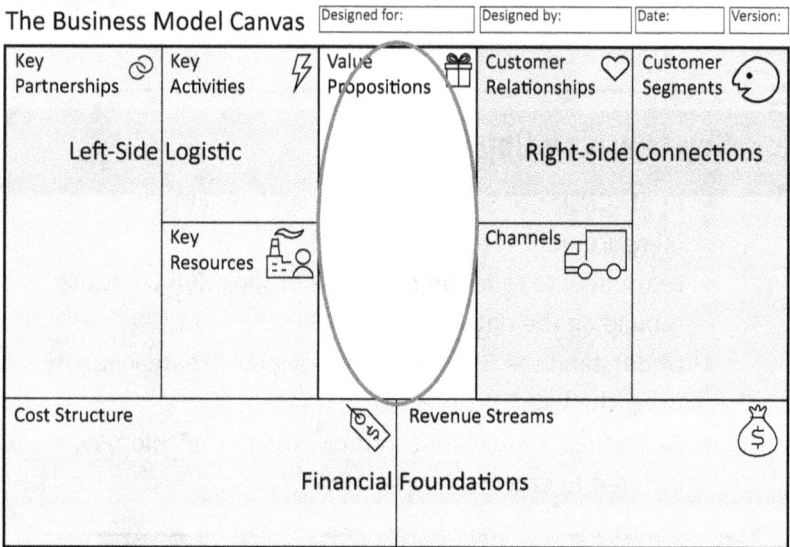

The Business Model Canvas

(Adapted from the Strategyzer BMC Model, 2025)

As an enterprise adds new sustainability practices, its Value Propositions increase, leading to new types of products and services it can sell and expanded markets to sell in.

In a competitive marketplace, it can be difficult for businesses to express and maintain new sustainability practices due to higher costs, consumer skepticism, communication challenges, pressure for short-term returns, operational complexity, and the lack of clear industry standards. Circles of Sustainability is a UN-based social measurement concept that can provide a birds-eye-view of an enterprise, delivering a clearer assessment of where it is, and identifying strengths and weaknesses in its sustainability journey. This helps enterprises to guide goal setting, connect with new allies (Key Partnerships), and measure tangible wins while further clarifying and promoting the Value Proposition.

5.1 Circles of Sustainability: The Bird's Eye View

Created through a series of United Nations Development Program conferences starting in 2012, the Circles of Sustainability is a participant-based method of understanding sustainability. Now largely managed through the University of Melbourne, it approaches sustainability from a stakeholder perspective, looking at the ecological, cultural, political, and economic impacts of practices (James, 2023). It is based on the Circles of Social Life survey tool for measuring place-based sustainability.

On an enterprise level, the Circles of Social Life survey can be applied to stakeholders, including workers, contractors, consumers, and internally, to understand an enterprise's sustainability impacts and continued needs. The result is a clearer view of the Value Propositions and a baseline measurement of progress that can be used for future planning and assessment.

There are many sustainability solutions focused on people, planet, and markets. Enterprises seek to have smaller environmental footprints, more meaningful trade, and expanded access for customers. These actions exist within the context of a society. Therefore, it's important to note that how society is experienced affects how sustainability is felt as well.

For example, a person might not appreciate receiving a beautifully hand-crafted, fair-trade garment made of organic fibers if it does not reflect their gender identity or personal preferences. Or a worker being given a flexible, half-day job share option might have transportation problems, which makes the flexibility difficult to manage. These reflect societal mismatches of sustainability practices. Enterprises with their ability to create change through how and what they produce have the power to influence sustainability in societies, too.

Figure 5.2 The Circles of Sustainability

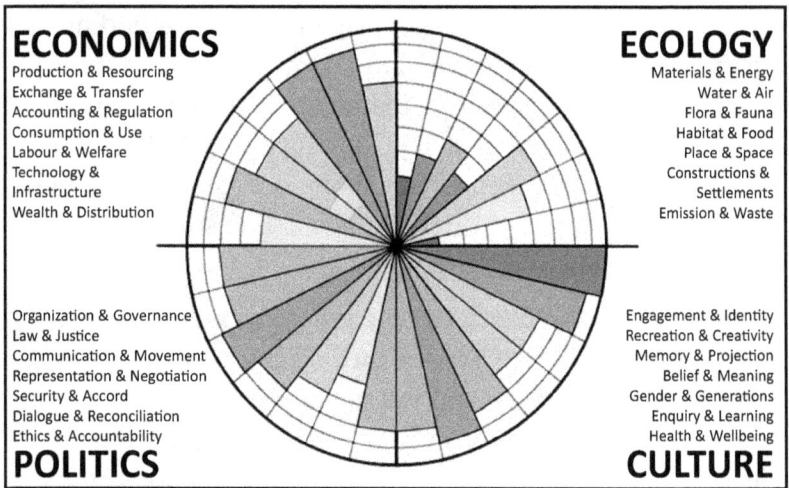

ECONOMICS
Production & Resourcing
Exchange & Transfer
Accounting & Regulation
Consumption & Use
Labour & Welfare
Technology &
Infrastructure
Wealth & Distribution

ECOLOGY
Materials & Energy
Water & Air
Flora & Fauna
Habitat & Food
Place & Space
Constructions &
Settlements
Emission & Waste

Organization & Governance
Law & Justice
Communication & Movement
Representation & Negotiation
Security & Accord
Dialogue & Reconciliation
Ethics & Accountability
POLITICS

Engagement & Identity
Recreation & Creativity
Memory & Projection
Belief & Meaning
Gender & Generations
Enquiry & Learning
Health & Wellbeing
CULTURE

(Circles of Sustainability, 2025)

The Circles of Sustainability measure enterprise or societal well-being in Ecology, Culture, Politics, and Economy.

5.1.1 Measuring Well-Being Beyond Traditional Indicators

The Circles of Sustainability concept captures crucial aspects of politics, culture, justice, and social meaning for creating transformational sustainability focused on the four domains: ecology, economy, politics, and culture (Fig. 5.2). It is an interrogative approach that helps businesses and stakeholders to reflect and analyze practices together, making sustainability something that is done with instead of done for.

This approach relies on people's interpretations of their own lived experiences in physical, social, political, and economic environments. By collecting data that reflects how a population is feeling at the moment, a snapshot of personal well-being is formed. This offers a different perspective from "traditional" well-being measurements of income levels or disease rates. Through a survey, stakeholders give input on their personal experiences in relation to the enterprise, society, and sustainability practices:

- **Ecology:** How do enterprise operations impact the environment beyond efficiency metrics (i.e., biodiversity, land use, cultural landscapes)?
- **Economy:** Are economic practices inclusive, equitable, and sustainable over the long term?
- **Politics:** Does the enterprise foster democratic participation, transparency, and accountability in its governance and supply chains?
- **Culture:** Are enterprise products and services culturally appropriate, respectful of local identities, and supportive of human flourishing?

Using the Circles of Sustainability approach, enterprises can broaden their sustainability vision beyond efficiency and profitability, and strengthen stakeholder relationships through dialogue, co-creation, and feedback loops. They can also enhance resilience and legitimacy by being culturally attuned and socially embedded, and verify their operationalization of the SDGs.

Revisiting the lemonade stand at the farmers' market with the plethora of new sustainability practices added using Suma Qamana, Permaculture, and Solidarity Economy frameworks creates new transformations. The following is a chart summing up many of the innovative and fun changes happening at the stand (Table 5.1).

Table 5.1   **A summary of key lemonade stand sustainability practices and their impact**

Dimension	What's changing	How it matters
Consumer engagement	• Access has widened: Pay-What-You-Can cups, time-bank hours, farmers-market tokens, and bartering make lemonade available to cash-poor customers; refillable jars and bring-your-own (BYO) cup discounts reward low-waste habits. • Co-creation and storytelling: "Heritage" flavors are co-designed with elders and beekeepers; chalkboards and QR codes reveal the whole supply chain; kids decorate cups, and buyers vote on how enterprises use surplus revenue, such as donating 1% of profits to environmental protection, education, or community development.	Converts purchasers into partners, deepens trust, and generates a steady stream of user-generated marketing content while reinforcing Suma Qamana values of *Munay* (love) and *Ruray* (doing together).

Dimension	What's changing	How it matters
Production	• Raw-materials loop is closing: Cosmetically "ugly" lemons, herb trimmings, and local honey are upcycled into micro-batches, while peels and meltwater are composted or reused for planter irrigation. • Energy is shifting to renewables (portable solar panel/ planned solar fridge) and low-carbon logistics (cargo bike, pooled market deliveries). • The labor model has moved from casual hires to a youth worker-co-op where members earn wages *and* ownership shares.	Cuts input costs and waste, lowers emissions, builds soil health and food security, and distributes production decision-making to workers, an explicit SE goal.
Financials	• Front-loaded, community-based capital: Season-long "Lemonade Community Sponsored Agriculture" pre-orders and a solar-juicer crowdfunding round replace interest-bearing debt. • Cost difference: Bulk-buying compostable cups with peer stalls, barter for ice, and sourcing "seconds" fruit cuts per-unit costs 30-40 %. • Recurring and diversified revenue: Subscription growlers, jar-deposit returns, royalty flavors, and patronage rebates tie customers to future cash flow.	Liquidity is improved up-front, operating costs fall, revenue becomes more predictable, allowing the stand to finance further ecological upgrades out of cash rather than loans.

(Continued)

At the same time, SDGs are being addressed on many different fronts. The following are the top four SDGs the new lemonade stand model achieves and how (Table 5.2).

Table 5.2 **Sustainability practices support four main SDGs**

SDG	Mechanism	Examples
(7) Affordable and Clean Energy	Community-financed on-site solar for juicing and cooling.	Crowdfunded solar juicer naming rights, with consumers given the opportunity to collectively choose a name for the juicer; reinvest 10% of profits into purchasing a solar fridge.
(8) Decent Work and Economic Growth	Worker-co-op model, fair-price grower contracts, skill-building via time-bank gigs.	Youth co-op shares, a graphic-design student paid in time credits, and a contract that stabilizes orchard income.
(12) Responsible Consumption and Production	Closed-loop sourcing and waste prevention across every stage.	Upcycling imperfect fruit, composting peels, a jar-return program, ingredient transparency board.
(13) Climate Action	Localized supply chain, solar power, cargo-bike deliveries, and pooled trucking.	Portable solar fridge investment, shared refrigerated truck, BYO-cup uptake, cutting single-use plastics.

5.1.2 Circles of Sustainability Survey

The Circles of Sustainability survey collects relevant demographic data, including the social group the person affiliates with, and asks questions in four realms: ecology, culture, politics, and economics. Respondents answer using a Likert scale method based on their own opinions. This reflects how an individual perceives their well-being in the social realm.

The survey follows the philosophy of Amartya Sen, Indian economist, philosopher, and 1998 Nobel laureate, noted for his work on welfare economics and the capabilities approach. It captures how people are able to live the life they have reason to value (Sen, 2009). A person may have a modest income yet feel fully satisfied economically because they have a different value opinion towards wealth. Or a wealthy person may feel lonely or isolated and report being unsatisfied with their community.

The Circles of Sustainability survey could show a lower-income person reporting being satisfied economically and a wealthy person being unhappy socially. Having people value their own places within the social sphere captures the well-being they are experiencing themselves. This gives a more accurate view of how sustainability is working for them.

Role of stakeholders in conducting the survey:

The survey is conducted via stakeholders, not the enterprise itself. Stakeholders could be workers, customers, suppliers, producers, and the Key Partnerships the enterprise may have with cooperatives, barter clubs, towns, civic groups, or other organizations outside of the enterprise.

It is important to have a stakeholder-centered approach for two reasons. One is to get a more authentic response, and the other is to have enough respondents. Stakeholder communities are better at reaching their members than an outside organization. People trust and feel comfortable within their stakeholder communities and are more apt to participate when the survey is presented by their known community.

Another benefit of having a stakeholder-driven survey is the chance to bring disparate stakeholders together on a mutual project, creating new points of collaboration as organizations disperse, collect surveys, and share results. Surveys can be anonymous, unless a participant wishes to be contacted. An incentive, such as a product discount, drawing for a larger prize, or other types of recognition, can be given so that more surveys are completed.

The following is an example of a Circles of Sustainability survey (Fig. 5.3). It can be customized slightly, but the central categories and format should stay the same. This helps the surveys to be comparable across industries. This example is based on a decade of survey development by the Circles of Sustainability group.

Figure 5.3 A sample of the Circles of Sustainability survey: Enterprise version 2025

Stakeholder Group: ____________

Surveyor Name: ____________

Date: ____________

Participant Name (optional):

____

Contact (optional):

____

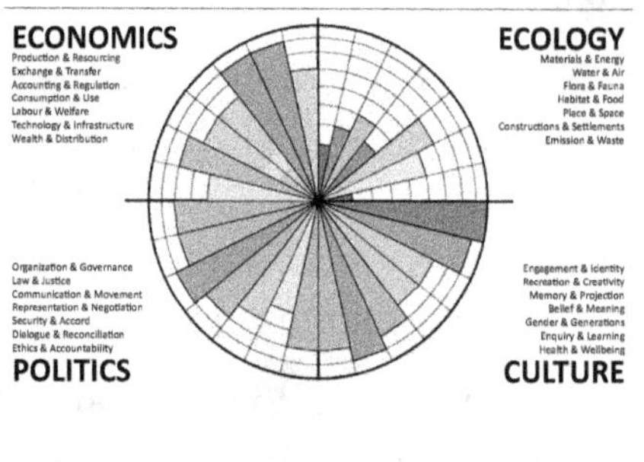

(James, 2018)

Survey demographics:

1. Gender: Male / Female / Other
2. Age (in years): 20 and under, 21-30, 31-40, 41-50, 51-60, 61-70, 71+
3. Year(s) at enterprise/ community: Less than 1, 1-5, 6-10, more than 10 years

4. What is your role/ affiliation at the enterprise/ community?
   Worker, Supplier, Customer, Resident/ Member
5. Annual income: Less than $49,999, $50,000 - $99,999, $100,000 - $100,499, more than $500,000
6. Do you own a home? Y / N
7. Demographic question relevant to the sustainability project/ outcome
8. Demographic question relevant to the sustainability project/ outcome
9. Demographic question relevant to the sustainability project/ outcome
10. Demographic question relevant to the sustainability project/ outcome

Table 5.3 **Opinion Questions**

1	2	3	4	5	6	7	8	9
Critical	Bad	Highly Unsatis-factory	Unsatis-factory	Basic	Satis-factory	Highly Satis-factory	Good	Vibrant

Survey Questions	Rating (1-9)

SOCIAL

1. The political environment is?
2. How do you consider your access to health services?
3. How is the health of your community?
4. How is the education in your community?
5. How well are you able to influence or participate in decision-making?
6. How well does your community make decisions?

(Continued)

Survey Questions	Rating (1-9)
7. How is the confidence between members of your community?	
ENVIRONMENT	
8. The natural environment is...	
9. How is the physical climate in your community?	
10. How is the food quality in your community?	
11. How is the wildlife around your community?	
12. How is your community's access to energy (gas and electricity)?	
13. How is your community's access to meeting and recreation spaces?	
14. How clean is your community in relation to environmental contaminants and garbage?	
ECONOMIC	
15. The opportunities to improve one's economic well-being are...	
16. How are your own economic earnings (financial well-being)?	
17. How is your market access for sharing products or services?	
18. How is your access to the products you want to consume?	
19. In general, how is the technology and infrastructure in your community?	
20. In general, how is the economic production in your community?	
21. How are your conditions for work and access to jobs?	
CULTURE	
22. How is/ are your cultural identity(ies)?	
23. The community values your culture...	
24. How is your participation in the customs of your culture?	

Survey Questions	Rating (1-9)
25. How is your participation in religion?	
26. How is your participation in local community festivals?	
27. How is your participation in family traditions?	
28. How is your sharing of ancestral stories/ beliefs/ wisdom?	

(James, 2018)

Once surveys are completed, averages are tallied, and the Circles of Sustainability online data mapping tool: https://www.circlesofsustainability.com/tools/rapid-assessment-tool/ is used to create a sustainability profile, inputting data in each quadrant in a clockwise manner.

5.1.3 Evaluating Survey Outcomes

Looking at the results by domain highlights where a balance or an imbalance exists.

- Full, lightly shaded: Strong areas with very positive responses. These are opportunities to celebrate successes, share best practices, and build on what works well.

- Partially full, dark: Weak areas with the lowest responses. These signal unmet needs and opportunities for change or innovation.

The profile can also be broken down by stakeholder groups or demographics to reveal differences in perspectives. The Circles profile represents an overview of sustainability at a particular point in time; it reflects the broader social environment in which the organization operates, not the organization itself.

Let's use the lemonade stand example. The stand could enlist farmers' market volunteers or students from a local high school math class to ask patrons to complete surveys in exchange for a free lemonade sample. Modern tools could be used to create the survey and analyze the resulting insights. The survey would be customized with demographic questions 6 through 10 reflecting the specific data needs of the lemonade stand, such as family size and make-up, reason for shopping the market, and frequency of shopping.

After administering surveys during the market, students would later study the survey data as part of a classroom statistics unit. Demographic data would be categorized into patron categories or "avatars." An example of a patron category could be a 30-40 -year-old woman visiting her local farmers' market lemonade stand in Boston, with her partner and small children during a time of sustainability challenges—from the natural environment, political stressors, and the economy (Table 5.4). The avatar of the person could be named "Jean," and this could be her Sustainability Profile. "Jean" would be representative of the range of people who fit into this patron category.

Table 5.4 Patron category: "Jean's" experience of a farmers' market lemonade stand using sustainability practices

#	Question	Rating	Brief reflection from today's visit
POLITICS	Average rating	5.7	
1	The political environment is...	4	National tensions feel heavy, though the stand's inclusive signage ("Pay-What-You-Can" cup) hinted at grassroots hope.
2	Access to health services	7	Boston's hospitals are world-class and nearby.

#	Question	Rating	Brief reflection from today's visit
3	Health of your community	6	Rising asthma rates worry me, yet the market's fresh produce and low-sugar lemonade are positive signs.
4	Education in your community	7	Strong public and charter schools; kids got a quick "how we squeeze lemons" demo.
5	Ability to influence/ participate in decision-making	5	I vote and attend precinct meetings, but city processes feel complex. The stand's chalkboard invite to "suggest flavors" felt empowering.
6	How well your community makes decisions	5	Mixed—bike-lane expansions go well, housing policy drags.
7	Confidence (trust) among community members	6	Farmers-market vibe fosters trust; neighbors chatted while kids sampled lemonade.
ECOLOGY	**Average rating**	**6.4**	
8	The natural environment	6	Charles River is cleaner than a decade ago, but urban heat islands persist.
9	Physical climate	5	Hotter, stormier summers; today was muggy even at 10 a.m.
10	Food quality in your community	8	Abundant local farms; the stand's organic "ugly-fruit" citrus upcycling impressed me.
11	Wildlife around your community	5	Squirrels and sparrows thrive, but pollinator loss is noticeable.
12	Access to energy (gas and electricity)	8	Reliable grid; stand displayed a mini-solar panel—loved that.

(Continued)

#	Question	Rating	Brief reflection from today's visit
13	Access to meeting and recreation spaces	7	Parks, libraries, and the market plaza are accessible; stroller-friendly, too.
14	Community cleanliness (contaminants and garbage)	6	Street trash after Red Sox games is an issue, but the market's compost stations help.
ECONOMICS	**Average rating**	**7.1**	
15	Opportunities to improve economic well-being	7	Robust biotech and education sectors; vendors accept Supplemental Nutrition Assistance Program (SNAP)/ Massachusetts' Healthy Incentives Program (HIP) benefits.
16	Your own economic earnings	6	Dual income is stable, yet childcare and housing costs pinch.
17	Market access for sharing products/ services	7	Pop-ups, Etsy locals, and this market give side-hustlers visibility.
18	Access to products you want to consume	8	From zero-waste shops to specialty grocers, selection is broad.
19	Technology and infrastructure	8	Fast internet, decent public transit; the stand's QR code receipt was seamless.
20	Economic production in your community	7	Start-ups abound; still worry about manufacturing decline.
21	Work conditions and job access	7	Strong labor market, though gig-economy precarity looms; the youth co-op staffing the stand felt hopeful.

#	Question	Rating	Brief reflection from today's visit
CULTURE	Average rating	6.0	
22	Your cultural identity(ies)	7	Proud of Latin-Irish heritage; bilingual signs at the stand felt welcoming.
23	Community values your culture	7	City festivals celebrate diversity; the market hosts a "Global Flavors" day.
24	Participation in customs of your culture	6	Cook family recipes, join Día de los Muertos events; limited time with toddlers.
25	Participation in religion	4	Spiritual but attends church rarely.
26	Participation in local community festivals	6	We hit Somerville PorchFest and now this farmers-market tasting.
27	Participation in family traditions	7	Weekly Sunday dinners, kids help bake.
28	Sharing ancestral stories/ beliefs/ wisdom	5	I tell bedtime stories from Abuela, but I want to record them for the kids.

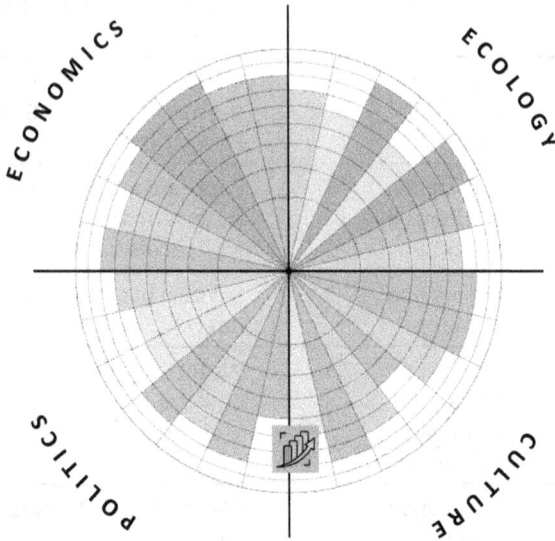

Figure 5.4 Mapping the Circles of Sustainability profile of Jean, a farmers' market patron

(Stenn, 2025)

The response in Table 5.4 is an example of what the user experience and outcome could be when using a Circles of Sustainability approach. In this case, the patron showed a strong sense of economic grounding but felt key cultural and political elements were missing. Referencing the original survey questionnaire shows exactly which question corresponds to each segment of the circle, arranged in clockwise order.

Ideally, dozens of surveys would be completed by stakeholders engaging with actual members, creating a diverse dataset to more accurately identify successes and needs. Enterprises cannot solve all problems, but having a baseline measure of the social environment in which they and their stakeholders operate builds a better understanding of strengths and opportunities.

Circles of Sustainability data helps enterprises to better connect with stakeholders, building stronger allies and markets. Applying what is learned by the Circles of Sustainability back to the Value Proposition helps an enterprise expand its mission, learn what is working well, and get new ideas. It helps businesses identify where further changes can be made and gain a baseline measure against which future efforts can be measured. It also sets an example for the community, building goodwill with customers and workers.

FUN FACTS

- Every Circles of Sustainability profile is built from four core domains (ecology, economy, politics, culture) with 7 sub-domains inside each one, equalling 28 pie-like segments in total. When the segments are filled from grey to black, the result is a personalized profile that instantly shows where an enterprise's stakeholders are thriving and where they need help. The more full and light each slice is, the more vibrant the people feel in that segment.

- The city of Milwaukee used the Circles framework to tackle water-quality issues; two years later, in 2011, it won the United States Water Prize and even landed a $500k IBM "Better Cities" award for its integrated approach—proof that mapping sustainability holistically can unlock real-world accolades (and cash!). (Western Sydney University, n.d.; Clean Water America Alliance, 2011).

TIPS

- Let stakeholders lead the survey. Having workers, customers, or community partners administer questionnaires boosts trust and response rates.

- Offer small incentives. A free lemonade sample or product discount encourages people to participate in the Circles of Sustainability survey.

POINTS TO REMEMBER

- Circles of Sustainability gives a "bird's-eye view" of an enterprise, highlighting strengths and weaknesses in ecology, economy, politics, and culture.

- Applying sustainability frameworks such as Suma Qamana, Permaculture, and Solidarity Economy often expands the Value Proposition.

- The resulting data can guide a pivot, refining the value proposition without rebuilding the enterprise, while verifying progress toward the SDGs.

DISCUSSION QUESTIONS

- How might an enterprise use feedback from the Circles of Sustainability survey to re-align its value proposition without disrupting existing operations?

- In what ways can the stakeholder-driven approach strengthen relationships and uncover new market opportunities for a social enterprise?

5.2 The Pivot: When to Change

As an enterprise engages in sustainability practices, its mindset, mission, and values may shift. New products and sales opportunities emerge, and the value proposition of current products and services expands.

Change is not easy for enterprises, and it might not always be what customers want. While it is exciting to identify new markets and features, knowing which changes to make and how is key. The Lean Startup Framework, developed by entrepreneur Eric Ries, takes the uncertainty out of change and helps to verify ventures on a small scale, or pivot, before large-scale implementation (Ries, 2011).

Based on Reis' failure to grow his own enterprise, the Lean Startup Framework draws from lean manufacturing's checks and balances systems to test the hypothesis of a new idea using Build-Measure-Learn (BML) loops (Ries, 2010). This enables enterprises to collect data before spending time or resources on an idea that is missing its mark, thus reducing waste and guesswork.

The Lean Launchpad is presented visually as a pyramid with the enterprise vision as its base, followed by a strategy to realize that vision, and a product which is the result of the vision-driven strategy being implemented (Fig. 5.5). The pivot, or place of change, occurs at the strategy point with the product being optimized.

| Figure 5.5 | The Lean Launchpad Change Optimization Model |

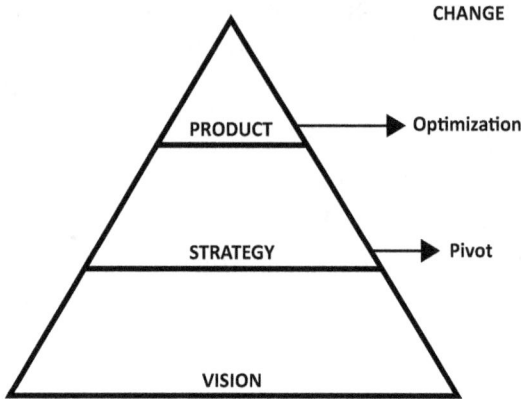

(Ries, 2011)

The Lean Launchpad visually shows the power of the vision to drive an innovation; it is the base of the idea pyramid. How that vision is realized leaves room for flexibility. Strategies to realize the vision are somewhat flexible and can pivot if they are proving ineffective. However, the product itself, the outcome of that vision, is where the most flexibility happens, with constant optimization and revision taking place.

5.2.1 Reaching the Pivot: Leveraging MVP and the BML Loop

Strategy is a measurable hypothesis, based on the belief that an action taken will result in a desired outcome. Product development occurs when the strategy is implemented on a small scale, in the form of a minimum viable product (MVP) (Ries, 2011). The pivot happens when the strategy and product are misaligned; the customer is not reacting as expected, or the product is underperforming.

The pivot gives the enterprise permission to start again, try things differently, and change. It is an iterative process that continues until vision, strategy, and product align, and optimization takes place. With optimization, there is a new Value Proposition, one that has proven meaning and impact and is ready to be launched and scaled. Pivots are meant to be agile and quick, something to check out briefly through a quick study, such as a tabling event, focus group, survey, or initial sales observations. In this way, the lean launchpad mindset is both scientific and flexible.

Optimizing sustainable solutions through quick experiments:

A Build-Measure-Learn (BML) loop is used to navigate the change management process towards sustainable changes. Build begins with the MVP, the smallest unit of a product or service that can be used to test the idea. The MVP could be a proof-of-concept prototype, a small first run of a few test samples, a test trial, or a small-scale version of the larger idea.

The MVP is used to verify the falsifiable hypothesis (one that can be proven wrong) or a quantifiable hunch the enterprise has about its sustainability solution, and is then presented to the market in a measurable way. Being measurable is important for verifying if the intended outcome is feasible or not. Often multiple outcomes can be explored at once, for example, different flavors, different prices, different sizes, with a determination of which one is optimum to scale and go into full production (optimize).

Different measurement metrics include conversion rates, repeat purchases, Net Promoter Scores (NPS) for customer recommendations, or how the sustainability solution affects the company's environmental, social, and governance reputation.

Learning happens when the data is analyzed. Enterprises ask, "What is working, what is not? Is the correct audience being addressed? Is the correct messaging being used? Are the features meeting customer needs and resolving pains?" The BML is a loop that brings enterprises back to the drawing board. If a solution is not hitting the mark, it can be simply tried again, and again, from different approaches until the right solution is found. This is the pivot.

The following are examples of common mismatches (pivots) that a Lean Startup framework uncovers and the solution (learning) that comes from it.

- **Feature-benefit pivot:** Though a feature may reduce carbon, the customer might be more interested in its cost savings. Solution: focus on the feature as a money saver with carbon offsets as a secondary benefit.

- **Customer-segment pivot:** The best customer may be a corporate bulk buyer rather than an individual consumer. Solution: switch to a Business-to-Business (B2B) sales model and packaging.

- **Problem-space pivot:** Customers might be more interested in the transparency of all processes and not just the new waste management efforts. Solution: Prioritize full supply chain transparency.

- **Engine-of-growth pivot:** Membership or green bonds investment fund scaling up better than profit margin alone by providing revenue up-front where it's most needed. Solution: adjust the revenue model.

Applying the Lean Startup framework to the lemonade stand in the farmers' market starts with a vision: "Serve delicious lemonade that leaves the planet and our community better than we found them." And it then moves to strategies asking, "Which green practices create enough customer value to sustain the stand financially?" The next step is to form a falsifiable hypothesis that can be tested within one or two weekend markets. Thus, four possibilities are:

- Shoppers will pay a 10% premium for lemonade made from cosmetically imperfect local lemons because they like the food-waste story.

- A refillable mason-jar program will boost repeat visits by at least 25%.

- People will crowdfund a solar-powered juicer if they receive naming rights and a "founder-edition" bottle.

- Offering a $0.25 BYO-cup discount will cut disposable-cup purchases by 40%.

The following is a BML loop for each of the falsifiable hypotheses (Table 5.5).

Table 5.5 | **The BML model tests different hypotheses, identifying possible pivots**

Hypothesis	Build (MVP)	Measure	Learn (pivot)
#1 Waste-wise recipe	Batch "Ugly-Lemon" lemonade with seconds from nearby growers, highlight the story on a chalkboard.	• % of cups sold at premium price • Customer interviews on taste and ethics	Pivot? If full-price buyers ≤ 50%, reframe the benefit from "planet-saving" to "farm-fresh taste" or seek a different customer segment (ie, zero-waste club).

(Continued)

Hypothesis	Build (MVP)	Measure	Learn (pivot)
#2 Container loop	Sell 24 refillable mason jars with a $1 deposit: track return rate next week.	• Return/ refill ratio • Repeat-purchase revenue	If refills < 15%, run a zoom-in pivot: keep the jar idea but narrow to weekly subscribers who get local growler deliveries by cargo bike.
#3 Energy story	Launch a one-week go-fund-me for the solar juicer; offer supporters a named bottle and free first refill.	• $ pledged vs. $ goal • Number of social-media shares	If funding stalls at < 60% halfway, switch to a problem-pivot: maybe customers care more about cold drinks than solar tech. Redirect funds to a solar-powered fridge that eliminates bagged ice costs.
#4 Cup savings	Post BYO-cup discount and stock compostable cups; track daily cup inventory.	• Disposables per 100 sales • Coupon redemption rate	If the waste reduction target is missed, test a channel pivot; sell insulated branded mugs at neighboring zero-waste shops to seed BYO behavior.

Based on the measured results, a pivot may be needed. The following are possible actions an enterprise could take in response to the lemonade stand BML and pivot types (Table 5.6).

Table 5.6	The BML response triggers a pivot type that results in vetted sustainability actions

BML response	Pivot type	Sustainability action
Customers applaud the waste story but won't pay more.	Value-proposition pivot	Emphasize super-fresh flavor and show a juice-time-to-cup countdown.

BML response	Pivot type	Sustainability action
The BYO program is embraced only by cyclists.	Customer-segment pivot	Target bike-commuter groups and local racing events.
Crowdfunding succeeds, but on-site sales plateau.	Engine-of-growth pivot	Shift to a subscription CSA model—prepaid weekly lemonade shares.
The solar juicer idea lacks draw, but cold drinks fly off the shelf.	Technology pivot	Reallocate funds to a solar fridge and market it as "sun-chilled."

If it works, do it again! Once an idea passes the Build-Measure-Learn loop, try it again to make sure it is solid. If so, keep going. Adopt it as a new practice, scale it, and start thinking about the next hypothesis and BML when ready. Using quick experiments, clear metrics, and evidence-based pivots, an enterprise maximizes both its social-environmental impact and its profitability, one cup (and one BML cycle) at a time. This is how a sustainable enterprise can grow in a measured, surefooted way.

Lean Startup reframes sustainability efforts as a series of evidence-based bets rather than one-shot, top-down programs or untested innovations. By treating the value proposition itself as a testable hypothesis and being willing to pivot when the data says so, enterprises can accelerate both their environmental impact and their return on sustainable investment, turning good intentions into competitive, resilient business models. Running sustainability ideas through the Lean Startup framework moves an enterprise away from idealistic but unfeasible or costly initiatives towards practices that connect with customers and create value.

Besides helping our lemonade stand example, Circles of Sustainability style surveys and Lean Startup pivots work with "real-world" enterprises, too. Enterprises collect plenty of data on current users through sales records and social media engagement. Getting to know non-users and the broader community where one operates creates new opportunities for sales and connection, targeting the Value Proposition in new ways. Taking the time to use a tool such as Circles of Sustainability to gather data on a community one may not know well but is a part of is not easy, but the insight one gains from community studies pays off.

5.2.2 Using Community and Demographic Data to Redesign a Product and Expand Market Impact: Nintendo's Wii

A compelling case of community and demographic-based product transformation can be seen in the development of the Nintendo Wii. In the early 2000s, Nintendo faced intense competition in the gaming industry from technologically superior systems offered by Microsoft and Sony. Rather than competing on graphics or hardware specifications, Nintendo conducted in-depth research into a lesser-understood demographic: people who did not identify as gamers. These individuals, referred to as "non-gamers," were often intimidated or disinterested in traditional video games due to complex controllers, aggressive content, or steep learning curves (Avery & Norton, 2017).

How Nintendo differentiated itself from competitors:

By gathering data on the behaviors, preferences, and barriers experienced by this cohort, Nintendo discovered a significant opportunity to engage new users through inclusive, intuitive, and socially engaging gameplay. This research informed a strategic pivot: instead of trying to outperform competitors technically, Nintendo would prioritize accessibility and simplicity. The result was the Wii, a radically different game console that used motion-sensitive controllers, interactive graphics, and straightforward user interfaces. These design features were specifically tailored to users who had been excluded from the gaming experience: older adults, young children, families, and people with limited gaming experience.

The Wii's market performance was staggering. It sold over 100 million units worldwide, making it one of the most successful gaming consoles in history (O'Gorman, 2008). More importantly, it broadened the definition of a "gamer" by welcoming new users into the gaming ecosystem. Nursing homes hosted Wii bowling tournaments, families played together in living rooms, and schools used the Wii for fitness and movement-based activities. This demonstrated how a value proposition, when informed by demographic and community insights, can expand and evolve to serve more diverse audiences.

A multi-perspective sustainability approach:

From a sustainability perspective, Nintendo's approach mirrors many of the principles seen in stakeholder-based frameworks such as the Circles of Sustainability. By focusing on user needs from multiple perspectives, ecological (simplicity, reduced components), cultural (inclusive gameplay), political (democratizing access), and economic (affordability and mass appeal), Nintendo effectively shifted the social role of gaming. The result was not only commercial success but also broader societal engagement and inclusion.

Nintendo's Wii story illustrates how listening to larger communities can catalyze a value proposition pivot, open new markets, and generate meaningful impact. It shows how sustainability, when viewed through a stakeholder lens, can inform innovation in ways that are culturally embedded, economically viable, and socially transformative.

HIGHLIGHTS

- The Lean Startup method was born out of Eric Ries' failure to grow his own enterprise, turning mistakes into a model for innovation.

- When Nintendo launched the Wii in 2006, it redefined who could be a gamer. The Wii invited grandparents, parents, and children to play together, even turning living rooms into fitness centers and physical therapy clinics. In fact, doctors began prescribing the Wii for patient rehabilitation, making it the first game console to be used as medicine (O'Gorman, 2008).

TIPS

- Always make hypotheses falsifiable; if you can't measure it, you can't improve or pivot from it.

- Don't fear the pivot; it's not failure, it's feedback that helps refine your sustainable value proposition.

POINTS TO REMEMBER

- Build-Measure-Learn is a looped process for testing ideas quickly and effectively.

- The pivot happens at the strategy level, when there's misalignment between customer response and the product.

- Optimization begins only after product, strategy, and vision are in alignment and validated through data.

- How does the Lean Startup approach reduce risk and increase success for sustainability-focused enterprises?

- In the lemonade stand case, which pivot example do you think had the most impact, and why?

5.3 Building Your Blue Ocean: Outperforming the Competition

Building sustainability into goods or services expands an enterprise's value proposition and opens new markets. The Blue Ocean Strategy helps sustainability-minded enterprises to recognize and connect with these markets, drawing on the value of their innovation practices.

The premise of the Blue Ocean Strategy was developed in 2004 by W. Chan Kim and Renée Mauborgne. After 15 years of research into 100 years of strategic business approaches across 30 industries, they found a common premise: enterprises either competed in red oceans, crowded and bloody with competition, or created blue oceans with relatively few players and lots of room for growth (Kim & Mauborgne, 2004).

Kim & Mauborgne favored the blue oceans and created a map for enterprises to get there. Suma Qamana, Permaculture, and Solidarity Economy frameworks help enterprises to succeed in increasingly competitive global markets by differentiating their strategies and forming their own blue oceans.

More specifically, red oceans are existing industries where the rules are known, and competition is fierce. Enterprises fight to gain a bigger share of limited demand, which leads to crowded markets, lower profits, and products that all start to look the same. In contrast, blue oceans are new or undiscovered markets with little or no competition. In blue oceans, enterprises create demand instead of competing for it. There's more room for fast, profitable growth. Blue oceans can be formed by creating entirely new industries or by redefining the boundaries of existing industries. Sustainability solutions give enterprises the option to do either or both.

The Strategy Canvas is a diagnostic action framework for defining and building blue oceans. It is a five-step visual tool that helps organizations understand how to create new markets by redefining value (Fig. 5.6).

Figure 5.6 **The five steps of the Blue Ocean Strategy Canvas**

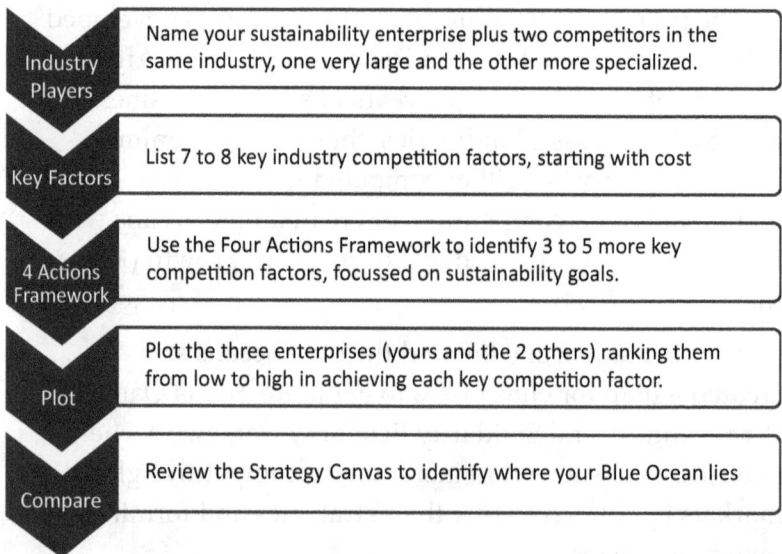

Industry Players — Name your sustainability enterprise plus two competitors in the same industry, one very large and the other more specialized.

Key Factors — List 7 to 8 key industry competition factors, starting with cost

4 Actions Framework — Use the Four Actions Framework to identify 3 to 5 more key competition factors, focussed on sustainability goals.

Plot — Plot the three enterprises (yours and the 2 others) ranking them from low to high in achieving each key competition factor.

Compare — Review the Strategy Canvas to identify where your Blue Ocean lies

(Adapted from The Blue Ocean Strategy, Kim & Mauborgne, 2004)

Step 1: Industry players

The Strategy Canvas starts with an enterprise naming key players, or competition, in its industry on either end of a spectrum. On one end is a large, popular competitor, and on the other is a more specialized one.

Step 2: Key factors

Next, seven or eight key factors, or industry norms, that the enterprises compete for are identified. The first key factor is always price. Others can be product access, product quality, or location—it depends on the industry. The result is a chart that shows the key factors of competition in the industry on the horizontal axis and the level of offering an enterprise provides for each factor, from low to high, on the vertical axis.

The two competitors and the sustainability enterprise are plotted on the chart, based on how high or low they are in each key factor. The objective is for the sustainability enterprise to plot differently than the competition, to eke out its own blue ocean.

Step 3: Four Actions Framework

Next, a Four Actions Framework is applied. This framework is like a design-thinking lens for creating a strategy that aligns with your ethics. When used with the Strategy Canvas, the Four Actions Framework becomes a powerful blueprint for inventing regenerative, inclusive markets that align with the SDGs, not just beating the competition, but changing the game entirely. The framework expands key factors to create blue oceans by asking questions illustrated in Figure 5.7:

Figure 5.7	The Four Actions Framework for strategizing industry conditions

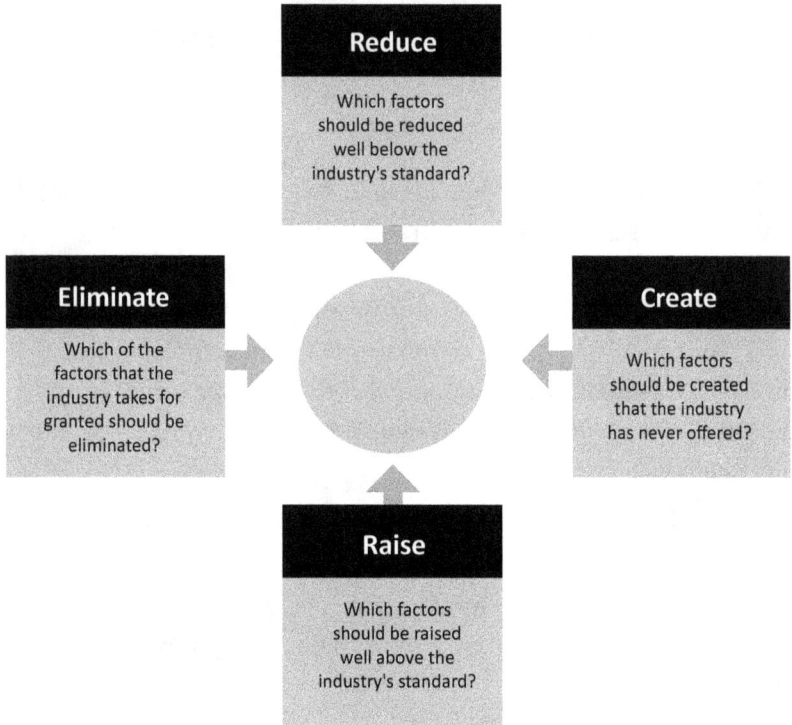

Reduce

Which factors should be reduced well below the industry's standard?

Eliminate

Which of the factors that the industry takes for granted should be eliminated?

Create

Which factors should be created that the industry has never offered?

Raise

Which factors should be raised well above the industry's standard?

(Kim & Mauborgne, 2005).

Step 4: Plot

This is where sustainability values come in. Enterprises working with sustainability frameworks are well-positioned to respond to the Four Actions Framework in unique ways. They are already considering the full lifecycle of products, the impacts of their enterprise on the community, collaborations with suppliers, and new ways of engaging customers.

The work enterprises do to develop sustainable solutions to meet and expand SDGs creates new key factors, too. Sustainability-focused key factors can include community ownership, cultural preservation, environmental regeneration, living wages, long-term well-being, and local value creation. Further, using the Four Actions Framework adds three to five additional key factors to the chart.

Step 5: Compare

The last step in creating a Strategy Canvas is to re-plot the competition and the sustainability enterprise on the chart, including the new key factors, creating a new value curve. Comparing a sustainability enterprise to mainstream competitors visually shows the distinct value offered. This strategy canvas visually demonstrates an enterprise's unique value proposition and shows how it breaks away from the red ocean to create a new, ethical, blue ocean market space.

Applying these five steps of the Blue Ocean Strategy Canvas to the farmers' market lemonade stand example creates new ways to market and present the enterprise. Industry competition can include a mass market canned lemonade and a powdered mix.

The result is a way to identify new product creation where there is no competition, a way to reposition old products, a strategic reinvention of an older enterprise escaping from outdated industry norms, an alignment with social enterprises, SDGs, and innovation, and new best practices in sustainability. Refer to Figure 5.8 and Table 5.7. Finally, Figure 5.9 illustrates the Blue Ocean Strategy Canvas for the lemonade stand market.

Figure 5.8   The five steps of the Blue Ocean Strategy for the farmers' market

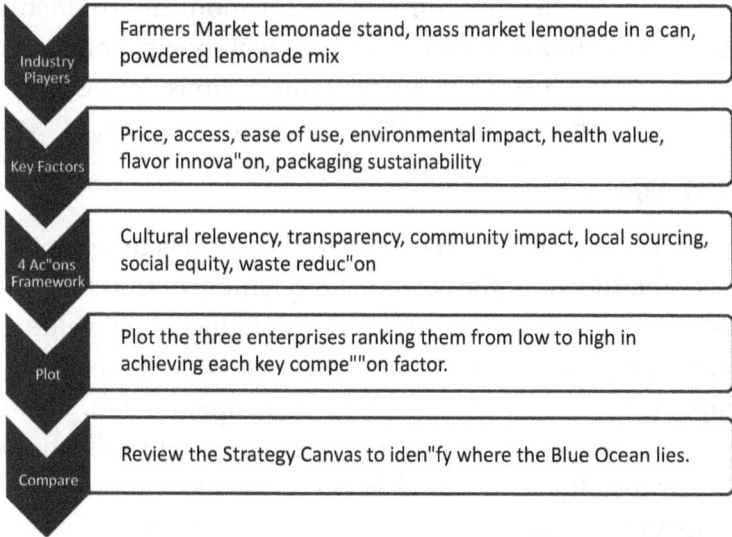

Industry Players	Farmers Market lemonade stand, mass market lemonade in a can, powdered lemonade mix
Key Factors	Price, access, ease of use, environmental impact, health value, flavor innova"on, packaging sustainability
4 Ac"ons Framework	Cultural relevency, transparency, community impact, local sourcing, social equity, waste reduc"on
Plot	Plot the three enterprises ranking them from low to high in achieving each key compe""on factor.
Compare	Review the Strategy Canvas to iden"fy where the Blue Ocean lies.

(Adapted from The Blue Ocean Strategy, Kim & Mauborgne, 2004)

Following these steps guides one to best understand their competition and market in order to carve out a unique niche, one's own "Blue Ocean."

Table 5.7   Lemonade stand: Four Actions Framework

Action	Lemonade stand: Four Actions Framework
Eliminate	Artificial ingredients, plastic packaging, bank-financed startup costs, and reliance on industrial supply chains
Reduce	Inconvenience (slower service, limited hours), cost sensitivity (low price preferences), disposable materials
Raise	Transparency, cultural connection, community involvement, health benefits, and environmental impact
Create	Heritage flavors, refillable jars, youth co-op jobs, CSA-style subscriptions, barter systems

Figure 5.9 Blue Ocean Strategy Canvas: Lemonade market comparison

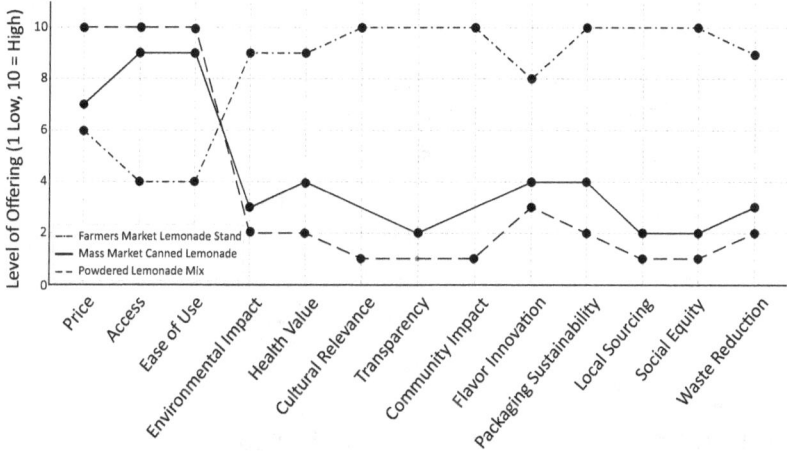

FUN FACTS   Entertainment company Cirque du Soleil is the poster child of Blue Ocean Strategy. Instead of trying to outdo traditional circuses with better clowns or more animals, Cirque du Soleil eliminated animals entirely, added theater, storylines, and high-end aesthetics, and created a new category blending circus, opera, and Broadway. This let them charge much higher prices, and people gladly paid (Blue Ocean Team, 2022).

TIPS

- When using the Strategy Canvas, always start with price, then add 6 to 7 other key industry competition factors.

- Use sustainability values, like environmental regeneration and community ownership, as your added key factors in the Four Actions Framework.

- The Strategy Canvas and Four Actions Framework were designed for businesses and can also help social enterprises to align with SDGs.

POINTS TO REMEMBER

- Red oceans are crowded markets with known rules and high competition.

- Blue oceans are new, uncontested market spaces where demand is created, not fought over.

- Sustainability-focused enterprises are well-positioned to leverage the Strategy Canvas and Four Actions Framework to unlock new ethical markets.

DISCUSSION QUESTIONS

- How can your enterprise use sustainability values to "raise" or "create" new key factors in its industry?

- In your sector, what are examples of red ocean competition, and how could you redefine those norms to create a blue ocean?

5.4 Case Study: Tony's Chocolonely

Bittersweet Success: Tony's Chocolonely and the Struggle to Stay Slave-Free

Introduction:

Founded in 2005 by Dutch journalist Teun van de Keuken, Tony's Chocolonely emerged as a pioneering social enterprise with a bold mission: to eradicate modern slavery and child labor from the chocolate supply chain (Holmes, 2025). What started as a journalistic investigation into abuses in West African cocoa farms evolved into a full-fledged chocolate business that challenged industry norms.

Based in the Netherlands and now expanded to the U.S., Ireland, and the UK, Tony's works directly with over 20,000 cocoa farmers in Ghana and the Ivory Coast. Its signature chocolate bars, with uneven segments symbolizing the unfair cocoa trade, represent more than just sweets; they are a platform for activism and ethical supply chain reform.

Figure 5.10 The Tony's Chocolonely logo includes its mission, "Together we'll make chocolate 100% slave free."

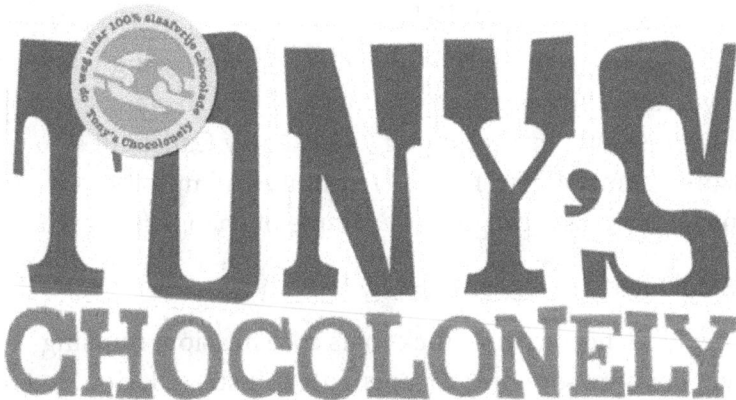

(Tony's Chocolonely, 2025)

The Challenge:

In 2021, Tony's Chocolonely celebrated a revenue milestone of €100 million (approximately $157.3 million), yet this success was marred by financial and reputational setbacks (Holmes, 2025). Despite strong market expansion, including a 45% increase in sales in the UK and Ireland, the company posted its second consecutive annual loss, totaling $6.5 million, a 40% increase over the prior year's losses.

At the core of the financial crisis were rising cocoa prices and low yields, both of which squeezed margins for a business already committed to paying above-market rates to ensure a living wage for its partner farmers. In addition, the company faced a legal challenge from the U.S.-based Slave Free Chocolate Coalition, which accused Tony's of false advertising due to its partnering with Barry Callebaut for chocolate processing.

Barry Callebaut was a major chocolate processor implicated in child labor abuses. Tony's did not have the resources to build its own chocolate couverture processing plant, so it rented separate equipment and space in the Barry Callebaut factory—dedicated solely to their chocolate so their slave-free chocolate did not mix with Barry's. But that was not enough for the Coalition.

The industry and public alike began questioning whether Tony's radical transparency model and ethical claims still held water. Would continuing to use Barry Callebaut's facilities compromise Tony's credibility and mission? Or could it serve as a pragmatic example of change from within?

The Solution:

Tony's Chocolonely stuck to its core mission, refusing to cut costs by sourcing cheaper cocoa. Instead, it doubled down on its five sourcing principles: full traceability, higher prices for farmers, long-term contracts, strong farmer relationships, and productivity-enhancing investments.

To mitigate operational burdens, Tony's had partnered with larger producers like Barry Callebaut, whose facilities could handle the industrial-scale processing Tony's needed. While controversial, this move allowed Tony's to scale without building its own expensive couverture plant. The company ensured segregation of its ethically sourced beans during processing and used the partnership to showcase how large-scale, slave-free chocolate production could be possible.

At the same time, Tony's launched the Open Chain initiative, inviting other chocolate companies to become "Mission Allies" and adopt its sourcing standards. Companies like Aldi (with its Cocoa Changer line) and Holland's Delicata brand signed on, helping Tony's grow cocoa sales without shouldering additional production and marketing expenses.

The Impact:

Tony's Chocolonely's efforts yielded tangible social impact. The rate of child labor among its partner farms dropped to below 4%, compared to an industry average of 47% (Holmes, 2025). The company also succeeded in reshaping market conversations around ethical sourcing and supply chain transparency.

However, financial losses and public scrutiny around its partnership with Barry Callebaut cast shadows over its success. Critics like Ayn Riggs of Slave Free Chocolate argued that Tony's could not claim to be slave-free while outsourcing to a facility associated with unethical practices (Kenber, 2021). Nevertheless, Tony's Director of Impact, Paul Schoenmakers, defended the move as part of the company's commitment to showing the big players that change was both possible and scalable.

Conclusion:

Tony's Chocolonely stands at a crossroads. It has proven that ethical chocolate can be profitable and impactful—but only if stakeholders accept a nuanced view of systemic change. The next steps will determine whether Tony's remains a pioneer or falters under the weight of its idealism and public scrutiny.

Discussion Questions:

- Is outsourcing processing to Barry Callebaut compatible with Tony's slave-free mission, or does it undermine the brand's integrity?

- Could Tony's maintain its mission and restore profitability by pivoting to a new customer segment or revenue model?

- How might Tony's use Blue Ocean Strategy to create a new market space focused on transparency and ethical sourcing?

- What metrics would be most important if Tony's were to pursue public investment through an Initial Public Offering (IPO)?

Activity:

Conduct a comparative analysis of three chocolate companies (Tony's Chocolonely, Hershey's, and Divine Chocolate). Use the Strategy Canvas to map competitive factors such as pricing, ethical sourcing, transparency, and product innovation.

In Chapter Five, we explored the evolving role of the Value Proposition in a sustainable enterprise. We saw how sustainability practices transform what a business offers, how it connects with stakeholders, and the systems it interacts with. As businesses adopt frameworks like Suma

Qamana, Permaculture, and the Solidarity Economy, their Value Propositions expand beyond price and performance to include social, ecological, political, and cultural dimensions.

This transformation not only broadens market opportunities but also enhances trust and resilience. However, expressing this layered value to consumers, partners, and investors can be complex, especially in competitive marketplaces that favor quick returns and cost efficiency.

To support this complexity, we explored how the Circles of Sustainability framework offers a stakeholder-based, multidimensional measurement tool. It helps enterprises see themselves in relation to their broader social context by assessing well-being across ecology, economy, politics, and culture. By mapping data visually, enterprises gain a bird's-eye view of their strengths and opportunities. This equips them to refine their Value Proposition and track their impact in real time.

In the case of the lemonade stand, applying these tools helped to generate innovative, community-rooted strategies, from barter systems and CSA pre-orders to youth co-op employment and energy self-sufficiency, while advancing SDGs like Clean Energy, Decent Work, and Climate Action.

In this chapter, we also discussed the importance of agility and feedback in sustaining value. Through the Lean Startup's Build-Measure-Learn loop, enterprises test and refine their sustainability hypotheses before full-scale rollout. This minimizes risk and maximizes alignment with market demand and stakeholder priorities. Whether it's identifying which flavor of innovations resonates or testing consumer support for eco-friendly packaging, the pivot becomes a vital moment of learning, not failure. Enterprises move toward optimal, sustainable solutions through this iterative process.

Finally, the Blue Ocean Strategy highlighted to us how sustainability itself can create entirely new market spaces, turning ethical practices into competitive advantages. By redefining industry norms and focusing on unmet needs, businesses position themselves not just to compete but to lead transformative change. The Tony's Chocolonely case illustrates both the promise and challenge of this journey. Even in the face of financial strain and ethical scrutiny, Tony's commitment to its mission and its innovative Open Chain model shows how stakeholder-centered values can shape entire industries.

Together, these frameworks, Circles of Sustainability, Lean Startup, and Blue Ocean Strategy, empower enterprises to reimagine their Value Propositions in ways that are grounded, adaptive, and visionary. They remind us that sustainability is not a destination, but a dynamic process of listening, learning, and aligning enterprise goals with the evolving needs of people and the planet.

Chapter Summary

- The Value Proposition evolves when sustainability frameworks like Suma Qamana, Permaculture, and Solidarity Economy are applied, expanding to include social, ecological, cultural, and political impact.

- The Circles of Sustainability provides a holistic, stakeholder-driven tool for assessing an enterprise's strengths and weaknesses across four domains: ecology, economy, politics, and culture.

- The Lean Startup Framework enables enterprises to manage change through small-scale testing (Build-Measure-Learn loops), allowing for evidence-based pivots that improve alignment between strategy, product, and stakeholder needs.

- Blue Ocean Strategy helps sustainability-focused enterprises break away from competition by redefining value and creating new market spaces rooted in ethics, inclusivity, and innovation.

- Case studies like Tony's Chocolonely and Nintendo's Wii demonstrate how stakeholder feedback and community engagement can drive powerful transformations in both mission alignment and market performance.

QUIZ

1. The Circles of Sustainability framework evaluates practices across which four domains?
   a. People, Planet, Profit, Purpose
   b. Ecology, Economy, Politics, Culture
   c. Environment, Ethics, Equity, Economics
   d. Resources, Relationships, Revenue, Regulation

2. Which set of models was applied to different enterprise areas before the Circles of Sustainability was introduced?
   a. Triple Bottom Line, Doughnut Economics, ISO 14001
   b. Fair Trade, Impact Investing, SDG Compass
   c. Suma Qamana, Permaculture, Solidarity Economy
   d. Life-Cycle Analysis, Lean Manufacturing, Cradle-to-Cradle

3. What online resource does the text recommend for creating a Circles of Sustainability profile?
   a. GRI Standards Portal
   b. SDG Tracker Dashboard
   c. Global Compact Self-Assessment Tool
   d. Circles of Sustainability Rapid Assessment Tool

4. What does the Lean Startup framework use to manage the change process in enterprises?
   a. SWOT Analysis
   b. Triple Bottom Line
   c. Build-Measure-Learn (BML) loop
   d. Customer Journey Map

5. **When does a pivot occur in the Lean Launchpad model?**
   a. When profits exceed projections
   b. When the product sells out
   c. When the strategy and product are misaligned
   d. When a new competitor enters the market

6. **What is an example of a customer-segment pivot in the lemonade stand case?**
   a. Marketing to bike-commuter groups and racing events
   b. Offering solar-powered juicers
   c. Reducing the price of compostable cups
   d. Selling lemonade from locally grown, imperfect lemons

7. **What is the main purpose of the Blue Ocean Strategy Canvas?**
   a. To find cheaper suppliers
   b. To outperform competitors in existing markets
   c. To define and build new markets by redefining value
   d. To eliminate all forms of competition

8. **Which is always the first key factor in a Strategy Canvas?**
   a. Location
   b. Environmental Impact
   c. Community Ownership
   d. Price

9. Which framework is used to expand key factors to help create blue oceans?

   a. SWOT Analysis
   b. Four Actions Framework
   c. BMC
   d. Value Chain Analysis

10. What is the primary benefit of stakeholder-led administration of Circles of Sustainability surveys?

    a. It increases costs but ensures data privacy.
    b. It guarantees accurate government compliance.
    c. It improves trust and response rates among participants.
    d. It reduces the number of required survey questions.

Answer Key				
1 – b	2 – c	3 – d	4 – c	5 – c
6 – a	7 – c	8 – d	9 – b	10 – c

CHAPTER 6

Leading the Change

Key Learning Objectives

- Use the Sustainability Lens to create possibilities and build new stories.
- Explore transformational leadership: Learn how to be at the helm and share the change.
- Make it palatable. Communicate the message and bring a change in others.
- Case study of Patagonia: Leading with purpose in sustainable business.

Leadership moments can be beneficial for the enterprise and an example for others. Exploring communication and messaging helps make leadership moments more powerful and meaningful.

This chapter explores the ways the Sustainability Lens Game is experienced and how it can be part of a sustainability building arsenal for any organization. It then delves into leadership roles and the ways that sustainability naturally leads to leadership moments. The chapter concludes with a case study about Yvon Chouinard, the founder of Patagonia clothing and a leader in sustainability practices.

6.1 The Sustainability Lens: Pulling It All Together

This book introduced a range of rich and sometimes complex sustainability concepts, including Suma Qamana, Solidarity Economy, Permaculture, and Circles of Sustainability, which can be challenging to explain and apply in organizational settings. To address this, the author developed the Sustainability Lens Game as a way to make these ideas more accessible, engaging, and inclusive.

The game empowers leaders and teams to collaboratively develop a common language and a unified vision using creativity and mutual understanding. Purpose-driven leadership and meaningful messaging are essential to fostering engagement and change. Prompts are supplied in the game to help spur on new ideas and approaches.

The Sustainability Lens Game provides a dynamic platform for exploring sustainability in action, helping participants not only understand key concepts but also actively participate in the development of impactful, SDG-aligned initiatives. The game supports transformational leadership by encouraging individuals to step into roles where they can guide, communicate, and co-create sustainable enterprise strategies.

The game starts with the Sustainability Lens, which is a tool that compresses the ideas of Suma Qamana, Permaculture, Solidarity Economy, and Circles of Sustainability into a guiding framework that can be used to glide over the BMC like a magnifying glass. Myriad sustainability possibilities become clear as one reviews an enterprise looking at it from the Right-Side Connections, Left-Side Logistics, and Financial Foundations perspectives.

The four quadrants of the Lens (Fig. 6.1) reflect the lessons carefully laid out in this text.

1. Resources: Where things come from.
2. Health: Human engagement and community.
3. Policy: Set the example, be the change.
4. Exchange: Accessibility and distribution.

Figure 6.1 **The Sustainability Lens Tool**

(Sustainability Lens Game, 2025)

Over time, the Sustainability Lens tool has become an interactive game, the Sustainability Lens Game, designed to be played both by people with little experience in sustainability or enterprise development and those who study it deeply.

Games such as board and simulation games have proven to be effective and engaging tools for raising awareness and promoting education around the SDGs. (Senka et al., 2024). Studies find that games can foster understanding, provoke critical reflection, and inspire behavioral change in both formal and informal educational settings (Katsaliaki & Mustafee, 2015).

The Sustainability Lens Game is about making change through enterprise development. In this way, it is different from other sustainability games that focus on place-based environments, energy, or social challenges without the enterprise perspective. The rationale behind the Sustainability Lens Game and the materials in this book is that the enterprise is the most powerful and accessible source of power for change. Enterprises are independent, versatile, nimble, and innovative.

The Sustainability Lens Game enables players to discover and apply sustainable thinking to unleash enterprises' power for good. It operates in the following three areas:

1. Enterprise orientation: Focusing on organizational strategy and business operations.
2. Interdisciplinary systems thinking: Integrating environmental, social, and economic decision-making in an enterprise context.
3. Stakeholder engagement: Building collaboration and shared understanding amongst diverse team members.

| Figure 6.2 | The four quadrants of the Sustainability Lens explained |

RESOURCES	HEALTH
Understanding where things come from	**Human connection and community**
Supply Chain Management:	**Participatory Democracy:**
• Knowing exactly where materials come from, down to the soil.	• Working together to build a supportive community.
• Acknowledging every person involved along the way.	• Involving everyone—customers, contractors, and employees—in important decisions, risk-taking, and planning whenever possible.
• Considering how local communities are affected.	• Finding ways to create opportunities, foster inclusion, and celebrate together.
• Tracking the energy used to produce and deliver it.	
Important: This requires suppliers to be fully transparent.	
POLICY	EXCHANGE
Set the example. Be the change.	**Accessibility and Distribution**
Engagement:	**Abundance:**
• Leading by example with strong sustainability policies inside your business.	• Using many ways to share value, such as barter, volunteering, cooperatives, profit sharing, local currencies, time trades, or community lending.
• Asking suppliers to meet the same standards.	• Slowing down to match the speed of available resources and labor.
• Encouraging customers to join in.	• Staying open to dialogue and new ideas.
• Involving the wider community in these efforts.	
• Staying open to dialogue and new ideas.	

(Sustainability Lens Game, 2025)

The Sustainability Lens Game's focus on resources, health, policy and exchange in all nine areas of the BMC create 45 new sustainability possibilities and mindsets for people to recognize problems and think of solutions (Fig. 6.2). Since solutions are not always known and take time to discover, the Sustainability Lens Game includes 64 "Gold Coin Ideas" valued at one to three points each, to provide viable solutions.

The gold coin ideas introduce players to new sustainability approaches while also gamifying the gameplay: the more ideas applied, the more points earned. The result is that people from all backgrounds and experiences can contribute meaningfully to sustainable development solutions in an accessible, inclusive, and fun way.

The following sections demonstrate real-world examples of how the Sustainability Lens Game was played at Bridgewater State University: as a facilitated board game, an asynchronous online workshop, and as a self-guide card game, along with the results of the play.

6.1.1 The Board Game

It was a warm summer day at Connecticut's Bridgewater State University. Members of a Sustainability Stewards Grant were gathered, a mix of students, faculty, and local sustainability supporters. They were part of an ongoing dialogue and workshop to explore how to build more sustainable systems in their community. They came from all walks of life, including environmental sciences, psychology, education, research, undeclared undergraduates, and community organizers.

Some had a business background; most did not. They formed teams and assembled around the game boards with a brightly printed BMC on them. One by one, they choose Sustainability Lens Cards, Gold Idea Coins, and roll a 10-sided die as they move around the BMC.

Each participant had two minutes to make an imaginary Farmers' Market Lemonade Stand more sustainable. Sipping hand-squeezed lemonade, they pondered possibilities, reading coins that said things such as "barter and trade," "Do it yourself (DIY)," and "closed-loop production." The accompanying game booklet was often consulted for definitions of these coins (Fig. 6.3).

Figure 6.3 The SL Game booklet

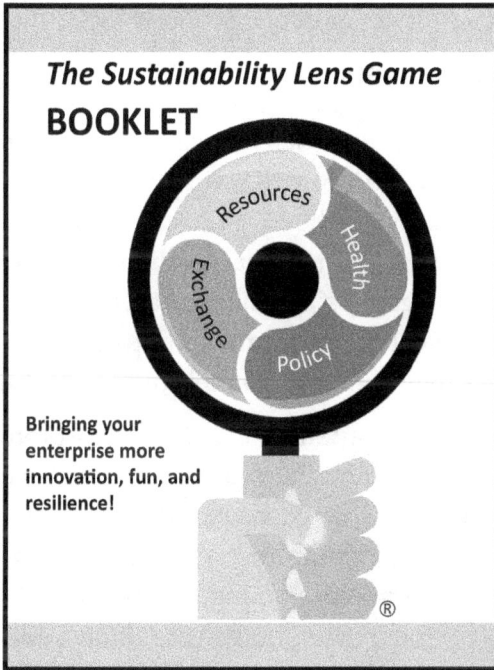

The Sustainability Lens Game
BOOKLET

Resources
Health
Exchange
Policy

Bringing your enterprise more innovation, fun, and resilience!

®

(Sustainability Lens Game, 2025)

The SL Game booklet includes definitions and tips so people of all backgrounds and experiences can participate in creating new solutions.

The clock was ticking. For each turn, participants tried to earn as many gold coins as they could by building more solutions into their BMC challenge area. The fast pace made the ideas flow. One team member was the scribe, keeping track of the innovation and creativity. After 20 minutes, teams shared their stories, transforming the lemonade stand into so much more: a carbon-free sailboat providing refreshments to beach goers, an after-school skill-building and revenue-generating project for the local Boys and Girls club, and more.

"I like the creative aspects and the game. It's not just about winning; it's a fun way to develop a new mindset," said Amy Smith, a student at Bridgewater State University.

6.1.2 The Online Game

On a cold winter day, the Connecticut Main Street Center hosted an online cohort for its Main Street Accelerator. They, too, were playing the SL game, but a facilitated online version attended by Main Street merchants across the state. Introduced to the game's premise, given a virtual BMC, and issued coins and cards online, they jumped in as remote teams to build new solutions to their own downtown areas.

After 20 minutes, they shared ideas of cross-promotions of rotating monthly events, hosted in each other's stores; bulk buying of recyclable paper goods branded with their town's name and their logos; a local currency or buying card they could all participate in—promoting downtown shopping. As ideas unfolded, other teams "borrowed" them, adding to their arsenal of downtown revitalization and sustainability solutions.

"It is a great way to connect with others and generate ideas," explained a participant on their feedback form. *"It triggered a good conversation and narrowed down priorities. The board was helpful from a visual point of view."*

6.1.3 The Card Game

On a rainy spring day in Boston, two undergraduate interns from Suffolk University met with the founder and director of a local NGO at their downtown office. With Martin

Luther King (MLK) Day fast approaching, they held a quick meeting with the agenda, "What can we do for MLK Day?" The students pulled out the Sustainability Lens Game card deck and began collaborating with the NGO team. Using the Business Model Canvas and the Sustainable Development Goals as their foundation, they selected cards and idea coins, sometimes at random, to spark creative thinking.

As they worked together, ideas started flowing. They told stories, recorded them on their phones, and later reviewed the ideas for concrete actions. The founder of the NGO ended up "winning" the game by generating the most ideas (and earning the most points), but the real success was the fully formed, budget-friendly MLK Day event that emerged. It aligned closely with SDG targets and brought their collective vision to life.

According to their notes, the final MLK Day concept looked like this:

- "An electric bus whisks students from the local Boys and Girls Club to the 'Embrace' Martin Luther King statue on the Boston Common. Stories, dreams, and SDGs are shared.
- Food trucks, or local families, serve celebratory meals in recyclable containers. These containers are saved and later filled with soil and sunflower seeds, symbolizing growth and rebirth."

The initiative addressed three SDGs:

1. Goal 15: Life on Land (supporting reforestation and biodiversity)
2. Goal 2: Zero Hunger (highlighting food accessibility)
3. Goal 12: Responsible Consumption (reducing waste and promoting circular systems).

This creative, community-centered event idea honored Dr. King's legacy while engaging the youth in sustainability.

It promoted reflection, inclusion, and action through storytelling and symbolic planting.

Whether used as a board game, an online version, or a card game, the Sustainability Lens Game brought innovation, playfulness, and resilience into the planning process. The BMC provided a visual, design-thinking structure to guide the conversation, while the Sustainability Lens cards helped focus on specific challenges. Gold Idea Coins introduced 64 fresh, accessible concepts that opened minds and expanded the group's problem-solving possibilities (Fig. 6.4).

Figure 6.4 Sustainability Lens Gold Coin Idea Cards

(Sustainability Lens Game, 2025)

The SL Game booklet includes definitions and tips so people of all backgrounds and experiences can participate in creating new solutions.

6.1.4 How Games Make Sustainability Simple and Powerful

Through these games, participants who do not know anything about business or sustainability create meaningful scenarios and solutions. The ease with which untrained participants make meaningful contributions speaks to the universality of sustainability for all people, where solutions become intuitive once the mindset is embraced. Enterprise innovation, creativity, and fun are explored through problem-solving storytelling.

Using games to better understand and achieve sustainable development is not limited to just the Sustainability Lens Game. There are many sustainability-themed games that take different approaches towards defining sustainability and engaging players in sustainability concepts.

Some games focus on energy, water management, climate change, place-based development, or enterprise development, with players taking on roles of antagonist, hero, or, as in the SL Game, collaborator (Katsaliaki & Mustafee, 2014). These games are considered "serious" or "teaching" games, based on reality, grounded theory, and facts, though sometimes applied in mythical worlds and simulations. A study of 49 sustainability-themed games online found them to be effective in growing players' understanding of sustainable development issues (AlQallaf et al., 2022).

The United Nations Educational, Scientific, and Cultural Organization (UNESCO) developed an educational framework for teaching Sustainable Development Education (SDE) with a goal of building awareness and engagement with SDGs. It integrates the three dimensions of cognition, affection, and skills, with eight core abilities: system thinking, anticipation, normative, strategic, collaboration, critical thinking, self-awareness, and comprehensive problem-solving (UNESCO, 2017). The result is an engaged, interactive, interdisciplinary educational approach, which is well supported through games and simulations (Chen & Ho, 2022).

Overall, serious or teaching games are a good medium for building awareness and engagement of sustainability and the SDGs. Their ability to simulate complex systems, encourage collaboration, and integrate experiential learning makes them well-suited for the multidimensional nature of sustainable development. They do not replace the depth and meaning of complex models and theoretical frameworks such as Suma Qamana, Permaculture, Solidarity Economy, and Circles of Sustainability, but they are effective in getting people engaged, on board, and moving towards a sustainability vocabulary and mindset.

Playing with purpose:

The Sustainability Lens Game is specifically designed to help business teams reflect on, analyze, and improve their organizational practices through a sustainability lens. The game can be situated within the context of an actual enterprise. This enables participants to assess enterprise decisions and value chains through economic, social, and environmental dimensions, making real-life decisions that have an actual impact on product, people, and planet.

This enterprise-level orientation makes it a powerful tool for professional development, strategic planning, and organizational change. The game facilitates internal dialogue across departments, helping organizations to identify trade-offs and synergies amongst sustainability goals. It also promotes systems thinking by having players consider complex interdependencies within business models. Lastly, it is a practical resource for enterprises to internalize and act on SDGs from a grounded, business mindset.

HIGHLIGHTS

- Serious games can be seriously fun and effective. Despite tackling "serious" topics like climate change and social inequality, sustainability games often boost engagement and retention far more than lectures or textbooks (Tsai et al., 2021).

- Serious games demonstrate real-world impact by supporting policymakers and diplomats in exploring complex global climate negotiations. Through the simulation of decision-making consequences, such games enhance understanding of long-term environmental trade-offs, illustrating the potential of game-based learning to drive meaningful change (Mendler de Suarez et al., 2012).

TIPS

Here are a few simple tips to help you get the most out of the Sustainability Lens Game:

- Use a timer to keep gameplay dynamic.

- Pair novice and expert players to enhance collaboration.

- Start with a familiar business idea, like a lemonade stand, to ease participants into systems thinking.

POINTS TO REMEMBER

- The Sustainability Lens integrates theory with action.
- Games promote systems thinking in fun, accessible ways.
- Enterprise development is a powerful tool for sustainable change.
- Leadership moments can emerge naturally from gameplay.

DISCUSSION QUESTIONS

- How might leadership styles shift when sustainability becomes part of the conversation?
- What role do emotions and storytelling play in sustainability education?
- How do you measure the "impact" of a game-based activity?

6.2 Transformational Leadership

The Sustainability Lens Game offers a practical and engaging way for leaders and teams to explore and shape their approach to sustainable enterprise. It helps create direction by focusing attention on key areas of the business model while introducing a shared language and framework that supports collaborative thinking. This structure encourages teams to reflect together, surface new ideas, and connect their efforts to broader sustainability goals.

Why it's important:

Transformational leadership is especially important in sustainability work because it involves guiding people through change, often in uncertain or evolving conditions. Sustainable practices require shifts in mindset, behavior, and operations, which are areas where strong, inclusive, and visionary leadership is essential. The Sustainability Lens game supports this by creating space for participation, creativity, and shared purpose. It equips emerging leaders and their teams to explore values and co-create actionable solutions. These early steps in engagement and collaboration lay the groundwork for transformational leadership to take root and grow.

Transformational leaders instill big ideas, build connections, and usher in change. They are at the helm of something new, with a clear vision, steering it forward and engaging others to try it out too. Transformational leaders are inclusive, creative, trust their organizations, and become social architects, setting the values and norms of an enterprise (Bass & Avolio, 2007). Managing an enterprise through change seems challenging and encompassing enough, but as one engages in new models of innovation and resilience, they naturally move into transformative leadership spaces.

Continuously evolving leadership roles:

Leaders are expected to speak up about enterprise operations, achievements, and new initiatives. They are called upon by the press and industry for guidance, looked up to by others as an example of good, and are expected to show up and shine. Internally, their enterprise needs to be on board with people believing and trusting in the mission and feeling committed to the cause. This section unpacks what it means to be a transformational leader and the skills and mindsets that can be built to inspire others and represent positive change.

Leading organizational change is demanding, especially when innovating toward resilience and sustainability. Sustainability solutions operate within transformative spaces, where expectations and unknowns are high both internally and externally. While externally, transformational leaders become spokespeople and models for the sector, often called upon by media and peers, internally, they must also cultivate a sense of shared purpose, trust, and mission alignment among team members. Balancing the message and pace of change while keeping the team on board is key.

For example, a change in the supply chain could trigger vast changes within the organization with new tracking codes, vendor files, design specifications, quality control mechanisms, labeling, and communications needing development. The leader and the enterprise team must set clear goals, celebrate achievements, and work together, supporting each other through action, feedback, and encouragement.

6.2.1 The Four Behaviors of Transformational Leadership

The transformational leadership model focuses on four key behaviors: influence, motivation, knowledge or know-how, and recognizing the individual (Fig. 6.5).

Figure 6.5 — Transformational Leadership encompasses several leadership styles and behaviors

The Four Behaviors of Transformational Leadership

1. **Idealized Influence** - Modeling behaviors that earn admiration and trust
2. **Inspirational Motivation** - Creating a compelling vision and inspiring others to act
3. **Intellectual Stimulation** - Encouraging creativity and innovation
4. **Individualized Consideration** - Attending to each person's development and needs

These behaviors overlap with:

- **Authentic leadership** - grounded in self-awareness and moral clarity
- **Ethical leadership** - focused on justice, values, and moral alignment
- **Servant leadership** - centered on empathy, healing, and altruism

(Deng, Gulseren, Morin, & Chou, 2023)

Being authentic, transparent, inclusive, and open to new ideas, as a leader, helps build the trust needed to sustain change. These behaviors are present in ethical and servant leadership methods. Together, they form a leadership profile well-suited for sustainability: one that empowers others, sets values-based direction, and holds space for uncertainty and adaptation.

Leadership is integrated with the entrepreneurial journey. Revisiting Figure 1.7, Seven Stages of Entrepreneurship from Section 1.3, Chapter One, in the following Figure 6.6, we see that the entrepreneurial journey is not just about business creation but personal and organizational transformation. These stages, from interest and opportunity recognition through innovation, are all moments that demand leadership.

Figure 6.6 — The Seven Stages of Entrepreneurship

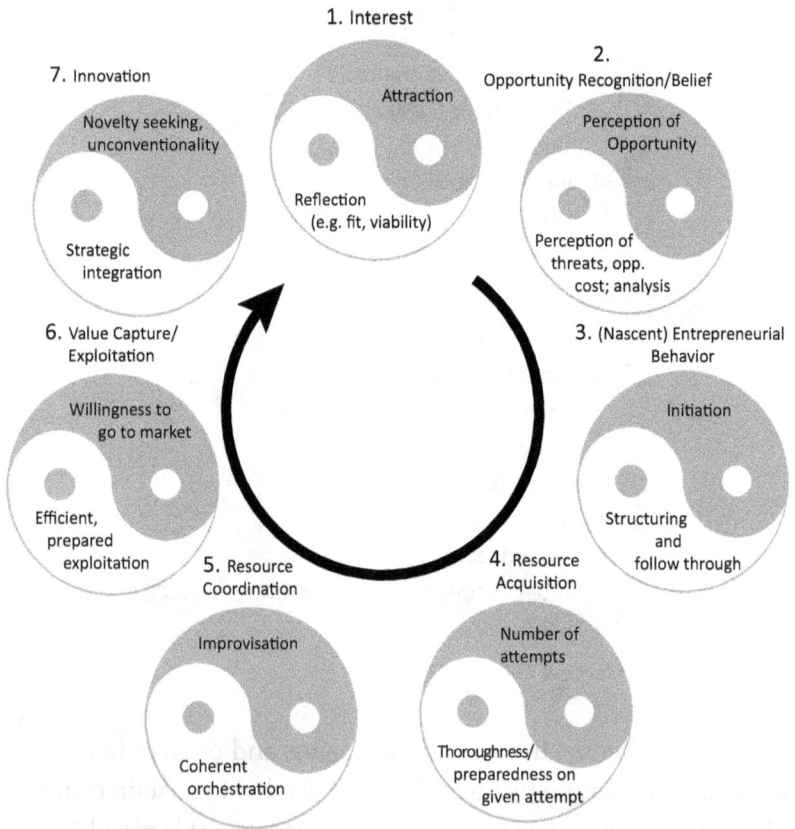

1. Interest
   Attraction
   Reflection (e.g. fit, viability)

2. Opportunity Recognition/Belief
   Perception of Opportunity
   Perception of threats, opp. cost; analysis

3. (Nascent) Entrepreneurial Behavior
   Initiation
   Structuring and follow through

4. Resource Acquisition
   Number of attempts
   Thoroughness/ preparedness on given attempt

5. Resource Coordination
   Improvisation
   Coherent orchestration

6. Value Capture/ Exploitation
   Willingness to go to market
   Efficient, prepared exploitation

7. Innovation
   Novelty seeking, unconventionality
   Strategic integration

(Lerner, Hunt & Verheul, 2017)

The Seven Stages of Entrepreneurship create key moments for Transformational Leadership practices to emerge.

- In Stage 1 (Interest) and Stage 2 (Opportunity Recognition), leaders set the vision for a sustainability approach.
- In Stage 3 (Nascent Behavior), leaders motivate and align teams.
- In Stage 4 (Resource Acquisition) and Stage 5 (Resources Coordination), leaders emphasize ethical practices and inclusivity.
- In Stage 6 (Value Capture) and Stage 7 (Innovation), leaders invite co-creation and shared ownership.

Through this journey to build a more sustainable enterprise, leaders grow alongside their enterprises. They evolve from founders into change agents, shaping the very culture and impact of their organizations. Self-assessment helps identify where transformational leadership skills exist and how others can be built. Revisiting one's scores on the seven stages of entrepreneurship assessment shows where ease and struggles exist in the journey.

A study of 300 companies engaged in sustainability transformation found that 98% of the sustainability initiatives failed at an organizational level (Davis-Peccoud, 2016). The 2% of organizations that achieved sustainability goals, continuing to innovate and grow, did so because of leadership support, employee buy-in, and effective communication (Fig. 6.7).

Figure 6.7 Leadership as a driver of sustainable initiatives

The largest barriers to change are lack of resources and competing priorities	Leadership support is the greatest factor in success
"Can you provide a concrete example of a barrier or other obstacle that threatened to derail your company's sustainability program?"	*"What has been the single greatest factor contributing to the success of your company's sustainability program to date?"*
25% Lack of investment or resources	**27%** Senior leadership support
15% Competing priorities	**11%** Employee engagement and interest
11% Culture change challenges	**8%** Clear goals and metrics
10% Organizational obstacles (e.g., structure, decision making)	**5%** Effective internal communication
6% Lack of a compelling case for change	**5%** Introduction of environmentally friendly policies/processes

(Davis-Peccoud, 2016).

Further, in sustainable enterprises, recognizing and including all stakeholders is essential. Providing stakeholders with a role in delivery, design, and reflection builds shared commitment and deeper knowledge. It helps to turn initiatives into movements and supports an enterprise in long-term, sustained transformation. The different sustainability frameworks in this book include internal and external stakeholder involvement with input from workers, vendors, contractors, producers, consumers, and the community.

As daunting as transformational leadership may seem, it is essential for enterprise success. Transformational leaders must actively build internal and external alignment and commitment.

Research shows that leaders who promote intellectual stimulation, transparency, a supportive learning environment, and individualized inclusivity can spark greater engagement and innovation (Bakker, Hetland,

Demerouti, & Olsen, 2023). These practices also foster psychological safety and trust (Fig. 6.8). When people feel safe and trusted, a culture of can-do positivity emerges, one that enables enterprises to navigate change and drive growth in new and innovative ways.

Figure 6.8 Key practices to building engaged, resilient, and transformational teams

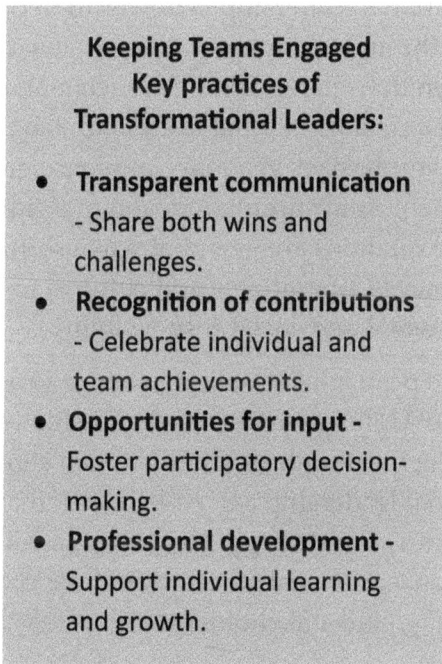

**Keeping Teams Engaged
Key practices of
Transformational Leaders:**

- **Transparent communication** - Share both wins and challenges.
- **Recognition of contributions** - Celebrate individual and team achievements.
- **Opportunities for input -** Foster participatory decision-making.
- **Professional development -** Support individual learning and growth.

(Bakker, Hetland, Demerouti, & Olsen, 2023)

The following practices help to build a positive, sustainable transformation culture:

- Reflect: Complete self-assessments on leadership style and entrepreneurial mindset.
- Observe: Identify role models of transformational leadership in your sector.

- Engage: Facilitate team meetings with inclusive input and vision setting.
- Invite: Ask team members how they'd like to be supported and challenged.
- Assess: Track engagement levels, innovation outcomes, and team alignment over time.
- Adapt: Use reflection and feedback loops to adjust your leadership approach.

Transformational leadership is powerful in guiding organizations through complex, values-driven change, especially when that change involves sustainability. As outlined in the transformational leadership model (Fig. 6.4), this approach emphasizes visionary influence, inspirational motivation, intellectual stimulation, and individualized support. These qualities are essential when shifting enterprise mindsets, operations, and cultures toward long-term environmental and social responsibility.

To see these principles in action, we turn to a real-world example: Unilever under the leadership of Paul Polman. During his decade as CEO, Polman showed how transformational leadership can embed sustainability into an organization's core strategy. He did this while managing internal resistance, external scrutiny, and the changing expectations of global stakeholders.

6.2.2 Ideas in Action: Transformational Leadership at Unilever

Unilever, a British-Dutch multinational consumer goods company, is one of the world's largest fast-moving consumer goods enterprises, operating in over 190 countries with well-known brands like Dove, Lipton, and Ben & Jerry's. By the early 2000s, Unilever faced increasing pressure to address environmental and social concerns within its global operations (Schawbel, 2017).

Need for a pivot:

Consumers were demanding more ethical and sustainable products, while investors remained focused on short-term financial returns. Simultaneously, the company's sprawling supply chains and complex organizational structure made coordinated sustainability efforts difficult to implement. Recognizing that its traditional business model was no longer viable, Unilever saw the need to embed sustainability directly into its strategy, not just as a compliance effort, but as a long-term value driver (Unilever, 2019).

The beginning of change:

The tenure of Paul Polman as Unilever's CEO from 2009 to 2019 marked a turning point. With a background at Nestlé and Procter & Gamble, Polman brought industry experience and a bold new vision. He eliminated quarterly earnings guidance and instead emphasized long-term value creation. In 2010, Polman launched the Unilever Sustainable Living Plan (USLP), a strategy designed to decouple business growth from environmental impact, increase social value across the value chain, and simultaneously double the company's size.

This vision aligned Unilever with global sustainability efforts, including the UN Sustainable Development Goals (Unilever, 2019). Polman's approach reflected transformational leadership in action: setting a clear and values-based direction, motivating and aligning teams around purpose, and fostering innovation through inclusion and trust.

Challenges:

The transformation was not without challenges. Internally, employees and managers accustomed to traditional metrics resisted the cultural shift. Polman addressed this by embedding sustainability into employee roles, offering training, and fostering internal dialogue. Externally, investors were initially skeptical of Unilever's move away from short-term financial reporting. Polman and his team met this challenge through consistent communication and transparent reporting that linked sustainability goals with business outcomes.

Operationally, embedding sustainability across hundreds of brands and supply chains was complex. The company overcame this by redesigning sourcing practices, leveraging partnerships, and empowering brand teams to innovate. Finally, as a public sustainability leader, Unilever had to maintain high transparency and accountability in the face of scrutiny (Schwabel, 2017).

Results:

Through strong transformational leadership, Unilever achieved notable results. By 2019, 28 of its sustainability-focused brands were growing 69% faster than the rest of the portfolio. The company had reduced CO_2 emissions from energy use by 65% and achieved 100% renewable grid electricity across its operations. Perhaps more importantly, Unilever emerged as a global benchmark for how sustainability can be integrated into core strategy to drive innovation, trust, and long-term growth (Unilever, 2019).

Their work is not done, though. In 2021, Unilever rose to be cited as one of the top three plastic polluters worldwide, and though they did pledge to reduce by half their use of virgin plastic by 2025, they missed that target and hoped to reach a 30% reduction by 2026 (Rachal, 2024).

Polman's work at Unilever illustrated the power of transformational leadership to guide organizations through complex change, build internal and external alignment, and position enterprises as sustainability leaders. The continued work and challenges Unilever faces demonstrate the tough work and ongoing demands of sustainability.

6.2.3 Measure Your Own Leadership Qualities

Transformational Leadership is a journey that can be undertaken by anyone, not just top management, but anyone interested in helping to facilitate lasting change. Where are you in your own Transformational Leadership development? Rate each statement below from 1 (Strongly Disagree) to 5 (Strongly Agree) to see where you are in the Transformational Leadership spectrum.

Use this self-assessment to reflect on your current transformational leadership practices. Make notes of where and how they can change. Use it alongside the Seven Stages of Entrepreneurship (Table 1.3 "Entrepreneurship Assessment") scores from Chapter 1 to identify alignment or friction points in your journey.

Table 6.1   Transformational Leadership Self-Check

Statement	Score (1–5)
I regularly communicate a clear and compelling vision.	
I encourage others to think creatively and offer new ideas.	
I recognize and celebrate individual contributions.	
I provide space for reflection and feedback in decision-making.	
I demonstrate moral consistency in difficult situations.	
I seek to understand and support others' development goals.	
TOTAL	

Understanding the scoring:

Each statement is rated on a scale of 1 to 5, where 1 = strongly disagree and 5 = strongly agree. Your total score reflects how consistently you demonstrate transformational leadership behaviors.

- **5–15: Growth opportunity**
  A score in this range suggests you are at the early stages of developing transformational leadership skills. You may be leading effectively in some areas but have significant room to grow in communicating vision, fostering creativity, supporting others, or modeling ethical behavior.

- **16–20: Developing leader**
  This score indicates you are building transformational leadership qualities but may not yet demonstrate them consistently. You are moving beyond basic management toward inspiring and empowering others, but you still have key areas to strengthen.

- **21–30: Emerging transformational leader**
  A score here shows you frequently display the core qualities of a transformational leader—vision, creativity, support, ethics, and inclusivity. You are likely fostering trust, engagement, and innovation within your team or organization.

Scoring explained:

A Growth Opportunity or Developing Leader score indicates there are still places where a different perspective could be taken towards leading and working with others.

Suggestions:

Look at some of the areas where you scored low, and think about how you could change the way you approach one of the low-scoring items. Make an effort to approach it differently next time and pay attention to how it felt and what the outcome was. A low-score area is also a good place to solicit feedback and guidance from others.

Transformation is difficult. Enlisting others to help you on that journey helps to build commitment, solidify relationships, create places for greater inclusion, and enables a leader to learn what their team needs.

HIGHLIGHTS

- Only a small fraction of organizational sustainability initiatives achieve long-term success. Research suggests that failure often stems from a lack of leadership commitment, poor communication, and insufficient employee engagement (Kiron et al., 2013).

- Transformational leaders are characterized by their ability to adapt and grow alongside the organizations they serve, often evolving from entrepreneurial founders into agents of systemic change (Bass & Riggio, 2006).

TIPS

- Celebrate achievements with your team. This builds morale and commitment.

- Create feedback loops to learn and adapt your leadership approach over time.

- Recognize individuals for their unique contributions to foster loyalty and engagement.

POINTS TO REMEMBER

- Transformational leadership is about instilling vision, fostering trust, and guiding change.

- The four transformational leadership behaviors are: Idealized Influence, Inspirational Motivation, Intellectual Stimulation, and Individualized Consideration.

- Sustainable transformation requires both internal buy-in and external engagement.

- Leaders should be inclusive, authentic, approachable, and transparent, especially during change.

- Transformational leadership is not restricted to those in executive roles. Individuals at any level within an organization can drive significant change by cultivating trust, encouraging innovation, and fostering a shared sense of purpose (Northouse, 2019).

DISCUSSION QUESTIONS

- How can you apply transformational leadership behaviors to a current team project or organizational challenge?

- In what ways does engaging external stakeholders, from outside the enterprise, strengthen the success and impact of a transformational leadership approach?

- How does individualized consideration contribute to an enterprise's long-term resilience?

6.3 Communicating the Sustainability Message

While transformational leadership sets the vision and motivates teams to pursue sustainability, it is through strategic communication that this vision becomes visible, understood, and supported, both inside and outside the organization. Leaders may inspire change and foster innovation, but without clear, authentic, and timely messaging, even the most compelling sustainability efforts can go unnoticed or misunderstood. Communication is the connective tissue that links leadership to action, aligns stakeholders, and builds the momentum needed to sustain long-term impact.

The role of communication in driving sustainability is powerful and essential. Getting the message out about an enterprise's sustainability impact is important for supporting the enterprise culture, celebrating wins, building networks, growing awareness and sales, and showing up as an industry leader and changemaker. Messaging builds allies and support that prove important when challenges and unexpected downturns arise. Messaging also helps to clarify and quantify the impacts of changes, and signals to others one's sustainability commitment.

Communication is a balance between transparency and optimism; not all news is good news. Being authentic by communicating gains as well as challenges builds trust and rapport. Knowing when and what message to send, how and to whom, is key in building a supportive network that expands sales, reaches new customer segments, and rewards the enterprise.

Overall, communication is a strategic celebration. It overlaps and intersects with marketing but is also an entity on its own. As an enterprise enters the sustainability realm, new places for participation and engagement arise. The sustainability community, due to its mindset and belief system, is naturally one of collaboration, not competition. Being a part of this community brings new access to events, conferences, trade shows, press, and organizations, creating more places for messages to be shared and amplified — building a strong community of support grounded in common goals and ideals.

In this section, we will look more specifically at the whole enterprise communication strategy, landscape for broadcasting sustainability success, and joining a new community of sustainability allies.

6.3.1 Sustainability Reports: What to Measure

Transformational leadership lays the foundation for sustainable change by inspiring purpose, aligning teams, and fostering a culture of innovation and accountability. Yet, vision alone is not enough. For sustainability to truly take root and deliver long-term impact, organizations must translate purpose into practice and language, and that requires measurement.

Once leaders chart the course, sustainability reports become essential tools for tracking progress, building credibility, and maintaining momentum. These reports help enterprises move from intention to action, offering a structured way to monitor results, communicate with stakeholders, and refine strategy based on real data.

As complicated as sustainability is, collecting and reporting data on it can become even more complex. Nevertheless, organizing and controlling sustainability data is key to keeping the sustainability momentum and morale going. Data is important for identifying wins, tracking and celebrating progress, and reassessing areas where impacts are not being met.

A sustainability report helps enterprises target and express sustainability actions, showing their progress in the sustainability journey. Reports set sustainability benchmarks, measure progress, and identify new goals. In 2022, 99% of all S&P 500 companies issued sustainability reports, with 70% of them providing outside assurance to verify accuracy in their reporting (CAQ, 2025).

Frameworks such as Suma Qamana, Permaculture, Solidarity Economy, Circles of Sustainability, and the Sustainability Lens identify many ways and mindsets to make holistic change for good. Once methods and mindsets are determined, their cost and effectiveness need to be captured. Some costs may be up front through capital investment, increased labor, and materials costs, or long-term, through loans and longer sales cycles.

Tracking these costs, setting goals, forecasting, and measuring outcomes are key to managing a healthy enterprise and ensuring an adequate ROI. Knowing what to measure and how involves setting key performance indicators (KPI) linked to sustainable actions backed by reliable and accurate numbers (Toikka, 2025). While there are no universal measurements of sustainability, there are some key areas for change metrics. Actions can include bottom-line savings, improved ESG performance, and streamlined budgeting and forecasting, as illustrated in Figure 6.9.

| Figure 6.9 | Details of ESG: Essential data areas for sustainability measurement and reporting |

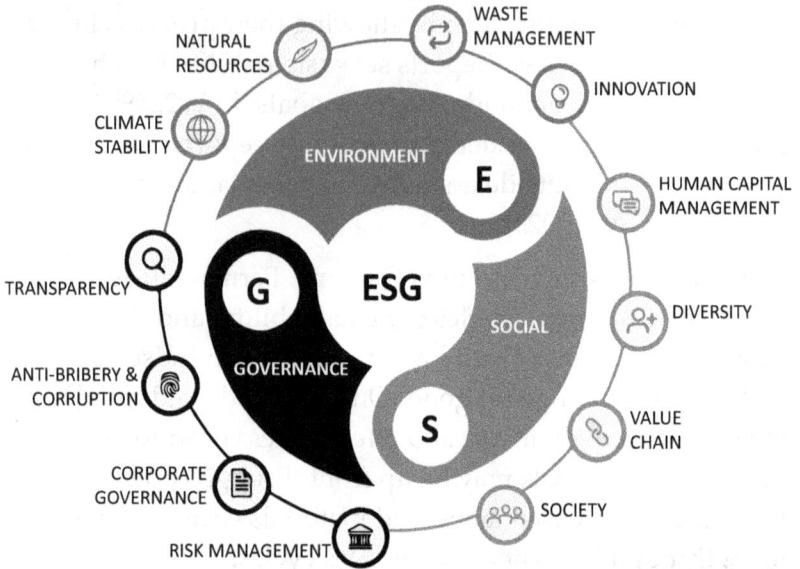

(Persefoni, 2025)

1. The Global Reporting Initiative (GRI) Standard

The GRI Standard, used by 73% of the world's 250 largest companies, provides 31 Topic Standards divided into three areas as illustrated in Figure 6.10 (Persefoni, 2025).

Figure 6.10 GRI Standards

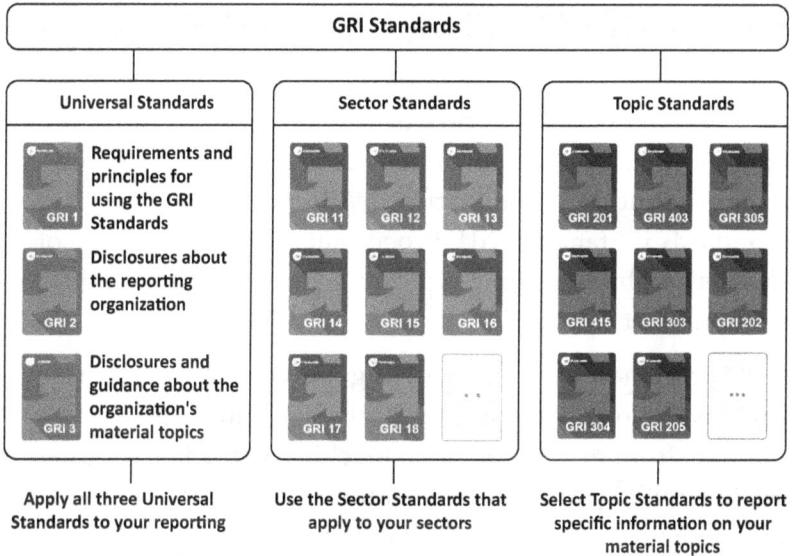

(GRI, 2025)

GRI standards offer three areas of sustainability focus and a common language and metrics for comparing progress across industries and over time.

The first area:

GRI Universal Standards are mandatory for an organization to disclose and cover foundational aspects like governance, strategy, and management, looking at economic, social, and environmental impacts.

The second area:

GRI Sector Standards provide additional guidance for enterprises that tend to have significant environmental impacts, especially in areas such as oil, gas, coal, agriculture, and fisheries.

The third area:

GRI Topic Standards offer detailed guidance on a wide range of sustainability topics, including climate change, human rights, and anti-corruption.

The benefit of GRI standards is that they create a common language and measurement metrics that can be compared over time and across industries. Within the GRI Topic Standards is Standard 204: Procurement Practices. Many of the sustainability actions explored in this text fall into the procurement category.

Procurement includes sourcing, purchasing, receiving, and inspecting all goods and services an enterprise uses to operate, from raw materials to machinery to office supplies. Sustainability procurement includes ESG impacts, looking at where procured materials were made, how they were sourced, the energy used to produce them, transportation, and carbon outputs for delivery, the social impact the materials had on producers, and their community impact. This is a lot of data to source and track.

Sievo is a procurement analytics software that follows the triple bottom line model to identify data areas to track (Figure 6.11). Using internal enterprise data, external industry data, and their own proprietary frameworks, Sievo helps enterprises to track sustainability efforts, costs, impact, and ROI by providing graphs, charts, and recommendations (Toikka, 2025). Sphera, Workiva, and IBM Envizi are other types of sustainability procurement software.

Figure 6.11	The Sievo software tracks organizations' sustainability practices through triple bottom line analysis

The triple bottom line of sustainable procurement

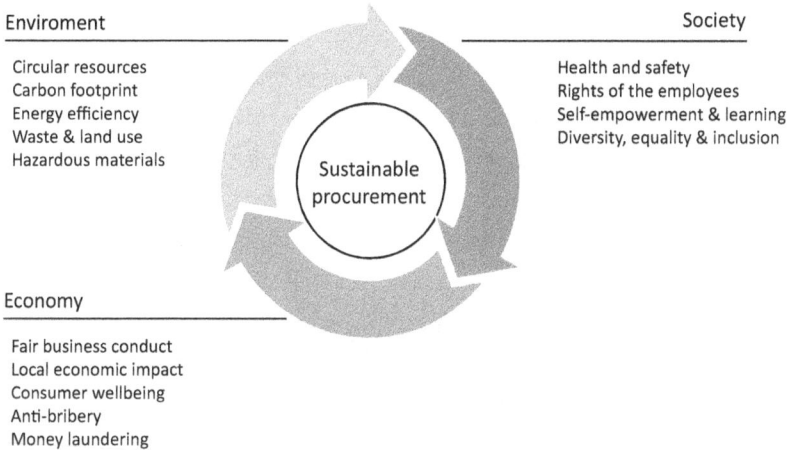

Enviroment

Circular resources
Carbon footprint
Energy efficiency
Waste & land use
Hazardous materials

Sustainable procurement

Society

Health and safety
Rights of the employees
Self-empowerment & learning
Diversity, equality & inclusion

Economy

Fair business conduct
Local economic impact
Consumer wellbeing
Anti-bribery
Money laundering

(Sievo, 2025)

2. B-Corp

One powerful tool for measuring, ensuring accountability, and communicating sustainability efforts is the B-Corp certification, provided by B Lab Global, a nonprofit network dedicated to building an inclusive, equitable, and regenerative economy (B-Lab UK, 2025). The B Lab Global certification offers a rigorous, standardized framework for evaluating and reporting an enterprise's social and environmental impact.

As a third-party certifier, B Lab Global uses its B-Impact Assessment (BIA) to measure ESG performance as well as impacts on workers, communities, and customers. Companies that receive a B Lab Global certification are called B-Corps.

B Lab Global was founded in 2006 with the mission to transform the global economy into one that benefits all people and the planet. The B-Corp model emphasizes that businesses should be a force for good, beyond just financial performance with a goal of collectively creating an equitable, inclusive, and regenerative economy for all.

There are over 9,893 B-Corp certified companies in 104 countries, across 160 industries, impacting 991,470 workers (B-Corp, 2025). The B-Lab Global goal is to improve performance to the level where the enterprise can apply for certification, with a focus on continuous improvement.

B Lab Global identifies five stakeholder areas: governance, workers, community, environment, and customers (Fig. 6.12). Together, these five areas create a comprehensive picture of a company's social and environmental performance and its long-term commitment to stakeholder value. Presented as a 1,149-page document, the B Lab Foundation Requirements (FR) take anywhere from three hours to three weeks to complete, depending on an organization's size and complexity; its purpose is to define and value the five stakeholder areas (B Lab, 2025).

| Figure 6.12 | The B-Corp five impact areas |

Our 5 impact areas

Governance	Workers	Environment	Community	Customers
· Mission & Engagement · Ethics & Transparency	· Financial Security · Health & Wellness · Career Development · Benefits	· Environmental Management · Air & Climate · Water · Land & Life	· Diversity & Inclusion · Workforce Development · Civic Engagement · Supply Chain Management	· Stewardship · Health · Education · Arts, Media & Culture · Economic Empowerment

(B-Corps, 2025)

A. Governance:

This area focuses on the company's mission, ethics, transparency, and accountability. It examines how the company integrates social and environmental performance into decision-making, how it communicates these impacts, and how it safeguards its mission over time, especially in the event of leadership changes or capital raises.

B. Workers:

"Workers" assesses how a company treats its employees. This includes compensation and benefits, training and education, worker ownership, job flexibility, satisfaction, and health and safety. A key emphasis is placed on creating a positive work environment and opportunities for professional development and economic security.

C. Community:

This area evaluates the company's impact on the communities in which it operates, hires from, and sources from. Important elements include diversity, equity, and inclusion; economic impact; supply chain practices; civic engagement; and charitable giving. It looks at both internal policies and external outcomes.

D. Environment:

Environment reviews a company's environmental performance through its facilities, materials, emissions, and resource and energy use. It also considers the company's impact on biodiversity, sustainable sourcing, and product lifecycle. Efforts to reduce carbon footprint and implement circular economy principles, which look at the whole product lifecycle from creation to waste, are key.

E. Customers:

This area analyzes whether a company's products or services create direct social or environmental impact, especially for underserved populations. It also considers data privacy, ethical marketing, customer feedback mechanisms, and product quality and safety.

Whether or not an enterprise chooses to become a B-Corp, these freely available FR guidelines can help any enterprise to identify measurable areas of sustainable development to focus on and help with goal setting and data gathering.

GRI focuses on reporting about sustainability impacts, while B Corp certification focuses on evaluating and managing a company's overall social and environmental performance over time. They can be used together to create a more comprehensive picture of a company's sustainability efforts.

Pros and cons of using Sievo for effective sustainability reporting:

Sievo provides a platform to manage, measure, and report on day-to-day sustainability performance, which is valuable for companies seeking to become B Corps and conducting GRI sustainability assessments. It facilitates data collection, analysis, and reporting in a way that aligns with the requirements of these frameworks.

Enterprises can take an integrated sustainability reporting approach using a GRI-B-Corps-Sievo approach. Benefits include a turnkey solution to building and maintaining sustainability with the support of industry experts, data professionals, and established peer members. The downside is that it can be costly, puts the work and effort of understanding and scrutinizing sustainability in the hands of others, and can lead to a disconnect between the organizational culture and its sustainability goals.

Benefits of a direct approach:

Taking a more direct, ‹boots on the ground' approach towards measuring and tracking sustainability helps an enterprise develop systems and methods more organically. This approach allows the enterprise to move at a pace that makes sense for them, keeping them aligned and constantly re-committed to their needs and methods. Drawing from the data types and measurement of GRI, B-Corps, and Sievo can help enterprises to frame their own metrics.

Following the goals and intentions created from Suma Qamana, Permaculture, Solidarity Economy, Circles of Sustainability, and the Sustainability Lens frameworks can also help identify areas to measure. Enterprises engage in sustainability practices within their organization, as demonstrated through the application of sustainability frameworks throughout the entire BMC. Sustainable procurement strategies are more present in the Cost Structure and Key Resources areas of an enterprise. Sourcing products from organizations that provide sustainability reports, transparency, and verified data helps to strengthen an enterprise's own practices, as positive social, environmental, and corporate governance impacts are amplified.

This information can be collected into an annual sustainability report with quarterly and monthly check-ins and updates shared with the public. Having a centralized report helps to keep messaging consistent and on track. It can show improvements over time and create a common enterprise language and structure in which to measure sustainability gains. It can also be branded with enterprise graphics and logos, which will help to create a strong, recognizable message as the data is shared throughout the enterprise, on social media platforms, and through marketing efforts.

Including quarterly and monthly updates keeps the data fresh, builds trust, celebrates wins, and shows places for improvement. This creates more sustainability news to be shared with stakeholders, building more brand value, authenticity, and customer commitment.

6.3.2 Six Lessons of Sustainability Communication

Building on the foundation of transformational leadership and strategic communication, enterprises must also learn how to effectively translate their sustainability goals and actions into messages that resonate with diverse audiences. Leadership sets the tone and direction, but it is through communication that stakeholders are engaged and impact is made visible. As sustainability becomes more integrated into core business practices, the ability to share progress, challenges, and successes, both internally and externally, becomes essential.

The following section outlines six key lessons in sustainability communication that help enterprises craft compelling messages, foster authentic engagement, and grow a community of support around their mission.

1. Craft a clear, engaging message:

Crafting a clear and engaging message in sustainability communication is crucial for raising awareness and motivating action among stakeholders. Let's see how this can be achieved.

A. Keep it simple.

Sustainability is multifaceted and highly technical. It is easy to get into the weeds explaining difficult processes to people who do not have experience in the area, creating meaning out of systems that are unfamiliar to others, or showing how a problem was solved that people did not even know existed.

There are also language and vocabulary barriers as sustainability terms are not universally known, understood, or applied. There is plenty of room for error; gains can be mismeasured or overstated, unintended impacts may arise from a sustainability action, and non-sustainability players can object to being called out for their shortcomings.

This presents a challenge for effective communication, both internally and externally. Complex concepts and information must be simplified to avoid overload, and audiences must be engaged and motivated to act. Refine the message, putting it into a familiar language for your target audience. Ask your audience to respond to the refined messaging. Ask how they understand the main points?

B. Make it human.

An emotional appeal is essential in building connection and commitment. Make sure there is emotion and a human connection in your message. Include a person or place that is relatable. Focus on a single producer story, worker background, or community detail to create that personal connection.

A micro story within a larger message helps to make the message relatable and shareable. A picture is worth 1,000 words. Having an image that supports the message's theme helps capture attention and emphasize what is being communicated.

C. Document the change.

Success starts as an idea that may never come to fruition. It is easy to skip documenting the start of something new when the end result is not yet clear. However, this "before and after" story is a compelling communication message.

Be sure to document the start of a new initiative in numbers, photos, and stories. That way, the change that ensues becomes more obvious, engaging, and meaningful.

D. Prove it.

Make sure your message is verifiable by offering real information and links to sources. When telling a story, use quotes from outside sources, photos, names, and titles. Take photos before engaging in a new initiative and then afterwards to show progress.

Share data, making simple charts and graphs to show how much change happened and when, building credibility and trust. Being open and accurate, providing context and content, while explaining the why and the how (substantiate claims), is key to crafting effective communication messages.

E. Be humble.

Acknowledge limitations. Showing where challenge areas still exist helps to bring people on board to chip in and support the goal. Sharing challenges also creates empathy while building credibility.

2. Tailor messages to and from stakeholders:

The most important part of sustainability engagement is getting the internal team on board and up to speed with what is happening and why. Sustainability initiatives work best as a top-down approach, with buy-in and commitment first from the top leaders and decision makers. They have the power to implement the change. This is why leadership is an important component of prolonged sustainability that is integrated over the long term in decision-making, mission, and culture.

Internally, sustainability efforts can create tension or disagreement as new systems and methods are introduced. Clear and consistent internal communication helps reduce confusion and resistance by keeping team members informed about what is changing and why. Strong internal messaging also builds more cohesive teams by recognizing contributions, celebrating successes, and encouraging innovative ideas from all levels of the organization.

While leadership is needed to drive sustainability, the innovative ideas and initiatives often come from people working at lower levels of the enterprise, who are closer to the processes where change is happening, from internal operations to supply chain sourcing (procurement). Create inclusive spaces where all voices of an enterprise can contribute to measuring and messaging sustainability. This helps to build pride and commitment amongst workers, create a more authentic communication message, and capture new places of change and impact that might be overlooked from top-level perspectives.

At the same time, input from suppliers and producers can be included to further highlight sustainability impacts. This is especially true for initiatives that suppliers and producers undertake, which are being supported by the enterprise through their buyer/ client relationships. Lastly, creating space for the consumer voice to be heard in messaging builds engagement, commitment, and helps spread the news about the goodwill and impacts made by the enterprise. Spaces for consumers to share their experiences with the product/ service and sustainability can be gained through social media posting, e-mail marketing, surveys, contests, tabling, and other interactive opportunities where sharing takes place.

3. **Share the story beyond the stakeholder circle:**

    Sharing the story beyond the stakeholder circle expands the impact of sustainability efforts, building

broader support and wider engagement. Here's how it
can be done:

A. Making new allies

There is growing awareness of and demand for
sustainability practices. Globally, 85% of people
indicate that they have shifted their purchase
behavior towards being more sustainable in the past
five years, with younger generations being more
committed to changing behaviors (Pope, 2021).
Thus, working in sustainability presents new areas
where messaging can be shared beyond immediate
stakeholders of current customers, suppliers, and
workers, expanding traditional areas of marketing.

Sustainability signals a commitment to
community, culture, alternative energy, ethical
procurement, environmentalism, and a care for
others. These messages evoke empathy, respect,
and support, reaching the hearts and minds of
people who are deeply committed and engaged with
caring for the planet and its people. In this way,
sustainability commitments make an enterprise's
work important with new communities ready
to embrace and support them, from academia to
activists to conscious consumers. These communities
present new areas for involvement and messaging,
including festivals, events, and classroom
collaborations. They support peer-to-peer learning in
sustainable business and brand positioning.

Further, working in sustainability makes
enterprises subject matter experts (SME) in a topic
that is garnering global attention and importance,
creating new leadership opportunities. This can feel
very new and different for an enterprise not used

to working in this way. Thankfully, sustainability is about cooperation, not competition. When working in the sustainability arena, one finds many eager and willing collaborators and an inner circle that is inviting and easy to access.

Participation spreads the message. Sustainability SMEs can present themselves as public speakers in the press, at events, and in classrooms. Numerous events centered around sustainability provide opportunities for tabling and speaking, including environmentally conscious festivals, conferences, eco-friendly product launches, and workshops on sustainable practices. Through active participation in these initiatives, businesses can establish themselves as leaders in sustainable development, fostering stronger relationships with environmentally conscious customers and partners.

Thus, making new allies is an inexpensive way to get in front of new consumers and share information, product samples, and stories while soliciting feedback and growing one's consumer base. Enterprises can also partner with university students as interns or as the subject of a case study. Authoring blogs or white papers with fact-based stories about the practices undertaken and their impacts adds to the academic study of sustainability while building trust and transparency.

B. Growing B2B sustainability demands

When entering B2B markets, sustainability provides a plus for buyers who are looking to "green up" their own supply chains and practices, building a new client base for sustainability enterprises. The search for suppliers who practice sustainability methods is on the rise, with 90% of business executives believing that consumers would hold businesses responsible for their environmental impact (EDF, 2019).

In addition, studies show that businesses are more willing to pay premium pricing for products and services created with sustainability methods and engage in longer-term relationships and buying commitments (Cassidy & Lie, 2023). Researchers Cassidy and Lie found that B2B buyers most actively seek branding that includes the supplier firm presenting itself as a good example of green behavior. This includes being clearly sustainable with established business initiatives that demonstrate a focus on the environment, and considering the environment, society, and economics in its decisions.

Keeping this in mind can help an enterprise to create a clear, consistent, fact-based messaging that appeals to the B2B community's needs for more sustainability in their supply chains and procurement. Many industry trade shows now feature special organic, fair trade, or eco-focused areas showcasing sustainable goods and practices.

4. **Amplify the message through social media marketing:**

With the world behind you, trumpet the news. Sharing messages internally, with stakeholders, and at targeted events, helps refine the message using feedback to focus directly on what has the most meaning and impact to consumers. It also helps to build a groundswell of supporters and influencers who will further amplify your social media messaging through re-posts, shares, and direct engagement.

Approaching public events strategically helps develop social media content. For example, an enterprise can have a photo booth with their product, brand, or mascot; record people engaging with the product, collecting testimonials; or invite producer guests to speak about the impact the enterprise has had on them, making sure to get participants to sign up for newsletters or join an action. The key is to gather and share sustainability metrics to create a consistent impact communication backed by data and facts, while also growing contact lists for targeted follow-up campaigning and customer growth.

Creating a clear outward-facing sustainability communication strategy helps to streamline the internal sustainability work. For example, a clear brand message can originate from the sustainability report and be utilized across all communications, until it is a tagline on the product packaging itself.

Expanding into the sustainability arena creates new opportunities and allies for communication. External communication should include a comprehensive sustainability marketing campaign, such as press and mailing lists, social media, business-to-business channels, broad and targeted messaging, brand and product/service promotion, and outreach through SME speakers. By engaging with sustainability-focused industries and consumers, an enterprise can broaden and strengthen its overall marketing reach.

5. Build sustainability allies:

Third-party validation and certification can be an important part of building and maintaining an enterprise's sustainability credibility. It is also a way to join a community of like-minded individuals working towards similar sustainability goals, facing similar challenges, and working in similar markets; building camaraderie and a supportive environment.

Remember, sustainability is about cooperation, not competition. There is strength in numbers. Working with third parties helps enterprises solidify their messaging in a cohesive way and collectively signal to consumers their commitments via familiar logos and programs. As was shown by the B-Corps example earlier in this chapter, certification organizations provide important infrastructure and support as enterprises navigate the complicated methods of establishing, measuring, and growing their sustainability practices.

A recent study found that 74% of consumers consider organic ingredients important in personal care products, with 62% of younger consumers, aged 19-21, willing to pay more for certified personal care products with organic ingredients (NSF International, 2025). They seek out familiar organic certification logos and wording on product packaging.

The four gains of joining a third-party certifying organization are as follows:

1. Infrastructure and guidelines for compliance.
2. Independent verification of reporting and claims.
3. Expanded consumers and markets that the certifier itself attracts.
4. Allies and peers committed to the same goals.

There are many different types of sustainability certifications on the organizational, industry, and consumer levels. The US Library of Congress lists the following standards and certification programs for businesses striving for sustainability (Table 6.2).

Table 6.2	Library of Congress Standards and Certifications	
Name	**Description**	**Website**
Certified B Corporation	Businesses verified for social, environmental impact, transparency, and accountability.	bcorporation.net
Cradle to Cradle Certified®	Product certification ensures safety, circularity, and social responsibility across five sustainability areas: Material Health, Product Circularity, Clean Air & Climate Protection, Water & Soil Stewardship, and Social Fairness.	c2ccertified.org
Forest Stewardship Council (FSC)	Certification for responsible forest management and supply chains.	fsc.org
Global Reporting Initiative (GRI)	Widely used standards for reporting on economic, environmental, and social impacts.	globalreporting.org
World Green Building Council	List tools to assess and certify buildings meeting green standards worldwide.	worldgbc.org
EPA Green Building Standards	U.S. EPA reference to major model codes and green building programs.	epa.gov/greenbuilding
Green Business Benchmark	Sustainability software and certification for measuring and improving business impact.	greenbusinessbenchmark.com
Green Business Certification Inc. (GBCI)	Administrator of Leadership in Energy and Environmental Design (LEED) and other sustainability certifications and credentials.	gbci.org

Name	Description	Website
FTC Green Guides	U.S. guidelines to prevent misleading environmental marketing claims.	ftc.gov/green-guides
Green Seal Certification	Certifies products/ services based on rigorous environmental and health standards.	greenseal.org
International Sustainability Standards Board (ISSB)	Develops International Financial Reporting Standards (IFRS) for sustainability disclosures to prevent greenwashing.	ifrs.org/issb
ISO 14000 Environmental Management	A family of standards for managing environmental responsibilities in organizations.	iso.org/iso-14001
Organic Certification (Rodale Institute)	Guides producers through the United States Department of Agriculture (USDA) organic certification process.	rodaleinstitute.org
Library of Congress Standards Collection	U.S. government archive of official standards, including sustainability.	loc.gov
U.S. Green Building Council (USGBC)	Developer of LEED, promoting sustainable, energy-efficient buildings.	usgbc.org

(Green Business: Sources of Information, 2025).

Other types of third-party certifiers and standards in areas of sustainability include the following:

Table 6.3 **Other Third-Party Certifiers**

Name	Focus area	Short description	Website
Fair Trade International (FLO)	Ethical Trade	Ensures fair wages, safe working conditions, and community development in global supply chains.	Fair Trade International. (n.d.). Retrieved from, https://www.fairtrade.net/
Fair Trade USA	Ethical Trade	U.S. version of fair trade certification with a focus on agriculture, apparel, and seafood.	Fair Trade USA. (n.d.). Retrieved from, https://www.fairtradecertified.org/
Fair for Life	Fair Trade/ CSR	Certifies fair trade and socially responsible practices across sectors and supply chains.	Fair for Life (n.d.). Retrieved from fairforlife.org
Rainforest Alliance	Agriculture & Forestry	Certifies farms, forests, and tourism operations that meet social, environmental, and economic criteria.	Rainforest Alliance (n.d.). Retrieved from rainforest-alliance.org

Name	Focus area	Short description	Website
Regenerative Organic Certified®	Regenerative Agriculture	Builds on USDA Organic with high-bar standards for soil health, animal welfare, and worker fairness.	Regenerative Organic Certified. (n.d.). Retrieved from regenorganic.org
Certified Naturally Grown	Local Food Systems	Peer-reviewed organic certification alternatives tailored to small-scale local farmers.	Certified Naturally Grown (n.d.). Retrieved from, certifiednaturallygrown.org
Real Organic Project	Organic Integrity	Farmer-led add-on label for U.S. organic farms that exceed USDA Organic requirements.	Real Organic Project. (n.d.). Retrieved from realorganicproject.org
Food Alliance Certified	Sustainable Food	Verifies sustainable practices in farming, ranching, and food handling.	Food Alliance Certified (n.d.). Retrieved from foodalliance.org
Equitable Food Initiative (EFI)	Farm Labor/ Food Safety	Combines farm labor protections, food safety, and pest management certification.	EFI. (n.d.). Retrieved from, equitablefood.org

(*Continued*)

Name	Focus area	Short description	Website
Child Labor Free Certification	Child Labor	Provides assurance that a brand or supply chain is free of child labor.	Child Labor Free (n.d.). Retrieved from childlaborfree.com
GoodWeave	Child & Forced Labor	Focuses on eliminating child and forced labor in the rug, fashion, and home industries.	GoodWeave (n.d.). Retrieved from, goodweave.org
Social Accountability International (SA8000)	Human Rights	Standard for workplace rights, including child labor, health and safety, and wages.	SA8000. (n.d.). Retrieved from, sa-intl. org
Ethical Trading Initiative (ETI)	Labor Rights	Alliance promoting ethical supply chains based on International Labor Organization (ILO) standards.	ETI. (n.d.). Retrieved from ethicaltrade.org
FairWild	Wild Harvest	Certification for sustainable and fair trade sourcing of wild plants and botanicals.	FairWild. (n.d.). Retrieved from fairwild. org

Name	Focus area	Short description	Website
Fairmined	Mining	Certifies responsibly mined gold with fair labor and environmental standards.	Fairmined. (n.d.). Retrieved from fairmined.org
Domestic Fair Trade Association (DFTA)	U.S. Fair Trade	Promotes equity in U.S. food systems through domestic fair trade partnerships.	DFTA. (n.d.). Retrieved from, dfta.org

It is often complicated and costly to choose which certifications to pursue. The best way to decide is to conduct an internal audit of an enterprise's strengths and weaknesses in its own sustainability practices. Where do they need more help? B-Corps and GRI are great for organizational support, while more targeted certifications such as GBCI, Farm Sustainability Assessment (FSA), and Fairmined are more materials and procurement focused, and Fair Trade and Goodweave look at labor and worker conditions.

Finding certification areas that can support an enterprise's sustainability weaknesses is a good strategy towards continuous improvement. At the same time, these certifications can be obtained through procurement and partnerships by working with suppliers to bring their certified goods and services to the enterprise. It is important to remember that certifications alone do not make for a sustainable enterprise; they help by providing the infrastructure, market, and validity, but sustainability is grown in the mindset, intention, and belief of the organization, embedded in its culture and mission.

6. Celebrate:

The most important aspect in sustainability communication and development is celebration. It is easy to get burnt out or overwhelmed and just stop. Sustainability practices are pervasive, appearing in every aspect of an organization. There are many moving parts, both internally and externally, and it takes a lot of extra work to get started and maintain. This is why sustainability is considered a work in progress, one of continuous improvement.

Celebrating builds momentum and energy, inviting allies to get involved, and lightening the load. A celebration could be a recognition of a new supplier, with a visit by the supplier, product samples, or a trip to see suppliers. It could be an open house inviting customers and the public to come and see how things are made or done, and include product sales, demonstrations, and testing. It could be a series of workshops that reward and engage customers and the public in sustainability efforts. And it could also be internal celebrations put on by departments.

The key to the celebration is to create an upbeat and festive atmosphere, reach a benchmark, offer rewards, try out new things, and get people engaged. Also, make it inclusive so entire families and whole communities can participate, building connections and strengthening people's understanding of and commitment to the enterprise.

Companies such as New Chapter and Equal Exchange offer producer tours to employees who have been at the organization for a certain number of years. Loyal employees travel to another country to see how product materials are produced, meet farmers, and enjoy a cultural, place-based educational vacation. Badger Products and Orchard Hill bakery host open houses with monthly potluck celebrations featuring local bands and product sampling.

Another way of celebrating sustainability is joining in on others' celebrations, either as a speaker, presenter, or attendee. The following is a list of celebratory sustainability events worldwide featuring speaker panels, workshops, networking, tabling, and trade show floorspace (Table 6.4). These are great for connecting with new allies and customers, learning about new tools and programs, and finding new sustainability initiatives, including funding and partnerships.

Table 6.4 **Sustainability Magazine's Top 10 Sustainability Events**

Event Name	Description	Focus	Location	Attendees
Sustainability LIVE London	London's largest sustainability and ESG summit featuring C-suite leaders, panels, and strategy sessions.	Sustainability	London	8,000
COP 29	The UN Climate Change Conference bringing together governments and global stakeholders to advance climate action.	Climate change	Baku, Azerbaijan	70,000

(Continued)

Event Name	Description	Focus	Location	Attendees
Climate Week NYC	A major global climate event with 600+ sessions mobilizing government and business leaders across New York and online.	Climate change	New York City	2,000
World Economic Forum Annual Meeting, Davos	Annual gathering of global leaders to tackle economic, environmental, and geopolitical challenges.	Global issues	Davos, Switzerland	2,800
International Conference on Sustainable Development (ICSD)	International platform for solutions to the UN Sustainable Development Goals through hybrid presentations and discussions.	Sustainable development	Grand Dakar, Senegal	2,000
Innovation Zero	A UK summit connecting leaders and innovators focused on achieving net zero emissions through technology and policy.	Net zero	London	10,000

Event Name	Description	Focus	Location	Attendees
VERGE	A climate tech event exploring convergence across energy, buildings, transport, and digital infrastructure.	Climate tech	San Jose, California	6,000
ACESD 2024	Asia Conference on Environment and Sustainable Development (ACESD) sharing the latest academic research and solutions.	Environment and sustainable development	Osaka, Japan	N/A
EarthX 2025	A massive environmental conference fostering global dialogue with business and policy leaders in Texas.	Environmental sustainability	Dallas, Texas	177,000
CleanTech Forum North America	Connects clean technology innovators and investors to scale solutions in energy, materials, and resources.	Climate tech	San Diego, California	700

(Jessen, 2024)

FUN FACTS

- Nearly all S&P 500 firms reported sustainability (ESG) data, and about 70% of those had at least partial third-party assurance of their sustainability disclosures (Center for Audit Quality, 2022; BDO USA, 2023).

- According to B Lab, as of 2025, there are over 9,500 Certified B-Corporations operating in 160+ industries across 102 countries (B-Lab, 2025).

- A 2021 global consumer sustainability study found that approximately 85% of consumers reported changing their buying behavior toward more sustainable choices in the preceding five years (Simon-Kucher & Partners, 2021)

TIPS

- Start documenting early: Capture the "before" phase of sustainability initiatives to showcase progress.

- Use simple, emotional messaging: Connect through relatable stories and clear visuals.

- Leverage internal voices: Sustainability innovation often originates from employees closest to the process.

POINTS TO REMEMBER

- Communication is strategic; it goes beyond marketing and plays a central role in sustainability success.

- Sustainability is collaborative; joining sustainability communities opens up support and partnerships.

- Frameworks like GRI and B-Corp offer valuable guidance but should be tailored to the enterprise.

- Celebration of wins and recognition of progress builds energy and momentum.

DISCUSSION QUESTIONS

- How can an enterprise balance optimism and transparency when communicating sustainability challenges?

- In what ways can sustainability messaging expand a business's customer base beyond its traditional market?

- How might participation in third-party certification impact internal culture and external perceptions?

6.4 Sustainability Leadership Mindset: Self-Assessment

Self-awareness is critical when undertaking leadership and change. The following is a self-assessment tool based on the *Sustainable Enterprise Fieldbook* (Wheeler, Blatnicky, et al., 2013).

Evaluate where you are in your sustainability mindset through Table 6.5. Think about places where you are strong, where there are areas for growth, and how you can help others in activating their sustainability leadership mindset. Use a 1–5 scale for each principle (1 = rarely, 3 = sometimes, 5 = consistently).

Table 6.5 **Sustainability Leadership Mindset Self-Assessment**

Principle	How I practice this	Enterprise outcome	Personal outcome	Score (1–5)
1. Holistic Thinking	I consider social, environmental, and financial systems together.	Strategic alignment drives long-term profitability.	Helps clarify life purpose and connect personal and professional goals.	
2. Collaboration & Inclusion	I invite diverse voices and build shared ownership.	Builds trust and innovation, enhances team productivity.	Deepens personal relationships and empathy.	
3. Inquiry–Action–Inquiry	I test ideas, reflect, and adapt constantly.	Leads to smarter risk-taking and faster learning.	Increases personal growth and resilience.	
4. Integrity & Respect	I act ethically and treat others well.	Builds brand reputation, reduces legal/ PR risk.	Builds trust and self-respect.	
5. Win–Win–Win Thinking	I look for solutions that benefit business, society, and the environment.	Creates strong partnerships and stakeholder value.	Boosts satisfaction and confidence in impact.	
6. Deep Listening	I listen without interrupting or judging.	Enhances stakeholder engagement and retention.	Strengthens emotional intelligence and connection.	
7. Boundary-Spanning	I engage across functions, sectors, or cultures.	Uncovers new markets and collaboration opportunities.	Expands worldview and adaptability.	

Principle	How I practice this	Enterprise outcome	Personal outcome	Score (1–5)
8. Purpose-Driven Focus	I align actions with a clear sustainability mission.	Aligns teams and improves brand loyalty.	Provides a sense of direction and meaning.	
9. Positive Influence ("Be an Attractor")	I lead by example, not force.	Builds a culture that attracts customers and talent.	Inspires others and reinforces self-worth.	
10. Clarity of Meaning	I ensure shared understanding in goals and communication.	Reduces costly misunderstandings and conflict.	Builds confidence and psychological safety.	
11. Mutual Interest Seeking	I seek shared value, not just compromise.	Strengthens negotiations and supplier/ customer ties.	Builds fairness and long-term trust.	
12. Empathy	I try to understand others' experiences and views.	Enhances employee retention and customer satisfaction.	Deepens relationships and self-awareness.	
13. Accountability	I follow through and own my impact.	Increases operational performance and trust.	Builds credibility and self-confidence.	
14. Embracing Difficult Conversations	I engage openly with tough topics.	Prevents dysfunction and enables real progress.	Builds courage and authentic connection.	
15. Embodied Leadership	I model what I value, not just preach it.	Increases alignment and motivation across teams.	Increases fulfillment and coherence.	

(Continued)

Principle	How I practice this	Enterprise outcome	Personal outcome	Score (1–5)
16. Tangible Actions & Quick Wins	I create momentum through visible results.	Improves ROI and staff morale.	Generates satisfaction and optimism.	
			TOTAL SCORE	

(Based on the work of Wheeler, Blatnicky, et al., 2013)

Reflections on outcomes:

Have I experienced or contributed to the following outcomes in myself or my team/ community?

(Check all that apply)

☐ A greater sense of energy and purpose

☐ Curiosity, humility, and fascination with new ideas

☐ A focus on individual potential and shared values

☐ Renewed belief in the power of sustainability to transform

☐ Conditions that allow people to feel fully alive and engaged

☐ Commitment to capturing and spreading our passion for sustainability

Table 6.6 Score interpretation: Sustainability leadership mindset self-assessment

Score Range	Interpretation
65–80	**Strategic Sustainability Leader**: You are well-aligned with a sustainable leadership mindset that fosters business growth and personal fulfillment. You're likely seen as an ethical, trusted, high-impact leader.

Score Range	Interpretation
50–64	**Emerging Leader**: You demonstrate many sustainable leadership traits, but have opportunities to increase your impact—especially in how your mindset supports enterprise and personal success.
35–49	**Developing Awareness**: You are beginning to explore how sustainability aligns with business and personal growth. Focus on 2–3 areas for immediate improvement.
Under 35	**Foundational Opportunity**: Ample room for growth. Consider coaching, peer learning, or mentorship to expand your mindset and impact.

6.5 Case Study: Patagonia

Leading with Purpose—Patagonia's Sustainability Lens and the Making of a Movement

Introduction:

Founded in the 1970s by climber and self-taught blacksmith, Yvon Chouinard, Patagonia began as a small gear company forged in the outdoor climbing culture of California. From repurposed rugby shirts to climbing pitons, the company evolved into a global outdoor apparel brand with a fiercely independent ethos (Chouinard, 2006).

By 2011, Patagonia was not only a $500 million business, but it was also recognized as a pioneer in environmentally and socially responsible business practices (Sundheim, 2023). Patagonia's journey was defined by one driving belief: business could be done differently, with nature, not against it.

Yet this evolution did not follow a traditional business trajectory. Guided by a founder who preferred surfing to boardrooms and a decentralized leadership model that empowered employees, Patagonia made a series of transformative decisions rooted in sustainability and values. This case explores how Patagonia's Chouinard

used Sustainability Lens concepts to build new possibilities and how leadership was shared and communicated.
It also highlights how the company created powerful transformational leadership moments that inspired change in its industry.

The Challenge:

As Patagonia grew, it encountered multiple moments of dissonance between its operations and its environmental values. Employees discovered harmful chemicals like formaldehyde in their cotton fabrics and witnessed pesticide-drenched cotton fields in California. They saw the harmful labor practices at overseas suppliers (Stanley & Chouinard, 2023). Rather than ignore these realities or simply fix them superficially, Chouinard faced a deeper challenge: how to align business growth with a commitment to environmental and social justice in a way that was transparent, authentic, and lasting.

This moment marked the emergence of Patagonia's own Sustainability Lens, a mindset that asked not only "What is?" but "What could be?" It forced Chouinard and the company to ask new questions and build new stories.

The Solution:

Patagonia's solution was not one singular initiative; it was a series of transformational leadership moments, shared across the company (Jones, 2023; Foley, 2019).

- **Leadership through a sustainability mindset**

  Chouinard, with his Patagonia staff, made bold choices, such as abandoning conventional cotton completely, even before customers asked for change or regulations required it. They retrained themselves and rebuilt supply chains. They worked closely with growers to produce organic cotton, despite increased costs and logistical headaches. The company also chose not to build a new warehouse on undeveloped land and instead repurposed an abandoned coal mine, because it fit their environmental values.

- **Shared leadership**

    Founder Chouinard's decentralized leadership style meant middle managers and employees were empowered to take initiative. Field visits to factories and cotton fields were encouraged. These trips turned into educational journeys that sparked empathy and ownership; employees were not just executing sustainability, they were discovering it. These were not top-down mandates, but genuine leadership moments shared by all.

- **Communicating the message**

    Patagonia made its values visible and palatable. Through compelling campaigns like "Don't Buy This Jacket" and transparent messaging about its challenges, the company invited customers into its sustainability journey. Messaging wasn't greenwashing; it was honest, imperfect, and powerful. In 2011, Patagonia became the first California company to become a registered Benefit Corporation and a certified B-Corp. The certification was a way to institutionalize their values and communicate their purpose externally while protecting it internally.

The Impact:

The impacts of Chouinard's sustainability-driven leadership are measurable, providing a pathway for others to follow (B-Lab, n.d.) (Fig. 6.13):

Figure 6.13 Patagonia's commitment to investing in climate and ecological causes

(Patagonia, 2022)

- **Industry transformation:** Patagonia became a model for ethical supply chain reform. It pioneered practices that are now industry standards, such as Fair Trade Certification and organic material sourcing.

- **Cultural shift:** Internally, Patagonia created a culture of moral agency and environmental citizenship where every employee saw sustainability as part of their job.
- **Consumer trust and reputation:** By 2023, Patagonia was ranked the most reputable brand in the U.S.
- **Legacy leadership:** Through its B-Corp Certification and the establishment of the Patagonia Purpose Trust, the company ensured that its mission would be protected in perpetuity.

Conclusion:

Chouinard didn't just build a successful business; he built a movement. By applying Sustainability Lens principles, sharing leadership, and communicating authentically, Chouinard turned everyday decisions into transformational moments. Patagonia's journey shows that sustainability is not a department; it's a worldview. And when that worldview is shared across an organization, it generates stories that not only build the brand but also inspire change far beyond the business itself.

Discussion Questions:

- How does Chouinard's use of Sustainability Lens thinking differ from traditional corporate sustainability approaches?
- What are the advantages and risks of decentralized leadership in driving sustainability?
- In what ways did Patagonia's messaging contribute to its impact and success? What made it effective?
- What leadership moments can you identify in this case that were turning points for Patagonia?

Activity:

Choose a product or service in your life and analyze it using the Sustainability Lens. Identify areas of hidden environmental or social costs. How could a company transform these issues into leadership moments?

In this chapter, we explored the critical role of leadership in driving sustainability within enterprises. Framed through the concept of transformational leadership, we learnt that sustainability is not just a goal. It is a process that invites vision, shared responsibility, and strategic communication. It begins with the Sustainability Lens Game, a creative and participatory tool developed to help individuals and teams explore sustainable possibilities within the Business Model Canvas.

The game promotes systems thinking, storytelling, and interdisciplinary problem-solving across key sustainability areas: resources, health, policy, and exchange. It serves as an educational and professional development tool. It also encourages leadership moments by engaging people from all backgrounds in innovation and collaboration.

Transformational leadership is a leadership style particularly well-suited to sustainability challenges. Transformational leaders guide change by inspiring vision and modeling ethical behavior. They also believe in stimulating creativity and recognizing individual contributions. We saw how transformational leaders set values-based direction, create inclusive decision-making environments, and establish trust within and outside the enterprise. Leadership moments occur at every stage of the entrepreneurial journey, and transformational leadership behaviors can be developed at all levels, not just at the top.

In the third section, we discussed strategic communication, emphasizing that powerful sustainability efforts can fall short without clear, authentic, and audience-aware messaging. Communicating the vision, progress, and setbacks of sustainability initiatives builds momentum, community, and credibility. It also empowers stakeholders, both internal and external, to see their roles in the enterprise's transformation. Tools such as sustainability reports, KPIs, B-Corp Certification, GRI standards, and software like Sievo help measure and share progress transparently and support strategic communication messaging.

Chapter Summary

- The Sustainability Lens Game fosters creativity, systems thinking, and collaboration. It turns complex sustainability theories into actionable enterprise strategies through accessible gameplay.

- Transformational leadership is essential in sustainability work. It builds trust, inspires vision, and engages teams in meaningful change through influence, motivation, stimulation, and individualized consideration.

- Communication is critical in sustainability leadership; without authentic, strategic messaging, even the most innovative initiatives risk being misunderstood or undervalued.

- Measurement and accountability tools such as GRI standards, B-Corp certification, and platforms like Sievo help track progress, maintain transparency, and guide sustainability strategies.

QUIZ

1. **What is the Sustainability Lens designed to do?**
   a. Replace the Business Model Canvas
   b. Rank sustainability programs globally
   c. Provide a guiding tool to generate sustainable possibilities within enterprises
   d. Evaluate only environmental initiatives

2. **Which of the following is *not* one of the four quadrants of the Sustainability Lens?**
   a. Resources
   b. Innovation
   c. Policy
   d. Exchange

3. **What distinguishes the Sustainability Lens Game from other sustainability games?**
   a. It focuses on government policy.
   b. It uses artificial intelligence simulations.
   c. It centers on enterprise development.
   d. It is based on fictional characters.

4. **Which of the following is *not* one of the Four Behaviors of Transformational Leadership?**
   a. Idealized Influence
   b. Inspirational Motivation
   c. Resource Allocation
   d. Individualized Consideration

5. **According to the chapter, transformational leaders are expected to:**
    a. Act as spokespeople and set enterprise values.
    b. Focus solely on profit generation.
    c. Remain behind the scenes during change.
    d. Avoid media attention and limit external engagement.

6. **What is one key reason sustainability initiatives succeeded according to the study cited (Davis-Peccoud, 2016)?**
    a. High marketing budgets
    b. Technology adoption
    c. Leadership support and employee buy-in
    d. Strict government regulations

7. **Why is authenticity important in sustainability communication?**
    a. It simplifies the messaging process.
    b. It improves internal efficiency.
    c. It helps avoid legal issues.
    d. It builds trust and rapport.

8. **What is a key benefit of third-party sustainability certifications like B-Corp?**
    a. They guarantee profitability.
    b. They eliminate the need for internal sustainability practices.
    c. They provide infrastructure and external validation.
    d. They reduce marketing efforts.

9. **What is the primary function of a sustainability report?**
   a. To attract investors through storytelling
   b. To measure progress, set benchmarks, and identify new goals
   c. To promote products to consumers
   d. To replace financial reports with environmental data

10. **Which of the following is *not* one of the four core behaviors of transformational leadership?**
    a. Idealized Influence
    b. Inspirational Motivation
    c. Transactional Oversight
    d. Individualized Consideration

Answer Key

1 – c	2 – b	3 – c	4 – c	5 – a
6 – c	7 – d	8 – c	9 – b	10 – c

Glossary

Acronyms and Abbreviations:

- **Benefit Corporation (B Corp):** A company that voluntarily meets higher standards of social and environmental performance, transparency, and accountability.
- **Business Model Canvas (BMC):** A visual tool used to describe and develop the key parts of a business. It includes nine sections, like customers, resources, partnerships, and revenue. This book uses it as a foundation for building sustainability.
- **Corporate Social Responsibility (CSR):** A company's responsibility to contribute positively to society and the environment, beyond making profits.
- **Environmental, Social, and Governance (ESG):** A way to measure a company's sustainability efforts in these three important areas.
- **Global Reporting Initiative (GRI):** A set of standards companies use to report their sustainability performance.
- **Key Performance Indicator (KPI):** A way to measure how well a company or project is doing against its goals.
- **Non-Governmental Organization (NGO):** A nonprofit group, often focused on social or environmental work.
- **Return on Investment (ROI):** A measure of the benefit or profit gained compared to the money invested.
- **Sustainable Development Goals (SDGs):** 17 global goals created by the United Nations to make the world more sustainable and fairer for all by 2030.

Key Concepts and Terms

- **Accountability:** Being responsible for one's actions, especially when those actions affect people or the environment.

- **Carbon Emissions:** The release of carbon dioxide into the air, mainly from burning fossil fuels. This contributes to climate change.

- **Circular Economy:** A system that keeps products and materials in use for as long as possible, reducing waste.

- **Climate Risk:** The potential problems caused by changes in climate, like floods, droughts, or rising sea levels.

- **Communication Plan:** A strategy for how and what a company shares with the public or stakeholders about its sustainability efforts.

- **Conscious Consumerism:** Buying products that are made ethically and sustainably, often by checking for things like fair trade or organic certifications.

- **Credibility:** Being believable and trustworthy, especially important when making sustainability claims.

- **Double Materiality:** The idea that sustainability matters both because it affects the company and because the company affects the world.

- **Entrepreneurship Spectrum:** A range of skills and traits that entrepreneurs may have. It helps people understand their personal strengths and where they may need support.

- **Greenwashing:** When a company makes misleading claims to appear more environmentally friendly than it actually is.

- **Impact Measurement:** A way to track the effects a business has on people, the planet, and communities.

- **Materiality Assessment:** A process where a company decides which sustainability issues are most important to its success and stakeholders.

- **Messaging:** The way information is presented or communicated to an audience.

- **Mission-Driven:** A business or organization that exists to accomplish a specific positive goal, not just to make money.

- **Neurodiversity:** The idea that people think and process the world in different ways (e.g., due to ADHD, autism, dyslexia). These differences can be strengths in entrepreneurship.

- **Planetary Boundaries:** The limits within which humanity can safely operate without causing severe damage to the Earth's systems.

- **Sustainability:** Operating a business in a way that meets current needs without harming the ability of future generations to meet theirs. It includes environmental care, social responsibility, and financial health.

- **Shared Value:** Business practices that benefit both the company and society at the same time.

- **Stakeholder:** Anyone affected by or interested in a company's actions—this includes customers, employees, investors, and the community.

- **Storytelling:** Using stories to help people understand and connect with a company's sustainability journey.

- **Sustainability Communication Pyramid:** A framework from the manuscript that shows how to communicate sustainability by moving from compliance (bottom) to inspiration (top).

- **Sustainability Lens Game:** A visual, interactive way to apply the Four Lenses of Sustainability to the BMC. It helps entrepreneurs "see" sustainability opportunities in each part of their business.

- **Triple Bottom Line:** A model for measuring success not just by profit, but also by how a company supports people and the planet.

Frameworks and Approaches

A. **Business Model Canvas (BMC):** A strategic tool divided into 9 parts:
  1. **Key Partners:** Who helps you run your business?
  2. **Key Activities:** What you do.
  3. **Key Resources:** What you use to create your product or service.
  4. **Value Proposition:** Why your product or service is valuable.
  5. **Customer Relationships:** How you interact with customers.
  6. **Channels:** How customers get your product or service.
  7. **Customer Segments:** Who your customers are.
  8. **Cost Structure:** What it costs to run the business.
  9. **Revenue Streams:** How you earn money.

B. **The Four Ps of Sustainability:** This is a model that expands on the Triple Bottom Line by including Purpose, which emphasizes genuine commitment.
  1. **People:** The social impacts of your business (workers, community).
  2. **Planet:** The environmental impacts (resources used, waste created).
  3. **Profit:** Financial success.

4. **Purpose:** The deeper reason why your business engages in sustainability.

C. **The Four Pillars of Fair Trade:** These pillars support strong, fair supply chains and responsible sourcing.

   1. **Institutions:** Organizations that create and enforce ethical standards (like fair trade certifiers).
   2. **Consumers:** People who choose to buy ethical products.
   3. **Producers:** The people who make or grow the products.
   4. **Governments:** The systems or groups of people that create laws and infrastructure that support fair trade.

D. **The Four Lenses of Sustainability:** This lens is based on indigenous and global knowledge and offers a holistic way to analyze sustainability across a business.

   1. **Resources:** Where your materials come from and their environmental impact.
   2. **Health:** The well-being of people in your business and community.
   3. **Policy:** Your internal rules and how you influence bigger change.
   4. **Exchange:** How your product or service is shared, sold, or accessed by others.

E. **The *Dueling Banjos* Model (Seven Stages of Entrepreneurship):** This model helps entrepreneurs understand where their natural strengths fit and where they might need help. It is a framework that links neurodiverse traits (like impulsivity or creativity) with different stages of growing a business:

1. Interest
2. Opportunity Identification
3. Nascent Entrepreneurial Behavior
4. Resource Acquisition
5. Resource Coordination
6. Value Capture
7. Innovation and Renewal

F. **SWOT Analysis:** A tool to reflect on:
   1. **Strengths:** What you're good at.
   2. **Weaknesses:** Where you struggle.
   3. **Opportunities:** What could help you grow?
   4. **Threats:** What could hold you back?

References

1. ACCO Brands Corporation. (2025). *ACCO Brands official site*. Retrieved July 6, 2025, from https://www.accobrands.com/

2. Adams, C. (2020, September 29). Here's why autistic people make efficient and logical workers. *World Economic Forum*. https://www.weforum.org/stories/2020/09/autistic-people-neurodiversity-at-work-benefits-everyone/

3. Akhtar, F., Lodhi, S.A., & Shah Khan, S. (2015). Permaculture approach: linking ecological sustainability to business strategies, *Management of Environmental Quality, 26*(6), 795–809.

4. AlQallaf, N., Chen, X., Ge, Y., Khan, A., Zoha, A., Hussain, S., & Ghannam, R. (2022, March). Teaching solar energy systems design using game-based virtual reality. In *2022 IEEE Global Engineering Education Conference (EDUCON)* (pp. 956–960). IEEE.

5. A Place at the Table. (n.d.). *A Place at the Table | A Pay-What-You-Can Café | Raleigh, NC*. Retrieved June 7, 2025, from https://tableraleigh.org/

6. Artaraz, K., Calestani, M., & Trueba, M. L. (2021). Introduction: Vivir bien/Buen vivir and post-neoliberal development paths in Latin America: Scope, strategies, and the realities of implementation. *Latin American Perspectives, 48*(3), 4–16.

7. Autism at Work. (2019). *About Autism at work*. Retrieved May 31, 2025, from https://www.autismatwork.org/about

8. Avery, G. C., & Bergsteiner, H. (2010). *Honeybees & locusts: The business case for sustainable leadership*. Allen & Unwin

9. Avery, J., & Norton, M. I. (2014). *Pay attention to your extreme consumers*. *Harvard Business Review*. Retrieved from https://www.library.hbs.edu/working-knowledge/pay-attention-to-your-extreme-consumers

10. Bakker, A. B., Hetland, J., Demerouti, E., & Olsen, O. K. (2023). The power of leadership: Inspirational, engaging, and supportive. *Journal of Occupational and Organizational Psychology, 96*(1), 1–23.

11. Bass, B. M., & Avolio, B. J. (2007). *Full range leadership development: Manual for the Multifactor Leadership Questionnaire*. Mind Garden.

12. B Corporation Europe. (n.d.). *3 steps to become a B Corp*. Retrieved June 21, 2025, from https://bcorporation.eu/blog_post/3-steps-to-become-a-b-corp/

13. B Corporation UK. (n.d.). *B Corporation*. Retrieved June 21, 2025, from https://bcorporation.uk/

14. B Lab. (2025). *BIA: Foundation Requirements (FR) and Body of Knowledge for the FR Impact Topic (Version 1.0)*. https://www.bcorporation.net/en-us/certification/

15. B Lab. (2025). Certified B Corporations. Retrieved July 8, 2025, from https://www.bcorporation.net/en-us/

16. B Lab. (n.d.). *Patagonia – Certified B Corporation – B Lab Global*. B Corporation. Retrieved July 21, 2025, from https://www.patagonia.com/b-lab.html

17. BDO USA. (2023). *99% of the S&P 500 is reporting on ESG and 65% are obtaining ESG assurance.*

18. Before Breakfast. (2025). Before Breakfast London. Retrieved July 6, 2025, from https://beforebreakfast.london/

19. Blue Ocean Team. (2022). *7 powerful blue ocean strategy examples that left the competition behind*. Blue Ocean Strategy. Retrieved from https://www.blueoceanstrategy.com/blog/7-powerful-blue-ocean-strategy-examples/

20. B the Change. (n.d.). *Best practices for communicating social impact*. B the Change. Retrieved June 21, 2025, from https://bthechange.com/best-practices-for-communicating-social-impact-81d70eb2647e

21. Branson, R. (2012). *Like a virgin: Secrets they won't teach you at business school*. Portfolio/Penguin.

22. Bryant, J., Ayers, J., & Missimer, M. (2023). What transforms? Transformative learning in a sustainability leadership master's program. *International Journal of Sustainability in Higher Education, 24*(9), 231–251. https://doi.org/10.1108/IJSHE-03-2022-0086

23. Cain, A. (2022, April 21). The world's favourite toilet paper brand is ready to clean up. *The Sydney Morning Herald.* https://www.smh.com.au/technology/the-world-s-favourite-toilet-paper-brand-is-ready-to-clean-up-20220419-p5aeix.html

24. California Certified Organic Farmers. (n.d.). *History*. Retrieved July 8, 2025, from https://ccof.org/about/history

25. Cassidy, R., & Lie, D. S. (2023). The effects of B2B sustainable brand positioning on relationship outcomes. *Industrial Marketing Management, 109*, 245–256. https://doi.org/10.1016/j.indmarman.2023.02.006

26. Carroll, D. (2024, July 19). *S&P 500 analysis: ESG reporting continues to evolve. Center for Audit Quality.* Retrieved from https://www.thecaq.org/aia-sp-500-analysis-esg-reporting-continues-to-evolve

27. Center for Audit Quality. (n.d.). *S&P 500 and ESG reporting*. The CAQ. Retrieved June 21, 2025, from https://www.thecaq.org/sp-500-and-esg-reporting

28. Circles of Sustainability. (n.d.). *Rapid assessment tool*. Circles of Sustainability. Retrieved June 9, 2025, from https://www.circlesofsustainability.com/tools/rapid-assessment-tool/

29. Chen, F.-H., & Ho, S.-J. (2022). Designing a board game about the United Nations' Sustainable Development Goals. *Sustainability, 14*(18), 11197.

30. Chouinard, Y. (2006). *Let my people go surfing*. Penguin Books.

31. Choquehuanca Céspedes, D. (2023). *Geapolítica del Vivir Bien*. Vicepresidencia del Estado Plurinacional de Bolivia.

32. Clean Water America Alliance. (2011). *U.S. Water Prize 2011 winners*. Retrieved from https://archive.jsonline.com/business/121425283.html

33. Commerce Institute. (n.d.). *Business failure rate statistics*. Retrieved July 8, 2025, from https://www.commerceinstitute.com/business-failure-rate/

34. Cradle to Cradle Products Innovation Institute. (n.d.). Home Page – FSC International. Retrieved July 8, 2025, from https://c2ccertified.org/

35. Craig, L. (2020). *Ugly food for thought: Ripple effects from a new food movement* (Senior capstone project No. 972). Vassar College Digital Window. https://digitalwindow.vassar.edu/senior_capstone/972

36. Creed, A., Ross, J., & Ross, J. (2021). *Storytelling for human sensitivity, compassion, and connection in corporate sustainability*. In S. H. Park, J. Zhang, & J. Zhang (Eds.), *The Palgrave handbook of corporate sustainability in the digital era*. Palgrave Macmillan

37. D'Ambrosio, D. (2023, June 6). *Green Mountain Power wants to eliminate the wait for Tesla Powerwalls*. Burlington Free Press. https://www.burlingtonfreepress.com/story/money/2023/06/06/green-mountain-power-wants-to-eliminate-the-wait-for-tesla-powerwalls/70289137007/

38. Dam, R. F. (2025, March 13). *The 5 Stages in the Design Thinking Process*. Interaction Design Foundation - IxDF. https://www.interaction-design.org/literature/article/5-stages-in-the-design-thinking-process

39. Davey, B. (2016, January 23). *How to barter art, make money and have fun*. Art Marketing News. Retrieved June 7, 2025, from https://artmarketingnews.com/barter/

40. Davis-Peccoud, J., Stone, P., & Tovey, C. (2016). *Achieving breakthrough results in sustainability*. Bain & Company.

41. Dean's Beans Organic Coffee. (n.d.). *Dean's Beans*. https://deansbeans.com/

42. Deleny, G. (2024, July). *In Ecuador's Intag Mountains, the value of nature far exceeds the risk of mining*. One Earth. https://www.oneearth.org/in-ecuadors-intag-mountains-the-value-of-nature-far-exceeds-the-risk-of-mining/

43. De la Garza, A. (2021, July 26). This Vermont Utility Is Revolutionizing Its Power Grid to Fight Climate Change. Will the Rest of the Country Follow Suit? TIME. https://time.com/6082973/vermont-electric-grid/

44. Deloitte. (2019, May 2). *Outsourcing and shared services market to soon exceed $1 trillion.* Consultancy-me. Retrieved July 8, 2025, from https://www.consultancy-me.com/news/2063/ outsourcing-and-shared-services-market-to-soon-exceed-1-trillion

45. Deng, Y., Gulseren, D., Morin, A. J. S., & Chou, Y.-L. (2023). Transformational leadership and employee outcomes: A meta-analytic path model. *Journal of Organizational Behavior, 44*(1), 58–82.

46. Designphil Inc. (2025). Designphil – English site. Retrieved July 6, 2025, from https://www.designphil.co.jp/english/

47. Doane, D. (2001). *Taking flight: The rapid growth of ethical consumerism.* New Economics Foundation.

48. Dr. Bronner's. (2025). *150 years and 5 generations of family soapmaking.* Retrieved July 8, 2025, from https://www.drbronner.com/blogs/ourselves/ the-dr-bronners-story

49. Eaton. (2016). Blackout Tracker annual report: United States 2015.

50. Egger, M., Booth, A. M., Bosker, T., Everaert, G., Garrard, S. L., Havas, V., Huntley, H. S., Koelmans, A. A., Kvale, K., Lebreton, L., Niemann, H., Pang, Q., Proietti, M., Puskic, P., Richon, C., Royer, S.-J., Savoca, M. S., Tjallema, A., van Vulpen, M., ... Mitrano, D. M. (2025). Evaluating the environmental impact of cleaning the North Pacific Garbage Patch. *Scientific Reports, 15*(1), Article 16736. https://research-portal.uu.nl/en/publications/ evaluating-the-environmental-impact-of-cleaning-the-north-pacific

51. Eldred-Cohen, C. (2021, August 12). How Satoshi Tajiri's autism helped create *Pokémon.* The Art of Autism. https://the-art-of-autism.com/ how-satoshi-tajiris-autism-helped-create-pokemon/

52. Elkington, J. (1997). *Cannibals with forks: The triple bottom line of 21st-century business.* Capstone.

53. Elkington, J. (2020). *Green swans: The coming boom in regenerative capitalism.* Greenleaf Book Group.

54. Ellen MacArthur Foundation. (2015). *Towards a circular economy* (pp. 11–13). https://www.ellenmacarthurfoundation.org/ towards-a-circular-economy-business-rationale-for-an-accelerated-transition

55. Environmental Defense Fund. (2019). *Business and the fourth wave of environmentalism.* https://www.edf.org/sites/default/files/Business-and-the-Fourth-Wave-of-Environmentalism_2019.pdf

56. Equal Exchange. (2025). *About us.* Retrieved July 8, 2025, from https://shop. equalexchange.coop/pages/about-us

57. Equal Exchange. (n.d.). *About us.* Retrieved June 3, 2025, from https://shop. equalexchange.coop/pages/about-us

58. European Parliament. (2020, December 8). The impact of textile production and waste on the environment [Infographic]. https:// www.europarl.europa.eu/topics/en/article/20201208STO93327/ the-impact-of-textile-production-and-waste-on-the-environment-infographics

59. Everlane. (n.d.). *Everlane.* https://www.everlane.com/

60. Fairtrade International. (2025, May 27). *Fair trade single origin coffee.* Fairtrade. Retrieved July 8, 2025, from https://www.fairtrade.net/us-en/news/fair-trade-single-origin-coffee.html

61. Fashion Revolution. (2024). *What fuels fashion? Global fashion transparency index 2024.* Fashion Revolution CIC. https://www.fashionrevolution.org/transparency/

62. Ferguson, R. S., & Lovell, S. T. (2014). Permaculture for agroecology: design, movement, practice, and worldview. *Agronomy for Sustainable Development, 34*(2), 251–274.

63. Fernández, H. (2009). *Suma Qamaña, vivir bien, el ethos de la nueva constitución boliviana.* OBETS. Revista de Ciencias Sociales, (4), 41–48.

64. Foley, K. (2019, May 27). *The certified B Corporation: A definition and brief history of how it all started.* Valley to Summit. Retrieved July 21, 2025, from https://www.valleytosummit.net/ the-certified-b-corporation-a-definition-and-brief-history-of-how-it-all-started

65. Forbes Communications Council. (2025, January 13). *20 expert tips for crafting brief but impactful marketing messages.* Forbes. https://www.forbes.com/councils/ forbescommunicationscouncil/2025/01/13/20-expert-tips-for-crafting-brief-but-impactful-marketing-messages/

66. Forest Stewardship Council. (2025). Home – FSC International. Retrieved July 8, 2025, from https://fsc.org/en

67. Fortune Business Insights. (2025, May 26). *Cocoa and chocolate market size, share & COVID-19 impact analysis, by type (cocoa ingredients …).* https://www.fortunebusinessinsights.com/industry-reports/ cocoa-and-chocolate-market-100075

68. Gerpott, T. J. (2017). Pay-what-you-want pricing: An integrative review of the empirical research literature. *Management Science Letters, 7*(1), 35–62.

69. Gillespie, B. (2022). Using digital storytelling and game-based learning to increase student engagement and connect theory with practice. *Teaching & Learning Inquiry, 10*(1), Article 14. https://doi.org/10.20343/teachlearninqu.10.14

70. Global Reporting Initiative. (n.d.). *Global Reporting Initiative standards.* Retrieved June 21, 2025, from https://www.globalreporting.org/standards/

71. Green America. (2011, May). *Green American, 83.* Retrieved July 8, 2025, from https://www.greenamerica.org/sites/default/files/2018-10/GAM83_2011April-May_DigitalReady_5-26-11.pdf

72. Green Mountain Power. (2023, August 18). *GMP's request to expand customer access to cost-effective home energy storage through popular powerwall and BYOD battery programs is approved.* https://greenmountainpower.com/news/gmp-requests-removal-of-cap-on-powerwall-and-byod-home-battery-programs/

73. Grove Collaborative Holdings, Inc. (2024). *Investor FAQs.* Retrieved July 8, 2025, from https://investors.grove.co/company-information/faq

74. Harvey, G. (2023, May). *Major win for the rights of nature: Constitutional court rules in favor of communities in Ecuador's Intag Valley.* Bard Center for Environmental Policy Blog. https://blogs.bard.edu/cepblog/?p=13961

75. Holmes, H. (2025, February 4). *Tony's Chocolonely sales hit €200 m but losses mount due to record cocoa prices.* The Grocer. https://www.thegrocer.co.uk/news/tonys-chocolonely-sales-hit-200m-but-losses-mount-due-to-record-cocoa-prices/700649.article

76. Holmgren, D. (2002). *Permaculture: Principles and pathways beyond sustainability.* Holmgren Design Services.

77. Hou, H.-T., & Keng, S.-H. (2021). A dual-scaffolding framework integrating peer-scaffolding and cognitive-scaffolding for an augmented reality-based educational board game: An analysis of learners' collective flow state and collaborative learning behavioral patterns. Journal of Educational Computing Research, 59(3), 547–573. https://doi.org/10.1177/0735633120969409

78. Hudson Valley Current. (n.d.). *Member businesses.* Retrieved June 7, 2025, from https://hudsonvalleycurrent.org/member-businesses/

79. Hunt, V., Layton, D., & Prince, S. (2015). *Why diversity matters.* McKinsey & Company. https://www.mckinsey.com/capabilities/people-and-organizational-performance/our-insights/why-diversity-matters

80. Hunter, K. (2023, January 9). *Unpacking the packaging potential of mycelium, the mushroom 'roots' of many uses.* Bulletin of the Atomic Scientists. https://thebulletin.org/2023/01/unpacking-the-packaging-potential-of-mycelium-the-mushroom-roots-of-many-uses/

81. Inc. (2020, February 6). *Bartering*. Inc. Retrieved July 8, 2025, from https://www. inc.com/encyclopedia/bartering.html

82. Interface, Inc. (n.d.). Interface – sustainability commitment and corporate overview. Retrieved July 6, 2025, from https://www.interface.com/US/en-US. html

83. James, P. (2015). *Urban Sustainability in Theory and Practice*. Earthscan from Routledge.

84. James, P. (2022). Re-embedding the circular economy in Circles of Social Life: Beyond the self-repairing (and still-rapacious) economy. *Local Environment*, 27(10–11), 1208–1224.

85. Jessen, J. (2024). Top 10 sustainability events. *Sustainability Magazine*. https:// sustainabilitymag.com/top10/top-10-sustainability-events-2024

86. Jesta Freak. (n.d.). *Indulge in chocolate knowledge*. Retrieved June 16, 2025, from https://jestafreak.com/indulge-in-chocolate-knowledge/

87. Johanisova, N., & Vinkelhoferová, M. (2019). Social solidarity economy. In A. Kothari, A. Salleh, A. Escobar, F. Demaria, & A. Acosta (Eds.), *Pluriverse: A post-development dictionary* (pp. 311–314). Tulika Books.

88. John, M. (Ed.). (2025). *The Routledge handbook of global sustainability education and thinking for the 21st century* (1st ed.). Routledge.

89. Jones, G. (2023, March 2). *Two centuries of business leaders who took a stand on social issues*. HBS Working Knowledge. Harvard Business School. Retrieved July 21, 2025, from https://www.library.hbs.edu/working-knowledge/ two-centuries-of-business-leaders-who-took-a-stand-on-social-issues

90. Katsaliaki, K., & Mustafee, N. (2015). Edutainment for sustainable development: A survey of games in the field. *Simulation & Gaming, 46*(6), 647–672.

91. Kawano, E., Masterson, T. N., & Teller-Elsberg, J. (Eds.). (2010). *Solidarity economy I: Building alternatives for people and planet – Papers and reports from the 2009 U.S. Forum on the Solidarity Economy*. Center for Popular Economics.

92. Kenber, B. (2021, February 13). *Anti-slavery chocolate is taken off ethical list*. The Times. https://www.thetimes.com/uk/article/ anti-slavery-chocolate-is-taken-off-ethical-list-ghsrh06vs

93. Kim, W. C., & Mauborgne, R. (2004). *Blue ocean strategy*. Harvard Business Review, 82(10), 76–84. https://hbr.org/2004/10/blue-ocean-strategy

94. Kim, W. C., & Mauborgne, R. (2005). *Blue Ocean Strategy: How to create uncontested market space and make the competition irrelevant*. Harvard Business School Press.

95. Koszewska, M. (2010). CSR standards as a significant factor differentiating textile and clothing goods. *Fibres & Textiles in Eastern Europe, 18*(6), 14–19.

96. Kuckertz, A., & Wagner, M. (2010). The influence of sustainability orientation on entrepreneurial intentions—Investigating the role of business experience. *Journal of Business Venturing, 25*(5), 524–539.

97. Kumar, N. (2025, January 15). *Outsourcing statistics 2025: Worldwide & US data.* DemandSage. Retrieved July 8, 2025, from https://www.demandsage.com/outsourcing-statistics/

98. Kurniawan, A., & Sunitiyoso, Y. (2024). New business model for sustainable retail company using design thinking concept. *International Research Journal of Economics and Management Studies, 3*(4), 287–296.

99. Lagorio-Chafkin, C. (2022). *What I Know: Stuart Landesberg, Grove Collaborative.* Inc. Magazine. Retrieved July 8, 2025, from https://www.inc.com/christine-lagorio-chafkin/grove-collaborative-stuart-landesberg-what-i-know-podcast.html

100. Laville, J.-L. (Forthcoming 2023). *Origins and histories of the social and solidarity economy.* In I. Yi, P. Utting, J.-L. Laville, B. et al (Eds.), *Encyclopedia of the social and solidarity economy.* Cheltenham & Northampton, MA: Edward Elgar Publishing Limited, in partnership with United Nations Inter-Agency Task Force on Social and Solidarity Economy (UNTFSSE).

101. Lerner, D., Hunt, R. A., & Verheul, I. (2017). *Dueling banjos: Harmony and discord between ADHD and entrepreneurship* [Working paper].

102. Library of Congress. (2025, May). *Standards and certifications – Green business: Sources of information.* Retrieved June 23, 2025, from https://guides.loc.gov/green-business/businesses-going-green/standards-certifications

103. Lidsky, D. & Mokwa, A. (2022, March 8). Most innovative companies: North America 2022. Fast Company. https://www.fastcompany.com/90724451/most-innovative-companies-north-america-2022

104. Lundberg, D., & DeVoy, J. (2022, September 22). *The aftermath of fast fashion: How discarded clothes impact public health and the environment.* Boston University School of Public Health. https://www.bu.edu/sph/news/articles/2022/the-aftermath-of-fast-fashion-how-discarded-clothes-impact-public-health-and-the-environment/

105. Market.us. (n.d.). *Green Technology Market Size, Share | CAGR of 24.0%.* Retrieved July 8, 2025, from https://market.us/report/green-technology-market/#overview

106. Max Havelaar. (2007). Retrieved July 8, 2025, from http://www.maxhavelaar.ch/en/maxhavelaar/index.php

107. MDG Monitor. (2025). *Millennium Development Goals.* Retrieved July 8, 2025, from https://www.mdgmonitor.org/millennium-development-goals/

108. Mendler de Suarez, J., Suarez, P., Bachofen, C., Fortner, R., Gordon, E., & Luu, K. (2012). *Games for a new climate: Experiencing the complexity of future risks.* Boston: The Frederick S. Pardee Center for the Study of the Longer-Range Future, Boston University.

109. M-KOPA. (n.d.). *Impact.* Retrieved July 6, 2025, from M-KOPA website: https://www.m-kopa.com/impact

110. Miller, E. (2010). Solidarity economy: Key concepts and issues. In E. Kawano, T. N. Masterson, & J. Teller-Elsberg (Eds.), *Solidarity economy I: Building alternatives for people and planet* (pp. 25–42). Center for Popular Economics.

111. Minkin, R. (2025, May 17). *Diversity, equity and inclusion in the workplace.* Pew Research Center. https://www.pewresearch.org/social-trends/2023/05/17/diversity-equity-and-inclusion-in-the-workplace/

112. Nguyen, A. (2020, September 29). Bitter origins: Labor exploitation in coffee production. The Borgen Project. https://borgenproject.org/labor-exploitation-in-coffee-production/

113. NSF International. (March 6, 2025). *Consumer personal care market insights and outlook: 2025 white paper.* https://www.nsf.org

114. The Ocean Cleanup. (2025). *We aim to clean up 90 % of floating ocean plastic pollution by 2040.* Retrieved from https://www.theoceancleanup.com \

115. O'Gorman, P. (2008). *Wii: Creating a blue ocean – The nintendo way. Palermo Business Review, (2),* 97–108.

116. Orfalea, P., & Marsh, A. (2007). *Copy this!: Lessons from a hyperactive dyslexic who turned a bright idea into one of America's best companies.* Workman.

117. Osterwalder, A., Pigneur, Y., Clark, T., & Smith, A. (2010). *Business model generation: A handbook for visionaries, game changers, and challengers.* Wiley.

118. Osterwalder, A., & Pigneur, Y. (2010). *Business model generation: A handbook for visionaries, game changers, and challengers.* John Wiley & Sons.

119. Osterwalder, A., Pigneur, Y., Bernarda, G., & Smith, A. (2014). *Value proposition design: How to create products and services customers want.* John Wiley & Sons.

120. Pannekoek, F., Breugem, T., & Van Wassenhove, L. N. (2023, September 11). *How Tony's Chocolonely created a purpose-driven (and profitable) supply chain.* Harvard Business Review. https://hbr.org/2023/09/how-tonys-chocolonely-created-a-purpose-driven-and-profitable-supply-chain

121. Parmley, S. (2024, April 2). Grove Collaborative refreshes core brand Grove Co. *Retail Dive.* Retrieved July 8, 2025, from https://www.retaildive.com/news/grove-collaborative-refreshes-core-brand-grove-co/712009/

122. Patagonia. (2022). *Ownership.* https://www.patagonia.com/ownership/

123. Patagonia. (n.d.). *Worn Wear*. Retrieved July 6, 2025, from https://wornwear.patagonia.com/

124. Persefoni. (2024, July 12). *What is ESG?* https://www.persefoni.com/blog/what-is-esg

125. Pope, A. (2021). *Recent study reveals more than a third of global consumers are willing to pay more for sustainability as demand grows for environmentally friendly alternatives*. Business Wire. https://www.businesswire.com/news/home/20211014005090/en/Recent-Study-Reveals-More-Than-a-Third-of-Global-Consumers-Are-Willing-to-Pay-More-for-Sustainability-as-Demand-Grows-for-Environmentally-Friendly-Alternatives

126. Prakash, S. (2024, August 30). *The role of communication in driving sustainable development*. Institute of Sustainability Studies. https://instituteofsustainabilitystudies.com/insights/guides/the-role-of-communication-in-driving-sustainable-development/

127. Rachal, M. (2024, April 25). Unilever reality-checked its 2025 plastic packaging targets. Will more companies do the same? *Packaging Dive*. Retrieved from https://www.packagingdive.com/news/changing-2025-plastic-packaging-goals-unilever/714063/

128. Ries, E. (2010, September 27). *Good enough never is (or is it?)*. Startup Lessons Learned. Retrieved from https://www.startuplessonslearned.com/2010/09/good-enough-never-is-or-is-it.html

129. Ries, E. (2011). *The lean startup*. Crown Business.

130. RIPESS (2024). *Activity Report, 2023*. https://www.ripess.org/about-ripess/?lang=en

131. RIPESS. (n.d.). *Intercontinental network for the promotion of social solidarity economy*. https://www.ripess.org/?lang=en

132. Robinson, P. (2023, February 23). *Reflections from Rink on the "Fair Trade Experiment"*. Equal Exchange Resource Center. https://www.info.equalexchange.coop/articles/the-fair-trade-experiment

133. Schawbel, D. (2017, November 21). Unilever's Paul Polman: Why today's leaders need to commit to a purpose. *Forbes*. Retrieved from https://www.forbes.com/sites/danschawbel/2017/11/21/paul-polman-why-todays-leaders-need-to-commit-to-a-purpose/

134. Schooley, S. (2024). *The benefits of highly motivated employees*. Business.com. https://www.business.com/articles/the-benefits-of-highly-motivated-employees/

135. SDG Academy. (2025). *SDG Academy: Free online education for sustainable development*. Retrieved July 8, 2025, from https://sdgacademy.org/

136. Senka, G., Tramonti, M., Dochshanov, A. M., et al. (2024). Using a game to educate about sustainable development. *Multimodal Technologies and Interaction*, *8*(11), 96. https://www.researchgate.net/publication/385575263_Using_a_Game_to_Educate_About_Sustainable_Development

137. Sentence, R. (2020, February 4). How Who Gives A Crap built a loyal following through feel-good branding and a commitment to CX. *EcoConsultancy*. https://econsultancy.com/how-who-gives-a-crap-built-loyal-following-feel-good-branding-commitment-customer-experience-cx/

138. Simon-Kucher & Partners. (2021). *Global sustainability study 2021: What role do consumers play in a sustainable future?* https://www.simon-kucher.com/en/insights/2021-global-sustainability-study-what-role-do-consumers-play-sustainable-future

139. Slave Free Chocolate. (n.d.). *Home*. Retrieved June 16, 2025, from https://www.slavefreechocolate.org/

140. Solon, O. (2012, January 17). *Interview: Eric Ries, author of* **The Lean Startup**. *Wired*. https://www.wired.com/2012/01/eric-ries-startup/

141. Stanley, V., & Chouinard, Y. (2023). The future of the responsible company. Patagonia.

142. Statista. (2024). *Revenue of Tony's Chocolonely worldwide from 2012 to 2023, by region (in million euros)*. Statista. Retrieved June 16, 2025, from https://www.statista.com/statistics/942652/revenue-of-tony-s-chocolonely-by-region/

143. Stenn, T. (2017). *Social entrepreneurship as sustainable development: Introducing the sustainability lens*. Palgrave Macmillan.

144. Stenn, T. L. (2013). *The cultural and political intersection of fair trade and social justice: Managing a global industry*. Palgrave Macmillan.

145. Stenn, T. L. (2018). US Fulbright scholarly research study, Bolivia. 2015-2018.

146. Stenn, T. L. (2019). Building resilient and meaningful enterprises with the Sustainability Lens. *Journal of Strategic Innovation and Sustainability*, *14*(3), 98–110.

147. Stenn, T. (2022). Harnessing Andean Spirituality and Entrepreneurship. In *World Scientific Encyclopedia of Business Sustainability and Entrepreneurship* (pp. 315-337). World Scientific.

148. Strategyzer. (2025). *Value Proposition Canvas*. Retrieved July 8, 2025, from https://www.strategyzer.com/canvas/value-proposition-canvas

149. Strategyzer. (n.d.). *Business Model Canvas*. Retrieved from https://www.strategyzer.com/canvas/business-model-canvas

150. Sundheim, D. (2023, December 12). *How Patagonia became the most reputable brand in the United States*. Forbes. https://

www.forbes.com/sites/dougsundheim/2023/12/12/
how-patagonia-became-the-most-reputable-brand-in-the-united-states/

151. Tarbi, L. (2023, December 6). *Case study: Tesla Powerwall installation*. EnergySage. https://www.energysage.com/blog/tesla-powerwall-installation-green-mountain-power-vermont/

152. Ten Thousand Villages. (2025). *Transforming lives through fair trade since 1946*. Retrieved July 8, 2025, from https://www.tenthousandvillages.com/

153. Ten Thousand Villages. (n.d.). *Ten Thousand Villages*. https://www.tenthousandvillages.com/

154. Tilda's Kitchen & Market. (n.d.). *Home – Tilda's Kitchen & Market*. Retrieved June 7, 2025, from https://tildaskitchenandmarket.com/

155. Tissue Online. (2024, June 19). Who Gives A Crap UK sees record sales surge post-global campaign. *Tissue Online North America* https://tissueonlinenorthamerica.com/who-gives-a-crap-uk-sees-record-sales-surge-post-global-campaign/

156. Toikka, J. (2025, May 5). *Sustainable procurement part 6: How to measure sustainable performance*. Sievo. https://sievo.com/blog/sustainable-procurement-part6

157. Tony's Chocolonely. (2011). *The story of Tony's Chocolonely* [Video]. YouTube. https://www.youtube.com/watch?v=kgwYcEabBls

158. Tony's Chocolonely. (2025). *Tony's timeline*. Retrieved June 16, 2025, from https://us.tonyschocolonely.com/pages/tonys-timeline

159. Tsai, J.-C., Liu, S.-Y., Chang, C.-Y., & Chen, S.-Y. (2021). Using a board game to teach about sustainable development. *Sustainability, 13*(9), 4942.

160. TST Technology. (2024, November 6). *The hard truth behind why 42% of startups fail. Medium*. Retrieved July 8, 2025, from https://medium.com/@tsttechnology/the-hard-truth-behind-why-42-of-startups-fail-ae4d9abe738c

161. UNESCO. (2017, January 1). *Education for Sustainable Development Goals: learning objectives*. UNESCO. (Last updated July 25, 2023). Retrieved September 10, 2025, from https://www.unesco.org/en/articles/education-sustainable-development-goals-learning-objectives

162. Unilever. (2019). *Unilever Sustainable Living Plan: The journey so far*. https://www.unilever.com/sustainable-living/

163. United Nations. (2012). *The future we want* (A/RES/66/288). Retrieved July 8, 2025, from https://sustainabledevelopment.un.org/futurewewant.html

164. United Nations. (2015). *Transforming our world: The 2030 Agenda for Sustainable Development* (A/RES/70/1). Retrieved July 8, 2025, from https://sdgs.un.org/2030agenda

165. United Nations. (n.d.). *The 17 Goals*. United Nations Sustainable Development Goals. https://sdgs.un.org/goals

166. United Nations Development Programme. (2025). *Human Development Report 2025*. United Nations Publications.

167. United Nations Global Compact Cities Programme. (2009, April 20). *Milwaukee 7 Water Council Global Compact Project: Briefing paper*. United Nations Global Compact.

168. United Nations Global Compact & Business for Social Responsibility. (2015). *Supply chain sustainability: A practical guide for continuous improvement* (2nd ed.). UN Global Compact.

169. United Nations Social and Solidarity Economy. (n.d.). *SSE and the SDGs*. Retrieved July 8, 2025, from https://unsse.org/sse-and-the-sdgs/

170. van Giezen, A., & Wiegmans, B. (2020). Spoilt - Ocean Cleanup: Alternative logistics chains to accommodate plastic waste recycling: An economic evaluation. *Transportation Research Interdisciplinary Perspectives, 5*, 100115. https://www.sciencedirect.com/science/article/pii/S2590198220300269

171. VBike. (n.d.). *Brattleboro E-Bike Lending Library*. Retrieved June 7, 2025, from https://www.vbikesolutions.org/brattleboro-e-bike-lending-library.html

172. Vitari, C., & David, C. (2017). Sustainable management models: innovating through permaculture. *Journal of Management Development, 36*(1), 14–36.

173. Western Sydney University. (n.d.). *Circles of Sustainability: Milwaukee case study*. Institute for Culture and Society. Retrieved July 21, 2025, from https://www.westernsydney.edu.au/ics/research/impact/circles_of_sustainability

174. Wheeler, D., Blatnicky, M., Edwards, M., & Howard, S. (2013). *The sustainable enterprise fieldbook: Building new bridges* (2nd ed.). Routledge.

175. Zorilla, C. (2014, April). *The struggle over Sumak Kawsay in Ecuador*. Upside Down World. https://upsidedownworld.org/archives/ecuador/the-struggle-over-sumak-kawsay-in-ecuador/

Bibliography

1. Food Empowerment Project. (n.d.). *Food Empowerment Project*. https://foodispower.org/

2. Lutheran World Relief. (n.d.). *About Lutheran World Relief*. Retrieved June 3, 2025, from https://lwr.org/about-lwr

3. Merrick, G. (2021, December 7). *The history of Equal Exchange*. Equal Exchange Resource Center. https://www.info.equalexchange.coop/articles/the-history-of-equal-exchange

4. Morrow, R. (2022). *Earth Restorer's guide to permaculture* (4th ed.). Melliodora Publishing.

5. Piema, C. (n.d.). Sustainable supply chain: What it is and how to create one. LinkedIn. Retrieved June 2, 2025, from https://www.linkedin.com/pulse/sustainable-supply-chain-what-how-create-one-carel-piema-msc-bsc-/

6. SAP SE. (n.d.). What is a sustainable supply chain? SAP. Retrieved June 2, 2025, from https://www.sap.com/products/scm/what-is-a-sustainable-supply-chain.html

7. United Nations. (1992). *Agenda 21: The United Nations Programme of Action from Rio*. United Nations Department of Economic and Social Affairs.

8. United Nations. (2000). *United Nations Millennium Declaration* (A/RES/55/2). Retrieved July 8, 2025, from https://www.un.org/en/development/devagenda/millennium_declaration.shtml

9. United Nations. (2025). *The 17 Sustainable Development Goals*. Retrieved July 8, 2025, from https://sdgs.un.org/goals

10. Walsh, Z., & Cordero, D. (2021). Buen vivir and other post-capitalist imaginaries: Alternatives to development in Latin America. *Latin American Perspectives, 48*(1), 17–35.

NOTES

www.ingramcontent.com/pod-product-compliance
Lightning Source LLC
Chambersburg PA
CBHW050331270326
41926CB00016B/3402